T0303372

Beast

WEREWOLVES, SERIAL KILLERS, AND MAN-EATERS

The Mystery of the Monsters of the Gévaudan

Gustavo Sánchez Romero & S. R. Schwalb

Foreword by Phil Barnson

Illustrated by Gustavo Sánchez Romero

Skyhorse Publishing

Skyhorse Publishing books may be purchased in bulk at special discounts for sales promotion, corporate gifts, fund-raising, or educational purposes. Special editions can also be created to specifications. For details, contact the Special Sales Department, Skyhorse Publishing, 307 West 36th Street, 11th Floor, New York, NY 10018 or info@skyhorsepublishing.com.

Visit our website at www.skyhorsepublishing.com.

10 9 8 7 6 5 4 3

Library of Congress Cataloging-in-Publication Data is available on file.

Print ISBN: 978-1-63220-462-2
Ebook ISBN: 978-1-63220-780-7

Cover design by Rain Saukas

Printed in China

Readers interested in the cryptozoological artwork of Gustavo Sánchez Romero may contact him at criptocriaturas@yahoo.es

Table of Contents

Part 1. The Never-Ending Night

(cont.)

Part 2. The Hunt for Truth

To the Reader

This book is inspired by true events that occurred in France from June 1764 to June 1767. The subject of this book is known as the Beast of the Gévaudan, but the Beast was actually two or more creatures that ranged south-central France in the Gévaudan and in neighboring Auvergne and the Vivarais. Something to keep in mind: *La Bête* (the Beast) is a feminine noun in French. Thus, in accounts quoted herein, such as that of the 1889 chronicle by the Abbé Pierre Pourcher, the Beast is referred to as female ("she attacked," "she devoured," and so on). For simplicity's sake, we refer to the creature or creatures described herein as "the Beast." Please note: To simplify comparisons of the animals discussed in this book, not all illustrations are to scale.

We are fortunate in this journey to have the company of respected Beast researcher, documentarian, and author Phil Barnson, from Béziers in the south of France. Phil maintains the website www.labetedugevaudan.com.

La Bête du Gévaudan identifiée, by Mademoiselle Marguerite Aribaud-Farrère. *Phil Barnson.*

Foreword

Once upon a time long ago in rural France, in a land known as the Gévaudan, a young shepherdess was found dead, slaughtered by a mysterious *bête féroce*, a ferocious beast. This bloodthirsty monster then attacked and killed others—children, women, and men—bringing about a never-ending night of dread that lasted three long years.

The peasants who eked out hardscrabble livings during this reign of terror came to wonder every single day: Would they know the next victim? Would they *be* the next victim?

***

I have been caught up in the clutches of the Beast since I was a boy growing up in the Languedoc region of France. Here, in the country of the Beast, the story has been passed from generation to generation since the occurrence of these horrifying events more than two hundred and fifty years ago.

My father possessed a booklet about the creature, called *La Bête du Gévaudan identifiée*, by Mademoiselle Marguerite Aribaud-Farrère. It was stapled, with a stark orange-yellow cover, upon which was a black-inked illustration of a man dressed from head to toe in wolfskin, his face leering out of the open jaws of the dead wolf.

I still have this booklet, and, as I look at it now, I recall poring over this picture many years ago, carefully studying the wolf-man who menaced readers with his claw-like fingernails and vampire-like teeth, ready to leap out of a foreboding forest. My hair would stand on end as I eyed the monster, recalling the stories of the Beast's ravages. It served as inspiration when I played in our family's attic, imagining hunting the werewolf myself, accompanied by my worthy companions, action figures G. I. Joe and Big Jim. I'd pretend we'd gone back in time to Old France to find the Beast, and I'd peer into the darkest corners, searching for our prey. But if there was a sudden sound, such as a creak of the house settling or a branch scraping a window, I'd freeze, eyes wide, heart pounding, clutching the grip of an antique saber I kept hidden under the eaves.

***

Years later, still on the Beast's trail, I decided to create a website that I call *In the Shadow of the Beast*, www.labetedugevaudan.com, that would make the facts about the monster and its world available to all who were interested. And when I began sifting through the stories, I was surprised to find that most were never verified.

So I decided to confirm as much as I could, with the help of as many professionals as I was able to contact. And I made the information available to all, with no need to register. Readers could also use the content freely; all I asked was that they just mention where it came from.

***

People are often surprised to learn this is a true story. In France, so many things have been said and written about the Beast over the years that many believe this simply is "a story." And those who are interested in the real account get lost in snarls of fact and fiction. They ask: *When did this happen? How poor were the people? There was a king at that time, right? What, you say there were no roads?*

I like to think they can find all they need to situate the case well enough in history, and, more importantly, in reality, on my site. I try to be as objective as possible so those who visit can find rational facts and "almost scientific" explanations for something that has become legend. Who wouldn't want to investigate a legend such as this?

Today, though I believe www.labetedugevaudan.com is the most complete site on the Web, it remains far from exhaustive.

For it does not solve the mystery.

***

What was the Beast of the Gévaudan?

Where did it come from?

You see, some say it was a wolf.

Some say it was a hyena or a lion, escaped from a menagerie.

Some say it was a man in wolfskin.

Some have said it was a scourge sent from God.

The only thing I am certain of is that no one will ever really know the answer, unless they could truly go back in time.

But perhaps, in the long run, it does not matter. What might matter more is the story told by the information contained within French archives and parish records. There is extensive documentation of the Beast, and it has been studied by specialists from the nineteenth century through today.

What the archives reveal is a story far bigger than one about a strange animal that killed children and women.

From the remote French countryside to the royal court in Versailles, it's about an entire microcosm with many components nested within each other, into which a number of complex agents were tossed: Social problems resulting from poverty in a land where justice was dispensed by religion, livestock succumbing to outbreaks of disease, a little ice age that made winter last from October to June, and a challenging landscape with no real roads of any kind.

There you have a thumbnail of life in the Gévaudan at that time.

Think things couldn't get any worse? That's what the peasants thought, too!

***

I admit I have favorite theories myself. But I have no answer. I only tell people what I know, what I've learned along the way, and then I propose solutions that are always open to any correction.

When Gustavo contacted me about this project, I wondered about there being one more book about the Beast. But this is not just "one more book." It is a book which shows the case in a new way. Bringing in other information and historical events, this readable account transports you to a world where magic and superstition live side by side with nature's "monsters."

A world where human hunters are outfoxed, shall we say, by other predators.

A world where humans are prey.

I will never say to anybody, "This is the answer," but I like to think the case is well presented here, with the story of the attacks, the major characters, the hunts, and then, the hunt for truth—theories about the identity of the Beast.

What you need to know to begin your own journey in the world of the Beast lies within these pages.

Now—do you have what it takes?

What will you find lurking in the darkest corners?

Keep your saber ready.

Phil Barnson
dans l'Ombre de la Bête (In the Shadow of the Beast)
www.labetedugevaudan.com
Béziers, France

The Main Characters

King, Court, Authorities:

Louis XV (1710–1774). **King of France.** A member of the Bourbon dynasty. Great-grandson of the Sun King (Louis XIV). Reign marked by the War of Austrian Succession and the Seven Years' (or French and Indian) War. Avid hunter. Queen: Marie Leszczynska of Poland (1703–1768). Mistresses: Madame de Pompadour and Madame du Barry, among others. Taken sick while hunting late in April 1774, the monarch was diagnosed with smallpox, horrifying and incurable. Louis, realizing his time had come, determined to die a Christian death, and sent Madame du Barry away. He passed on May 10. His highly contagious body was quickly transferred to a lead coffin and taken to the royal crypt.

Bishop of Mende (1688–1767), Gabriel Florent de Choiseul Beaupré. Co-ruler with the king of the diocese of Mende according to a *paréage*, or agreement, put in place four and a half centuries earlier. Member of an influential French family. Cousin of the secretary of state of foreign affairs. Conservative pro-Jansenist Catholic. Believed the Beast's appearance was auspicious. At the time of La Bête, the bishop was seventy-six years old; he passed away the month after Chastel killed the second Beast, on July 7, 1767.

Laverdy (1724–1793), Clément Charles François de Laverdy, or L'Averdy. Controller-General of France 1763–1768.

Choiseul (1719–1785), Étienne François, Duc de Choiseul. Secretary of state of foreign affairs. Cousin of the Bishop of Mende.

Saint-Florentin (1705–1777), Louis Phélypeaux, comte de Saint-Florentin. One of the King's administrators and a Beast communications coordinator. Also an avid hunter; lost his left hand as a result of a hunting accident.

Buffon (1707–1788), Georges Louis Leclerc, comte de Buffon. Prominent French naturalist. Curator of the Jardin des Plantes, Paris. Author of the multi-volume *Histoire naturelle*. According to the journalist Frédéric Melchior, Baron von Grimm, Buffon thought the Beast was several wolves.

Ballainvilliers (1721–1767), Simon-Charles, Baron de Ballainvilliers. Intendant of the province of Auvergne. Based in Clermont-Ferrand, France. The first Beast, the Chazes Wolf, would be destroyed within his jurisdiction, not in the Gévaudan.

Saint-Priest (1732–1794), Marie-Joseph de Guignard de Saint-Priest. Intendant of the province of Languedoc (which included the Gévaudan). Based in Montpellier, France.

Lafont, Étienne (1719–1779). Syndic or manager of the diocese of Gévaudan and subdelegate to province's intendant, Saint-Priest. Local boy. Formerly an attorney in Toulouse, France. Diligent caretaker of his district. Refereed hunters. Considered a thoroughgoing foe of the Beast, though he could not challenge king and court with regard to an apparent second Beast after the official destruction of the Chazes animal in September 1765.

Count Moncan. Jean-Baptiste Marin, comte de Moncan. Commander of military forces in the Languedoc.

Montluc. Pierre de Tassy Montluc. Subdelegate of the diocese of Saint-Flour to the intendant of Auvergne.

Morangiès, father and son. Father: Pierre Charles de Molette, Marquis de Morangiès (1701–1774). Son: Jean-François Charles de la Molette, comte de Morangiès, (1728–1791). At the time of the Beast, the Morangiès family was the area's most influential. Both father and son had served in the Seven Years' War, but the marquis had dishonored himself and retired afterward to the Morangiès home in Saint-Alban. The count, his son, had performed much better with regards to his military service, yet years later would become a human suspect responsible for the killings in the Gévaudan. His financial misdeeds caused him to be imprisoned in Paris's Conciergerie in 1773, but he was released. Voltaire among others came to his defense. Disgraced, he left France for the Netherlands and Metz, France, and became involved with an adventuress. He returned to Saint-Alban and died in 1801 after the woman hit him with a fireplace shovel.

The Hunters

Duhamel (Jean-Baptiste Louis François Boulanger Duhamel, born 1732). Captain and adjutant of the Clermont-Prince dragoon volunteers. First hunter of the Beast, from autumn 1764 through spring 1765. Dedicated yet heavy-handed. Once, in frustration, he broke the blade of his sword over the back of a peasant. He was made a knight of the Royal and Military Order of Saint Louis on December 9, 1771; he retired in 1788 with an annual pension of fourteen hundred *livres* (pounds).

The d'Ennevals. Father: Jean-Charles Marc Antoine Vaumesle of Enneval (1703–1769). Son: Jean-François Vaumesle of Enneval (born 1734). Court-approved wolf hunters from Normandy, France. Hunted the Beast after Duhamel, from spring 1765 through mid-summer 1765. Arrogant, taciturn. Afterward, the elder d'Enneval was said to have expressed that he believed there was something extraordinary in the Gévaudan.

François Antoine (1695–1771) and **Antoine de Beauterne, Robert-François Antoine de Beauterne** (born in 1748). Father-son hunters from the king's court. François Antoine was a knight of the Royal and Military Order of Saint Louis, the king's gunbearer, and a lieutenant of the hunt. His son was a cavalry officer. They hunted the Beast after Duhamel and the d'Ennevals. With the help of his nephew, **Rinchard**, gamekeeper of the Duke of Orléans, François Antoine destroyed the first Beast, the Chazes wolf, in September 1765. Though François Antoine is reported as being a gallant and kind gentleman, Beast chronicler Abbé Pierre Pourcher suspected him of trickery, of stealing the thunder and the reward money from local Jean Chastel.

Jean Chastel (1708–1789). Jean Chastel is credited with killing the second Beast. Husband of Anne Charbonnier, father of nine children, Chastel was an innkeeper, and said to be an excellent hunter. His enigmatic son **Antoine Chastel** has, in contemporary times, been connected with many stories pointing to his procuring and training a Beast to carry out the killings, either for himself or for a sadistic feudal lord, possibly Count Morangiès.

The Marquis d'Apcher (Joseph Jean Chateauneuf-Randon of Apcher, 1748–1798). A knight of the Royal and Military Order of Saint Louis, among other appointments. Eager young hunter of the Beast. In 1767, he hunted with Jean Chastel and led the hunts of June 18 and 19, 1767, in which Chastel took down the second Beast (the creature also referred to as La Ténazeyre canid). After pursuing a military career, becoming a *marechal du champ* (field marshal), followed by his election as a deputy of the Gévaudan, he fled France for Spain after the Revolution. He died in Barcelona in 1798.

Autopsy Reports:

The Jaladon report of the first Beast, or the Chazes wolf. Made by Charles Jaladon, local surgeon, in September 1765.

The Marin report of the second Beast, or La Ténazeyre canid. Made by royal notary Roch-Étienne Marin; autopsy performed by Boulanger, father and son, in June 1767.

Three Famous Survivors Of Attacks:

Portefaix (1752–1785). Jacques André Portefaix, twelve-year-old hero, leader of a group of children who defied the Beast in January 1765. The children were rewarded and Portefaix's education and military training were subsequently paid for by the state. He met King Louis XV in 1770, and went on to become a lieutenant before an untimely death in 1785 as a result of a shooting accident in Douai, northern France.

The *femme* Jouve. (Jeanne Jouve, born in 1732, wife of Pierre). Courageous mother who, unarmed, dared to brawl with the Beast to defend her children in March 1765.

Marie-Jeanne Valet. Young woman who rumbled with the Beast in August 1765, fighting the creature off with a bayonet. François Antoine, the king's gunbearer, compared her to Joan of Arc.

Priest-Historian:

Abbé Pierre Pourcher (1831–1915). Priest and "dean" of Beast chroniclers. Curate of Saint-Martin de Boubaux, diocese of Mende. His 1889 account, *Histoire de la Bête du Gévaudan,* *veritable fléau de Dieu* (*History of La Bête du Gévaudan: True Scourge of God)*, compiled from numerous official documents and letters (interspersed with commentary regarding the Beast as a creature used by God), is considered the bible of La Bête, and was approved by the Vatican. Pourcher's great-grandfather fought the Beast. Pourcher was also able to procure the gun of Jean Chastel, the local hero who killed the second Beast. English-speaking readers may enjoy Pourcher's work through British researcher Derek Brockis's translation.

An account of a locksmith from Langeac relates the story his father often heard his father tell, of two girls bringing food to their parents working in the wheat fields: "La Bête came out of the wheat and attacked one of the girls. She had time only to say to her companion, 'I am lost. *Adieu.*'"

—*Abbé Pierre Pourcher*

Prologue

In June of 1764, Louis XV had been the ruler of France for forty-nine years, since the age of five, when he succeeded his great-grandfather, Louis XIV, the Sun King. An orphan early on, with a youth that has been described as "six funerals and a wedding" (the wedding was his own, to Marie Leszczyńska of Poland; he was fifteen, she twenty-one), and surrounded by a gerontocracy of advisors, Louis XV was from a tender age a withdrawn and melancholy monarch. He avoided his subjects and rarely visited his capital city of Paris. He engaged a select circle of intimates and associated with many mistresses, the most famous being Madame de Pompadour, court "ringmaster" for twenty years. But Pompadour had died weeks before, in April of 1764, her passing compounding the king's moodiness. She would be replaced in due course by the bewitching Madame du Barry.

In later years, Louis XV preferred the country estate of Compiègne, north of Paris, its thirty-five-thousand-plus-acre oak and beech forest the perfect venue for hunting, his obsession. The king killed two to three hundred animals on a typical *chasse* (hunt) and knew all his dogs by name.

Still, Louis spent a great deal of his life at Versailles, his great-grandfather's palace complex and royal seat of power. Fourteen miles southwest of Paris and comprising, before the Revolution, thirty square miles, it included accommodations for a small city of people, as well as stables, kennels, and a ménagerie of exotic animals that evinced the crown's command of all things wild.

In winter, parties at Versailles were illuminated with three thousand candles. Masked balls were chic; the affair between Louis and Pompadour began with the king dressed as a yew tree and she as a shepherdess. Gambling, too, was popular; gamers spent the evening in armchairs known as *voyeuses*, the backs of which were specially upholstered so onlookers could more comfortably lean in.

In summer, the gardens of designer André Le Nôtre, disciplinarian of nature, impressed. Created over four decades from marshland, tracts of wooded fields, and, almost, a re-directed river, they included an orangery, lakes, and an open-air ballroom with marble flooring. Nautical spectacles were performed upon a Grand Canal. Fountains entertained with special effects and a plume of water that soared nearly ninety feet high.

***

Some three hundred and fifty miles south of these marvels, France was a primeval world of water and brimstone, where *aqua pura* ran its own course through yawning gorges thousands of feet beneath otherworldly volcanic peaks. Tangled forests were home to fearsome creatures, real and imaginary. Peasants resided in isolated villages, making their livings as weavers, lacemakers, farmers, and charcoal burners. Here children as young as five years old, lacking the royal security net provided to Louis as a lad, were put to work, often as caregivers of livestock. Herd girls and boys, sometimes with siblings or children of neighbors, would guide cattle and sheep to highland pastures and bring them home at day's end. Some might overnight in huts near their animals. Predators took livestock all too often, but youthful guardians learned they might fend off attackers with staffs or homemade pikes they made themselves by lashing knives to poles or branches.

One such herd girl was Jeanne Boulet of Les Hubacs, a hamlet lost among the mountains of the Vivarais, a province of Old France comparable to the modern district of Ardèche.

On the last day of June in 1764, Jeanne took a small flock of sheep to graze in an upland meadow.

She never came home.

Part 1
The Never-Ending Night

CHAPTER 1

The Apparition

June 30, 1764

In the light of the sun at the fall of day, at the edge of a wood on a rocky crag, lay the Beast, sphinx-like, scanning the countryside with panoptic vision.

Its nostrils flared, taking in an abundance of information: the odor of newly-turned earth in faraway fields, the fragrance of fir trees, the smell of sheep in a meadow below, and that of their attendant, a young woman.

The Beast had located its next meal.

The sheep, of the breed called Blanche du Massif Central, adapted to dizzying heights and tricky terrain, consisted of several four-month-old lambs, along with ewes and a ram, all cropping grass on the vertiginous hillside.

Their shepherdess, fourteen-year-old Jeanne Boulet, was singing, her adolescent voice afloat in the mountain air. "Eat your grass, sheep," she sang. "Eat your grass."

The Beast listened to her song, ears up, head tilted.

Stealthily, on its belly, it began to inch forward in the tall vegetation.

***

The day had gone by quickly for Jeanne Boulet. Early on, the shepherdess had used her staff to guide a lamb away from the peat bog at the bottom of the meadow.

"You want a drink? Come along."

She took it to a spring she'd known about since she was ten, when she first began caring for the animals on her own. The lamb drank, its tail switching to and fro. Thirsty herself, Jeanne crouched beside her charge, cupping the bubbling water in her hands. She tasted. *Cold!* She took off her bonnet, enjoying the warmth of the sun and the promise of summer after a long winter; the region was in the grip of a little ice age. She heard the sound of distant church bells announcing the noontime Angelus. She said her Hail Marys and ate the chestnut bread her mother had given her for her midday meal. She stood on a granite boulder, trying to see her family's little house far below through the emerging leaves of the trees along the mountain trail. She sat down and clomped her wooden *sabots* (clogs) rhythmically against the rock. She wondered what her friend Marie was doing. She would see her at mass tomorrow.

She watched a vulture coasting in the currents above.

The sun sank low in the sky.

"Oh!" said the shepherdess.

Shadows of tree limbs reached into the meadow. Tendrils of mist ascended from the bog.

Jeanne shivered.

She took up her bonnet and tugged it down over her ears.

"Come along, sheep," she sang. "Time to go home." She clambered off the rock, clutching her staff.

***

The Beast froze behind clumps of a flowering shrub called broom. Bright gold by day, its blooms in the waning light had become a jaundiced yellow.

Jeanne began shooing her animals to the stony path that led to the farm below. Some of the lambs stopped to steal last mouthfuls of grass.

"Come along!" Jeanne used her staff to manage the more wayward.

The Beast rose as if on command, riveted on its target. The sight of its prey decamping, turning tail, triggered a primal urge to pursue. A modern-day dog compelled to chase passing cars retains something of that instinct.

The Beast went after them.

At the head of the trail, Jeanne may have hesitated. From the corner of an eye, she may have caught an unexpected movement in the meadow. She may have wheeled, holding her staff before her, ready to defend herself against a village boy or vagrant man.

Maybe a wolf.

Blinded by the setting sun, Jeanne's eyes may have only registered the advance of a freakish silhouette.

Like a wolf. No. Not a wolf. Not a dog.

What?

The gap between them closed.

A monster.

"Run!" she screamed.

But the predator did not veer from its course and go after her sheep.

It was coming for her.

Apparitions galloped through Jeanne's head, creatures from fireside stories recounted by her grandmother on long winter nights.

A loup-garou! A werewolf!

Perhaps Jeanne tried to scramble after her livestock. Her sheep would have bolted helter-skelter, bleating in terror.

Sheep are not stupid. They are trainable. They will come when called by name. But even though there are accounts of Rambo-like sheep in the French mountains, and even though bacteria found in fleece is a source of the deadly substance anthrax (coincidentally, a pioneer in the study of anthrax and rabies, Pierre Victor Galtier, was born in nearby Langogne in 1846), sheep are for the most part defenseless when attacked by predators. Unlike cows, which can deliver disabling kicks, and, along with goats, can do serious damage with their horns, or pigs, which can bite viciously, the main defense of sheep is to run.

In their frenzy, some of Jeanne's flock may have run into the very boulder upon which their mistress had spent much of her day.

Jeanne shrieked, afraid for her life.

Afraid for her soul.

The Beast lunged.

It brought the girl down with a thud, her staff still within her grip. Pinned down, in shock, Jeanne would have been assaulted by a reeking stench, a slavering muzzle, and bestial eyes reflecting red in the last light of day. Snapping, the Beast sought the girl's throat.

It locked its jaws under her chin and shook, threshing her neck.

As if from far away, Jeanne may have been aware of her own blood ebbing away over her garments and the tang of copper mixed with the smell of heather, and the stink of the Beast.

Her staff slipped from her hand.

The creature clawed, shredding her simple frock, and fed greedily, carnassial teeth gutting her torso, mincing flesh and organs.

A tawny owl, *Strix aluco*, hunting mice nearby, called softly.

There was shouting from below. Men's voices. The Beast flattened its ears and bared its teeth. Snarling, it bit at Jeanne's shoulder, separating flesh from bone. It tore away a part of her and dragged its prize into the wood.

***

The sounds of screams and bleating had echoed down the mountainside, imaginably alerting the people of Les Hubacs that something was very wrong.

And so they'd come looking. In semidarkness and evening chill, they may have nearly stumbled over Jeanne's remains in the blood-smeared grass.

The horrified searchers would have gazed apprehensively into the now lightless forest beyond.

***

Little did anyone know that Jeanne Boulet's death, and those of approximately one hundred other victims over the next three years, would set in motion the mystery of a man-eating monster that would electrify all of France, from the Vivarais to Versailles.

CHAPTER 2

The Gévaudan

On that last day of June 1764, Jeanne Boulet's killer stole from the shepherdess not only her life in this world, but the blessings that would prepare her for the next. She was interred on the first of July, according to the official record documented by her *curé* or priest, Father Soucher, "without sacraments, having been killed by the ferocious beast."

Because of her sudden and violent end, she could not receive the traditional Catholic last rites, the sacraments administered to those who are seriously ill and presumed near death. These included a final confession of sins, receiving of communion, and anointing with blessed oil, or extreme unction.

Historians hold that the words "the ferocious beast" in Father Soucher's record suggest that the community was already acquainted with the brute that killed Jeanne, and that she was likely not its first victim.

As the story goes, more than two months before—about the time King Louis XV's mistress Madame de Pompadour passed away—a terrified young woman had returned home from attending her cattle to declare she'd had a hairbreadth escape from a "beast" that ignored the bovines in favor of her. Fortunately, the cattle had come to the damsel's aid—cattle were known to aggressively defend their caregivers, along with their own offspring, from danger. Still, the girl's clothes were in tatters and she was badly frightened.

She claimed the creature was "like a wolf, yet not a wolf."

This young woman was from Langogne, France, in the Gévaudan.

***

Missing from contemporary maps, and unknown to most eighteenth-century inhabitants of France, the Gévaudan is today asso-

Cattle grazing in the present-day region of old Gévaudan. *Photo Schwalb.*

ciated with the *département*, or administrative district, of Lozère, created at the time of the French Revolution. Something of the ancient Gévaudan subsists, however, in the mists of the undulating hills of Languedoc and Auvergne, among the Margeride mountains, and in the Cévennes range made famous by Scottish writer Robert Louis Stevenson. The Cévennes make up the southeastern rim of the enormous Massif Central, or central mountain mass, which is the source of several major rivers, including the Loire, the longest river in France.

These highlands feature a climate in keeping with the challenging terrain. At least one travel source has referred to the region as "The Scotland of France." Summers, especially in lower, Mediterranean-oriented valleys, are sunny, hot, and dry. But the Massif Central has a subalpine climate. Winters are long and harsh, with some of the snowiest conditions in the country. Daytime temperatures average minus six degrees Celsius, about twenty-one degrees Fahrenheit. *Sibères* or *burles* (biting winds) cause snowdrifts to accumulate at alarming rates.

Fir and beech trees clothe the mountain slopes. Chestnut trees have been cultivated for centuries. Peat bogs and moors provide additional habitats for flora and fauna. Plant life ranges from myriad varieties of wild orchids to the carnivorous sundew. Griffon vultures, recently reintroduced, circle the skies as they would have hundreds of years ago.

At the time of the Beast, the world was also in the grip of an exceptionally cold period, a little ice age that began in the 1500s. In addition, the plague struck here in 1720; well over two thousand people died in the Gévaudan capital of Mende and the nearby town of Marvejols. Poor harvests and subsequent famines affected the area from 1748 to 1750. According to seminal Beast chronicler Abbé Pierre Pourcher, writing almost a century and a half later, "The famine was so terrible that tales of the suffering are still recounted."

***

In antiquity, the Gévaudan was home to the Gabali, a tribe of the Celts, or Gauls, as their Roman conquerors deemed them. And the landscape is dotted with reminders of even more ancient predecessors: monuments known as *menhirs* (from the French; *men*, stone plus *hir*, long)—tall upright stones, erected alone as monoliths, or in groups, and dolmens—structures of upright stones capped by large flat stones; these are considered tombs. The menhirs were traditionally associated by locals with giants, the devil, fairies, and fertility gods into the Age of Enlightenment and beyond.

A pastoral people, the Gévaudanais were known for a long tradition of cloth making, especially for their serges, woolen fabrics. In the late 1700s, about three-quarters of local families kept flocks of sheep, along with goats and cattle. Locals' homes, humble *oustas*, held few furnishings.

***

In the twentieth century, this rugged world was the ideal base for the World War II guerrilla Resistance movement, the Maquis (referring to the *maquis*, the thickets or underbrush in which the Nazi fighters thrived):

> The narrow, winding gorges and the caverns of the limestone *causses* [limestone plateaus] of Quercy provided a labyrinth in which the hunted might hide. So, to the east, did the deep chestnut forests of the Ségala; the granite mountains of the Margeride in Auvergne, reforested with pine, spruce, and fir; the high desert of the Cévennes; the fastnesses of the Alps. Everywhere, there were potential lookout points on the high hills and dispersed hamlets and abandoned farms for shelter.

In June 1944, several thousand Maquis were able to hold back more than twenty thousand Nazi soldiers during a German drive to Normandy in the rugged area of Mont Mouchet. Today, there is a museum on the mountain which commemorates the remarkable achievements of the F.F.I. (*Forces Françaises de l'Interieur*).

More than two centuries earlier, the area served as a refuge for Protestants rebelling against King Louis XIV's revocation of the Edict of Nantes and reinstatement of Catholic control. King Henry IV of France had issued the Edict of Nantes in 1598 granting Protestant Huguenots—followers of Martin Luther and John Calvin—religious and political freedom following decades of persecution. Thousands of Camisards (referring to the Protestants' *camisos*, everyday shirts; they had no uniforms) were killed in the early 1700s.

***

Robert Louis Stevenson, the author of *Treasure Island*, *Kidnapped*, and *The Strange Case of Dr. Jekyll and Mr. Hyde*, came this way more than one hundred years after the time of the Beast in search of the homeland of Protestant heroes.

His sojourn through the countryside with four-footed companion Modestine became the basis for his *Travels with a Donkey in the Cévennes* (1879), from which comes his well-known quotation, "For my part, I travel not to go anywhere, but to go. The great affair is to move . . ."

Stevenson's journey is also the foundation for the modern footpath known as the GR70. GRs, *Grandes Randonnées*, are marked walking and hiking routes that trace timeworn roads and shepherds' paths.

The writer's account speaks of the "bleak fields" of Gévaudan and its "roaring blackness" at night, in which the author says, "I was sure of nothing but the direction of the wind."

Stevenson, who'd recently finished reading a novel about the Beast of the Gévaudan, writes of the creature,

> Wolves, alas, like bandits, seem to flee the traveler's advance; and you may trudge through all our comfortable Europe, and not meet with an adventure worth the name. But here, if anywhere, a man was on the frontiers of hope. For this was the land of the ever-memorable BEAST, the Napoleon Bonaparte of wolves. What a career was his! He lived ten months at free quarters in Gévaudan and Vivarais; he ate women and children and 'shepherdesses celebrated for their beauty'; he pursued armed horsemen; he has been seen at broad noonday chasing a post-chaise and outrider along the king's high-road, and chaise and outrider fleeing before him at the gallop. He was placarded like a political offender, and ten thousand francs were offered for his head. . . .

Stevenson traveled the Gévaudan in September of 1878.

A little over one hundred and a dozen years earlier, in August 1764, the Beast's second official victim would die.

CHAPTER 3

Lafont

August 1764

The summer of 1764 in south-central France advanced through July and into August, hastening toward its conclusion. The countryfolk continued with the farming and trade activities vital to their existence, most largely unaware of the Beast or its predations, owing to the region's sparse population residing in individual, isolated communities.

During the first week of August 1764, a little more than six miles from the site of Jeanne's death, but in the Gévaudan proper, a girl named Marianne Hébrard, from a tiny community called Cellier, went missing, but not as Jeanne had, at the close of day.

Marianne vanished in broad daylight.

Like Jeanne, however, Marianne was found "throttled and half-eaten." Searches were said to have turned up scattered remains and remnants of cloth. Official chronicles state that she was set upon by a roving beast that had recently encroached upon the area.

Forty-eight hours later, in another rural village named Masméjan, the Beast came out of nowhere to stalk, surprise, and savage another girl, her name unknown to historians. She was fifteen years old.

On August 30, two months after Jeanne Boulet's demise, a sunburned youth near Les Pradels, France, was keeping one eye on the family cattle as they grazed in the heat, snorting and swishing their tails, and the other eye trained on an insect struggling in the tentacles of a flesh-eating sundew plant.

The quiet landscape was shattered by another Beast attack. The boy was bushwhacked. The cattle's bellowing brought rescuers too late.

With the end of August and the arrival of September came sporadic violent storms, *épisodes cévenols*, the result of cold winds from the Atlantic Ocean in the west colliding with those of the warm Mediterranean to the southeast, causing alarming formations of clouds in the sky, torrential rain, and flooding.

There were also more deaths.

September 1764

Forty-five-year-old Étienne (Stephen) Lafont, knife in hand, reached for a goosefeather quill and began to trim it thoughtfully.

Lafont's office in Mende, France, was small but orderly. Tidy stacks of correspondence lay alongside maps, agricultural samples of grains and chestnuts, an inkwell, sealing wax, writing paper, and quills—he preferred quills made from shorter goosefeathers, with which he could write faster, as opposed to traditional quills from longer-length feathers. Bundles of letters, along with a coat and three-pointed hat, hung from pegs on the wall above a bookcase filled with leather-bound reference works.

Lafont was disturbed by the reports he'd been receiving of an animal which had attacked and killed several children in the Vivarais and the Gévaudan. The accounts did not ring true. It sounded as if the animal were something other than a nuisance wolf or pack of wolves. He knew of other instances where wolves had attacked people, but generally it was because they were rabid or famished from lack of prey during the region's harsh winters.

A former attorney who had practiced law in the Parliament of Toulouse in southern France, Lafont was a native of the Gévaudan; he'd grown up in Chirac, near Marvejols, with his brothers Jacques and Trophime.

Lafont put his quill knife away. Now, as a regional administrator with fifteen years in as trustee of the Gévaudan diocese, he was no stranger to the kind of persistent predators that made off with valuable livestock, affecting the local economy and its farmers' already tenuous livelihoods.

Lafont also served as a subdelegate to the intendant or supervisor of the province of Languedoc, Saint-Priest (full name: Marie-Joseph de Guignard de Saint-Priest), who was based in Montpellier, France, a city to the southeast, on the Mediterranean Sea.

Subdelegates were representatives of Louis XV himself on a local level, charged with disseminating state information. Their responsibilities also included monitoring of and reporting on issues and activities in their jurisdictions, including construction projects, agricultural practices, and homeland security. They spent much of their time on the road. Lafont also attended the annual meeting of the Estates of the Gévaudan, in which the landholders of the diocese conferred with their bishop in Mende.

When not traveling, subdelegates concerned themselves with the never-ending paperwork that came with their positions, writing letters, reports, and preparing accountings.

According to historian Jean-Marc Moriceau, a subdelegate received little rest. The better ones, like Lafont, were "selfless."

***

As trustee of the Gévaudan, Lafont reported to the bishop of Mende, Gabriel Florent de Choiseul Beaupré, now well into his seventies. A member of a well-connected French family, His Excellency was the cousin of King Louis XV's secretary of foreign affairs, Étienne François, Duc (duke) de Choiseul (whose implementations included the arrangement of the marriage of Marie-Antoinette of Austria to Louis-Auguste, grandson of King Louis XV). According to an unusual agreement called a *paréage*, put in place four and a half centuries earlier, the bishop of Mende was also Count of the Gévaudan, and co-ruled the diocese with the king of France.

Lafont was concerned. When Bishop de Choiseul Beaupré was informed of the man-eating beast now at large in his diocese, he stated that he believed its sudden appearance was "auspicious." Lafont responded with his usual tact. But he told the cleric he disagreed. The trustee's contention was that the creature was not a sign from God, but an aberrant animal with a taste for human flesh.

The bishop smiled.

"No, no, Lafont," said His Excellency. "Look at the signs. The Seven Years' War. Livestock succumbing to outbreaks of disease. Unfortunate meteorological events." He smoothed his robes with blue-veined hands. "This beast is yet another scourge. A reminder that we must heed the Commandments."

The bishop locked eyes with Lafont.

"It is an agent of divine wrath."

***

The majority of people within the universe of the Beast were Catholic, although, as mentioned earlier, the rugged countryside had long provided a haven for oppressed Protestants.

Villagers' lives revolved around the local church and parish priest. A parish is a district of the Roman Catholic Church under the charge of a local priest. Each parish was part of a larger diocese, overseen by a bishop. Dioceses were, in turn, divisions of provinces in France.

In the Gévaudan, the Catholic sacrament of penance or confession—disclosing to one's priest the sins one has committed to receive absolution and permit reconciliation with God—allowed the parish *curé* to conduct "ecclesiastical surveillance," with accounts of the most serious transgressions disclosed not to the local constabulary but to the seat of the diocese in the city of Mende.

Small but robust, the metropolis of Mende, situated on the river Lot, is dominated by its Nôtre Dame Cathedral, begun by Pope Urban V (1310–1370), a son of the Gévaudan. The cathedral was once home to *Non Pareille* (No Other), the largest church bell in the world. Its twenty tons were melted and made into cannons by Huguenots, French Protestants, in 1579.

***

His quill trimmed, Lafont selected a sheet of thick rag paper made by the craftsmen at the renowned paper mill in Auvergne.

Despite the isolation of the individual communities within his care, word of this *bête féroce* (ferocious beast) was surely spreading. People exchanged news after mass, and at markets and fairs. Muleteers leading pack mules, which were often bedecked with bells and pom-poms, transported foodstuffs such as beans, barley, bacon, and cheeses, as well as cloth and wineskins, throughout the region.

Surely they were recounting tales of the Beast at stops along the way. Printers and peddlers, sensing opportunity, would likely begin selling exaggerated likenesses of the creature to gullible peasants.

Lafont rubbed his brow.

Making the populace aware of the animal was positive; more would know to look out for it, and children might be protected.

On the other hand, stories of the Beast's atrocities would likely cause panic. Lafont could envision a disastrous abandonment of key enterprises requisite to the economy.

And it was September, time for harvest in the Gévaudan.

The Gévaudan.

The district for which he was accountable. To Bishop de Choiseul Beaupré. To intendant Saint-Priest. To King Louis XV himself.

Lafont reached for his inkwell.

The Beast must be destroyed. Immediately.

Quill in hand, Stephen Lafont commenced a retaliatory campaign.

CHAPTER 4

Count Morangiès

Lafont began by prevailing upon one of the area's most influential, yet troubled, families: that of the House Morangiès.

Pierre Charles de Molette, Marquis de Morangiès, and his son, Jean-François Charles de la Molette, *comte de* (count), were VIPS. Both had both served in the Seven Years' War (also known as the French and Indian War), but the marquis, a lieutenant general, had, with other leaders, brought dishonor upon France in the August 1, 1759, Battle of Minden, Prussia (in what is today Germany). In that conflict, seven thousand French troops had perished at the hands of Hanoverian and British opposition. At the direction of the court, the marquis retired to his estate in Saint-Alban, France, in the Gévaudan. Despite the disastrous outcome of his military career, the Morangiès family remained among the area's most powerful. Sixty-three years old in 1764, the marquis was known to be an aloof member of society.

His son, the count, now thirty-six, had joined the military early on, becoming a musketeer as a teenager. He had performed well in the War of the Austrian Succession (1741–1748), the conflict in which Maria Theresa of Austria (mother of Marie Antoinette), clashed with several rivals for the claim of the title of her late father, Emperor Charles VI.

In the Seven Years' War, as colonel of the infantry regiment from Languedoc led by Marshal Duke of Richelieu (friend of Louis XV, son of the famous Cardinal de Richelieu's great-nephew, and said to be the inspiration for the character Valmont in *Dangerous Liaisons* by Pierre Choderlos de Laclos), they took over the island of Minorca from the British, and Morangiès became governor of the island for a time. He became a brigadier in 1761, *marechal de camp* (field marshal) in 1762, and was eventually honored as a knight of the Royal and Military Order of Saint Louis.

In 1764, the count had been a widower for eleven years. His wife, daughter of a duke, had passed away just three years after they'd married in 1753, leaving him two sons. Though an enthusiastic hunter at the time of the Beast, the count was dealing with enormous debt and the wrath of his brothers for consuming the family fortune for his military expenses. (Military commands in France were almost exclusively purchased and sold among those members of the nobility which could afford them.)

After initial correspondence, Lafont visited the Morangiès estate in Saint-Alban.

The older marquis was napping by the fire. The count was sprawled in a large oak chair, his boys, nine and ten, in his arms on either side, their eyes wide with the subdelegate's accounts of the Beast and its horrors.

"Of course I will assist you, Lafont!" said the count, his eyes as wide as those of his sons. "When do we start?"

The boys exchanged glances.

"May we help?"

"*Non*, you stay with grandpapa."

Their faces fell.

"You must help him watch our home. Father, you will supervise?"

"Come on, Grandpapa!"

The marquis grunted, getting to his feet, a flicker of amusement in his eyes. "We might surprise you all if the Beast comes here," he said. "Fetch your sabers, young ones. And let me tell you a story about my first battle." The boys leapt to their grandfather's bidding.

As the marquis indulged his grandsons in an impromptu fencing lesson, Lafont and Morangiès made plans to enlist locals—both peasants and other noblemen—and begin initial hunts immediately, hoping to make short work of the crisis.

The Beast, meanwhile, emboldened by the helplessness and availability of its human prey, continued its offensive upon the people of the Gévaudan.

***

There are what may be considered a surprising number of records and documents related to the events in the Gévaudan from

1764 to June of 1767. Yet, despite the records that have survived, details of the deaths of some youngsters who may have perished in attacks by the Beast may not have been included in parish registers because they had not yet received their First Communion, the sacrament of the Eucharist in which the body and blood of Jesus are received as consecrated bread and wine.

But not all the victims were children.

The sleepy *hameau* (hamlet) of Les Estrets, France, is a stop along the Way of Saint James, the medieval pilgrimage route to the tomb of the brother of Jesus, in Compostela, Spain. Les Estrets, meaning "the straits," with its quaint bridge on the river Truyère, was a place where the priestly brotherhood of St. John approved the comings and going of travelers.

At about seven o'clock on the evening of September 6, the peace of the evening was overcome by a commotion in a local *potager*, or kitchen garden.

A French village garden might contain vegetables such as turnips, herbs for seasoning and for teas and remedies, and hemp, of the nettle family; from which rough cloth could be woven. Flax provided seeds for linseed oil and its fibers could be spun into linen thread. Fodder crops for animals. And, in some regions, a prize type of lentils, considered "poor man's caviar."

Known as the local witch—not non-Christian, but an herbalist and healer—a thirty-six-year-old woman had been harvesting rosemary to brew a tonic for her neighbor, a shy fellow who had a range of complaints; this time headaches and a too-fast heartbeat. It might help his thinning hair as well, she thought. Bent down, she collected leaves and flowering tops energetically, as the sun would soon be behind the mountains. *I should have picked them this morning*, she chastened herself, *after the dew had gone*. She would make a tea and was certain her neighbor would feel better in a day or two.

She stopped.

Someone or something was behind her.

But she felt she could not turn around.

The devil was surely near.

She began to shake. She could not cry out—fear had seized her vocal cords. The fingers of her right hand flew to her forehead, down to her heart, to her left shoulder. *In the name of the Father, and of the Son, and of the Holy . . .*

She was unable to finish the sign of the cross.

***

And so, unlike the Beast's younger victims, the thirty-six-year-old woman from Les Estrets did not meet her end in a remote pasture or far-flung meadow.

She was consumed in her own garden.

***

Ten days later, on September 16, a boy named Claude Maurines, twelve, took his family's cattle to graze in the vicinity of the village of Choisinets, part of the town of Saint-Flour-de-Mercoire, founded long before by a Cistercian order of nuns. The nunnery was located within the dense Forest of Mercoire, over twenty-seven thousand acres in size even today.

Claude knew of the Beast.

He'd heard its presence announced at Sunday mass.

In Old France, it was the parish priest's responsibility to share not only the Good News of the sacred, but news of the profane as well. On a recent Sunday in their modest church, peasants huddled in the somber chill of the stone-walled interior, their breath steaming, along with that of their dogs at their feet, the canines' claws scrabbling the slab floor.

The local curé warned his flock that a fierce animal, still at large, had attacked and killed people in the vicinity.

Continued the priest, "Subdelegate Lafont advises parents to keep young herders at home."

Stay at home? Claude was dumbfounded.

He turned to his parents. His mother put an arm around him; Claude, embarrassed, pushed her away.

Claude's father spat on the floor, narrowly missing their shaggy herding dog, Ruffe; the animal lifted an eyebrow, sighed, and rolled away.

Claude's father said, and not under his breath, "What does this curé want to do, vex us more than we are already vexed?"

It was still acceptable at that time to comment on a priest's messages during the service.

The priest, unflinching, went on. "Lafont is organizing hunts with Count Morangiès. Parishioners are expected to participate. We await their direction."

The men groaned.

"They mean to take us away from harvest?" demanded one.

The curé said, "There is talk of generous premiums to be paid for the creature's destruction, more than those usually paid for wolves."

A wolf carcass currently fetched six *livres*, or pounds, French units of currency at the time. A *livre* was said to contain about four and one half grams of silver.

The groaning stopped. "More?" voices asked in unison.

"And it may be that this animal *is* just a wolf or wolves," said the priest.

The male constituents of his flock regarded one another thoughtfully.

After the service, Claude's father told his son not to worry.

"I'm not," said Claude, one hand on Ruffe's head. "And I am not staying home. I can take care of myself and the cattle. Perhaps *I* shall claim the reward."

But Claude's mother was worried.

"This beast," she whispered to her husband later, as if she was almost afraid to speak her thoughts. "Could it be the one he has dreamed about since he was very small?"

Claude's father was silent.

That night, the boy carefully sharpened an old knife he'd inherited from his grandfather and tied it tight to the branch he used to guide his farmstock.

The next day, Claude, accompanied by Ruffe, took the cattle to their grazing area and stood watch.

Clouds, gray and black, churned above. The chilling wet of an autumn cloudburst drove Claude and his animals to take shelter beneath the trees, branches raining red and orange leaves upon them in bursts of wind.

***

Naturalists out of necessity, the young herders who spent much of their time outside were considered to be magical personages, "able to 'read' the 'book' of nature." It's easy to see why: Day after day, year after year, as they took their charges to the same heaths and meadows, they grew to know the ways of their world, to the families of wild creatures with which they co-existed to the individual rocks along the paths they traveled. Herders might sigh at midsummer, knowing the world was now back on the path toward winter and months of entrapment indoors. In autumn, as light decreased, they could predict when certain trees would begin to drop their leaves. They studied the skies, the phases of the moon, and marveled at shooting stars and other phenomena. Once Claude observed an entire hill illuminated with the greenish light of glowworms (which would be termed *Lampyris noctiluca*—"shining ones" and "night light"—by Swedish scientist Carl Linnaeus in three years). Once he watched a strange round white cloud float southward and suddenly fly apart, pelting stones as it vanished.

***

As the storm weakened, and slowing rain trickled through the trees and down Claude's back, the late afternoon sun emerged.

So did the Beast.

Its eyes blazed white, mirroring the last thunderbolt. It curled its lips and bared its teeth.

Ruffe barked furiously.

Claude, disbelieving, stared.

The stories were true!

His breath seemed to stop even as his heart accelerated to a gallop.

I know you.

You're in my dreams.

In my nightmares.

And here it was.

In reality.

He clamped his hands around his branch.

***

Claude was said to be small for his age. But he was a scrapper.

He'd bested bigger boys who taunted him at the weekly meetings after mass, and even started joining in the brutal fracases in which his *commune* (district) fought for honor over others.

He swallowed, straightened, and looked the Beast in the eye. If it was some sort of a wolf, Claude knew, you could sometimes face them down. They'd sit, do a turnabout, and leave, not really wanting much to do with people anyway. It was the livestock they were after.

As if on cue, a cow lowed in warning. Claude turned, seeking her calf.

It was his fatal mistake.

Muscle in motion, the Beast came on full bore, leaping for the youth's neck.

Claude leaned back, grunting, lashing out with his homemade pike. The Beast snapped the branch in two.

Ruffe charged, sinking his teeth into the Beast's side. The monster snarled. Claude watched in amazement as it twisted around in a way no wolf could and seized the herd dog by the scruff of the neck, slamming him into a large rock.

Ruffe yelped. Once.

"No!" Claude howled. He grabbed the knife end of his broken pike and shoved it into the Beast's flank.

Agitated, the cattle began to move toward the predator, bellowing and tossing their heads.

The Beast wheeled and charged the boy again, knocking him off balance. Claude fell. Before he could move again, the Beast wrapped its jaws around his neck, making guttural sounds. Claude croaked weakly and closed his eyes in agony.

The cattle were surrounding their guardian and his attacker, but they had not moved fast enough.

The Beast dragged its prey to the forest undergrowth where the bovines could not follow.

Later, Claude's people found his cadaver, torn limb from limb.

Dutifully, the priest recorded Claude's death and saw to the burial of his remains. The authorities pronounced this death, like the Beast's other fatalities, as *"non naturelle."*

At the next mass, the curé offered his condolences to the family and the community. Claude's mother wept. Claude's father, one hand on the empty space between them, the other on his knee, above Ruffe's place at his feet, spat.

CHAPTER 5

Le Petit Versailles du Gévaudan

Subdelegate Lafont now hunted the Beast himself while making his rounds, a heavy flintlock pistol holstered on his saddle. He also rode alongside Count Morangiès, who, despite his best intentions toward their quest, was distracted by his debts, his family, and his affairs in Versailles and Paris.

***

On September 20, a wolf of respectable size was destroyed by locals in the vicinity of Pradels, France. A reward of eighteen *livres* (pounds) was paid.

Lafont, and the locals who had destroyed it and hoped for a reward, marked time, as they waited to learn whether or not it was "the one who ate people." If the attacks ceased, it could be deduced that the killer had been caught.

It had not.

On the afternoon of September 29, 1764, Magdeleine Mauras, of the parish of Rocles, France, went to check on family cattle in their pasture.

A cheerful girl, Magdeleine, like Claude, was tough. Her father had passed away early, and at twelve, she found herself a working girl, fortunate to be employed by her uncle.

Magdeleine, in the manner of most peasants, believed a difficult life was all there was. The backbreaking labors required of her family were normal. She knew that sometimes boys got to go to school. But not girls. And not anyone in her immediate family. Her father, before he died violently at the hands of a beggar, signed his name when he had to with the symbol of a pitchfork.

Magdeleine's uncle, however, had learned to read and write. She hoped to learn something from him.

She never got the chance.

At about four-thirty that afternoon, when she went to check on his cattle, she was set upon, slain, and dismembered, her lungs and heart ripped from her chest, an arm torn away.

When he heard the news, Lafont's jaw tensed. He said nothing, but moved a hand across his desk for a quill and his knife. He would once more have to document for his superiors the loss of another young victim.

***

October 1764

It was becoming colder in the Gévaudan.

In October, there were about a dozen attacks—an average of four per week—and five deaths—more than one per week.

And this month would witness a new and more macabre development.

In consequence of laws put in place centuries earlier, nobles alone could possess and use firearms, but Lafont pushed for, and won, temporary legalization to bear arms in Langogne for the purpose of hunting the Beast.

The subdelegate also made arrangements for a fantastic reward—two hundred *livres*, equal to "a year's salary for a day laborer!"

In the Vivarais, Lafont's peer, a man named Lachadenède, was able to get permission for those of the town of Pradelles to carry weapons as well.

Hunts continued, but even with the enthusiasm that hefty rewards could muster, the wolf-stalks competed with the requirements of daily life, occurring intermittently at best. They would prove fruitless.

The Beast, meanwhile, wearying of unwanted attention, was on the move in search of a new lair. The afforested areas to the west/northwest, near Count Morangiès' own Saint-Alban, as well as Le Malzieu and Saint-Chely-de-Apcher, France, were promising.

The unflagging Lafont coordinated operations with his superior, Saint-Priest, and the hunters proceeded to Marvejols on October 5. Soon after, the Beast was seen ogling a young herder, but the peasant was protected from harm by his defiant bovines.

Two days later, however, the body of a young woman, twenty, was discovered near Prunières, France.

The following day, her head was found.

***

Could an animal cause a human decapitation? Yes. Experts tell us that large predators' teeth could destroy the fragile cervical articulation with which the head is attached to the body. The viciousness of the attacks, combined with the predator's hurried transport of the remains to a secluded location in which to consume their prey in peace might result in the dislodging of the head from the torso.

There is a contemporary documented case of a self-decapitation as a result of a suicidal hanging from a bridge. The head was separated from the body; both were located forty-eight hours later and identified.

***

On October 8, a twelve-year-old boy named Jean Rieutort was savaged, but survived. Rieutort lived on to age seventy-six, becoming a priest, his scars telling the story of his harrowing encounter with the Beast.

***

Later that day, an animal was discovered near a venerable estate, that of Château de la Baume.

With portions of its structure dating to the early 1600s, situated at an altitude of twelve hundred meters (nearly four thousand feet), Château de la Baume was originally the castle home of the barony of Peyre, the Gévaudan's most entitled, going back to the twelfth century. Constructed of granite and flagstone, the castle's substantial size—it is among the tallest in France—lent it the nickname, *"le petit Versailles du Gévaudan."*

Today this private home is a tourist attraction, a film set, and a location for weddings, Moët et Chandon Ferrari rallies, and other gatherings.

In late 1764, it was Beast Central.

On October 8, 1764, hours after mauling Jean Rieutort, the Beast was observed on the grounds of Château de la Baume, eyeing another young herdsman. Hunters trailed the animal into the estate's woods. Forced from its cover by dozens of "beaters"—peasant assistants tasked with beating through the brushwood with various implements, shouting, making noise, and in general creating an uproar to drive terrified game out into the open.

It worked.

The Beast was spotted and had at last become prey itself.

And so its hunters took aim, fired, and—hit their target. But to their astonishment, the animal fell, only to rise and run on. Another shot, and again success. The creature dropped. But through the thick white smoke of gunpowder, they witnessed the same phenomenon: the Beast scrambled to its feet and took off. The hunters pursued it until nightfall, anxious to finish off the wounded animal, and resumed the next morning, pre-dawn. Two hundred men scoured the woods of Château de la Baume, hoping to find a deceased Beast. It was not to be. Hours later, the creature, traveling with a limp, was observed by witnesses prior to attacking another herd boy of twelve years of age.

On October 10, a youth near Les Cayres, or Caires, was injured by the Beast. At dusk on that same day, the Beast ambushed three siblings, a boy of twelve, a boy of six, and a girl of about ten years of age. It seized the terrified girl and started to make off with her, when she was torn from its jaws by her brothers, who, Lafont reported to the governor, "pricked" La Bête, each armed with "a stick to which they had attached a knife."

A woman was killed on October 11, and a second decapitation occurred on October 15.

Chronicler Pourcher relates that during October 1764, his own great-grandfather, Jean Pierre Pourcher, was working alone in a barn near Julianges, France, shortly before nightfall, when he looked out a window and was struck with "a sort of fear" as "an animal arrived of a type he did not know." He grabbed his gun and fired. The creature fell, but got to its feet. Jean Pierre fired again, and the animal fell once more. But it got up for the second time, and, after "a wild cry," departed, "making a noise similar to that of someone who parts from another after a quarrel."

***

The animal was rapidly bringing local commerce to a halt. Peasants and tradespeople were afraid to venture out to their fields or go to market. A priest of Aumont named Trocelier reported, "There are those who have lost their minds and others who will have a lot of difficulty in ever getting up again." Pourcher comments, "In the face of such calamities the spread of terror was also added to [La Bête's] list of crimes."

An account of the Beast's predations published late in 1764 advised "fervent prayers" and "sincere conversion," "while waiting for some hero to present himself who will undertake to fight against such a monster . . ."

***

In his *History of the English-Speaking Peoples,* Winston Churchill labeled the Seven Years' War as "The First World War." A struggle for supremacy between the two most powerful countries in the world—France and Britain—the conflict involved Europe, North America, the Caribbean, Africa, and India.

Just prior to the time of the Beast, the conflict (1756–1763), also known as the French and Indian War, had proved disastrous for France financially and in regards to global influence. When it began, France was Europe's mightiest power. By war's end, Great Britain had become the predominant colonial empire of the world.

In the 1763 Treaty of Paris, a peace agreement under the management of Étienne François, Duc de Choiseul, secretary of state of foreign affairs (and cousin of the Bishop of Mende) of France, ceded immense holdings to Britain: Canada, the Great Lakes, Ohio, and Louisiana east of Mississippi. The rest of Louisiana went to Spain. France also lost Senegal in West Africa and some trade operations in India. It retained very little: fishing rights off Newfoundland (the Saint-Pierre and Miquelon islands remain a French territory today);

the island of Gorée, off Senegal; and the sugar- and coffee-producing Caribbean islands of Saint-Domingue, Guadeloupe, and Martinique.

In short, in post-war 1764, France was in the midst of a "hangover," according to historian Jay M. Smith.

As mentioned earlier, the Morangiès, father and son, were veterans of this conflict.

So was the first officially sanctioned Beast hunter—Captain Jean-Baptiste Duhamel.

***

A warrant officer and sergeant major, Jean-Baptiste Boulanger, Monsieur Duhamel, thirty-two years old, was eager, after sharing in the collective humbling of the French armed forces, to set something right. Specially requesting the mission to destroy the man-eater, Duhamel was convinced that, at this moment, his rightful place in the universe was that of champion-to-be of the ravaged Gévaudan.

Lafont had communicated information about the marauding animal to Count Moncan (Jean-Baptiste Marin, comte de Moncan), commander of military forces in the Languedoc, and also to the Marquis Saint-Florentin (Louis Phélypeaux, Marquis de Saint-Florentin), the French minister of state.

Moncan directed that more than fifty dragoons (in French, *dragons*, musket-armed soldiers on horseback and on foot) be sent to the area, captained by Duhamel. Authorities in the Vivarais, the Gévaudan, Velay (now part of the Haute-Loire department), and the Cévennes were to assist Mr. Duhamel "in achieving the destruction of the monster or leopard prowling for some time in the mountains of Vivarais and Gévaudan, and that almost always holds in the woods of Choisinèts."

The captain and his dragoons arrived in Saint-Chely-de-Apcher on October 15.

His cavalry unit, called the Clermont-Prince Volunteers, was an unusual one, not of King Louis XV, but a unit of princely light troops, the *dragons des troupes légères*, that had originated in Liège, Belgium, in 1758. Almost all were Germans. (About a quarter of the French army was actually made up of troops from other countries: Switzerland, Germany, Italy, Ireland, and Hungary among them. This was a result of recruiting difficulties, desertion, homesickness, and other issues.)

Duhamel was French, but their own versions of the *langue d'oc*, dialects spoken in southern France, from which comes the region's name: Languedoc.

Smartly outfitted in coats, vests, ties, gloves, boots, and helmets fringed with short horsehair "manes," these light troops likely carried sabers deemed "Hungarian," made by gunsmith Jean Knetch in Solingen, Germany, with curved blades measuring up to thirty-five inches in length. Some may have also carried a more basic 1750 standard-issue saber.

They were also equipped with .66-caliber flintlock pistols, with barrel lengths of about twelve inches, weighing about two and three-quarter pounds each. Brass embellishments on the pistols' grips allowed them to be used as clubs in close-quarter combat.

Most carried .61-caliber flintlock rifles, accurate within the length of an American football field. But Duhamel carried a more powerful, more accurate shotgun, which he claimed to load with three bullets; Researcher Phil Barnson wonders: Did the captain believe that so armed, he could better pierce the Beast's seemingly impermeable hide?

Early winter weather conditions prevented Duhamel from reaching the area immediately. He arrived in Langogne on October 31.

The peasants were hopeful the dragoons would put an end to their woes, but were unsure about having troops in their midst. Men and mounts would need food and shelter. Conflicts would arise over all of these necessities. Also, the term dragoons was still equated with the *dragonnades*, persecutions ordered by Louis XIV in the early 1700s in which military "missionaries" were billeted with Protestant families to convert them to Catholicism.

On October 22, a young herdswoman was slaughtered and decapitated in Grazières, in the parish of Saint-Alban. On that same day, minister of state Saint-Florentin, coordinating communications regarding the emergency in the Gévaudan, responded to letters from Lafont.

"There is no longer any doubt about this misfortune," Saint-Florentin wrote. "I have approved in general, Sir, the precaution which has been taken by multiplying the number of hunters in the woods and in the districts where the ferocious beasts have appeared. I don't think that there is only one beast and I suppose that they will soon be successfully destroyed by the means of the orders which the Count of Moncan has given to the hunters . . ." He cautioned against the use of *nux vomica* (the plant source of the deadly chemical strychnine) as the poison could kill other animals and cause disease. "The most common opinion," he states, "is that the ferocious beasts are either lynxes or wolves that have become man-eaters." The minister, like the king, was an avid hunter; however, he'd lost his left hand as a result of a hunting accident.

***

Count Morangiès led a series of hunts throughout October 1764, comprised of local nobles and *paysans* (peasants). In a letter to Lafont dated October 26, he comments on their lack of firearms: "Unfortunately there are very few guns in the parish of Saint-Alban or, at least, if there are, those who have them do not wish them to be seen." The hunter-peasants without guns felt so exposed, the count continued, that when they saw the Beast, one could not know if their descriptions of it "are true or crazy." Morangiès reluctantly advised that if the Beast killed again, the victim's corpse must be left where it was, as the creature returned to its kills. He suggested that troops were needed, "two hundred men," and that they would require a month to destroy it. He concluded: "If this animal was born in Africa, as has been presumed, . . . it will suffer . . . during the dead of winter." He stated that the harsh conditions might kill it, but they "could make it more wild."

After another disappointing wolf-stalk on Sunday, October 28, 1764, the count wrote, "Today's hunt, . . . has not had, Monsieur Lafont, all the effect I would have wished." A follow-up hunt for Wednesday, October 31—the day Captain Duhamel arrived—was canceled "because of the great quantities of snow."

Some of these first offensives included professional shepherds who accompanied vast herds of sheep during the traditional spring and fall movement of livestock between the Mediterranean and the mountains; they were accompanied by powerful *chiens de parc* (dogs of the sheepfold), mastiffs in studded collars, which protected the canines' necks from wolves' jaws.

CHAPTER 6

"Ferocious with Design"

November 1764

A total of nearly fifty official hunts would ensue from November 15, 1764. The first of these were made up of Duhamel, the dragoon unit, Morangiès, nobles, the peasantry, and fortune-hunting outsiders.

France's controller general Laverdy recommended that peasants assist on Sundays and holidays. Traditionally days set aside for worship, rest, and celebration, Sundays and holiday feast days were now commandeered for hunting, for two reasons: One, more people would be available; two, as they were not workdays, the local economy would be less disrupted.

Meanwhile, winter was setting in.

And the media was beginning to take notice.

***

It's true.

The time of the Beast was also the time of a growing commerce in news, information, human interest stories, and advertising. Understandably, the calamities caused by the creature in the Gévaudan began to attract the attention of fledgling print media in the region, in Paris, in Europe, and even across the Atlantic.

At that time, media consumption was, well, social. A single copy of a newspaper, newssheet, or a popular-press broadsheet or broadside—one-page publications featuring news stories, ballads, prayers, or advertising—was often circulated to many people. This was done in numerous ways: by subscription, via rental from news vendors, by being read aloud in cafés and other gathering spots, or through individual perusal in reading rooms.

Primary news outlets at the time included the *Courier d'Avignon* of Avignon, France, the closest major newspaper to the Gévaudan region (and perhaps one of the most inaccurate, according to sources). Its normal circulation might be as much as one thousand; at the time of the Beast, print runs were increased to three thousand. On November 23, the newspaper said it "did not have words sufficiently terrible to comment on this beast. She is ferocious with design . . ."

The *Gazette de France*, published in Paris, was the official newspaper of France. A subscription-based publication entitled *Correspondance Littéraire*, read by royal retinues on the Continent, was another influential outlet. These were supplemented by sensational broadsheets and newssheets produced by local printers for distribution by roving peddlers, shopkeepers, and festival hawkers.

***

Reward monies totaling four thousand *livres*, or pounds, for the Beast's demise were now being offered by various districts, the combined estates of the province, and the bishop.

As it would seem that several dozen dragoons should be able to make short work of a nuisance animal, their lack of success must have been embarrassing. To make matters worse, with winter arriving in the Gévaudan, many feared that the Beast—perhaps some kind of strange and terrible wolf—would be in its element in the extreme conditions of the Margeride and Massif Central.

The creature reappeared in mid-November, attacking four adults between the eighteenth and the end of the month.

On the twenty-fifth, it brought death to sixty-year-old widow Catherine Vally in Buffeyrettes, with another decapitation. Perhaps even more disturbing, Duhamel—as Morangiès had suggested—used her remains as bait, believing, as had been insisted, the Beast would come back for more. It didn't.

Accounts such as this only fueled public fear and speculation. The *Courier d'Avignon*, in its early days of coverage of the story, claimed, tabloid-like, that the Beast had so far taken thirty lives, more than twice the numbers of victims recorded in official reports. Exaggerated or not, word was quickly spreading that a monster roamed the French countryside.

CHAPTER 7

"Inconsolable"

December 1764

Duhamel, frustrated by a lack of results as well as the oncoming winter season, yet faithful to his call of duty, kept his hunters on the trail through snow- and fog-obscured conditions. In mid-December, the Beast commenced a concentrated series of attacks, beginning with the decapitation of forty-five-year-old herder Catherine Chastang in Vedrines Saint-Loup. It then set upon a sixteen-year-old boy and a forty-year-old woman before decapitating a twelve-year-old girl. Her body, like Catherine Vally's in November, was used as a lure. A twenty-one-year-old woman, a young child, and a teenage boy perished next, the last another decapitation.

The Beast ended its first year of terror by attacking yet another small child, followed by a young male. It then killed a fifteen-year-old in Rieutort-de-Randon, attacked a twelve-year-old girl, and finally assailed an adult male.

Alas, it seemed that if Duhamel did not have bad luck, he had no luck at all. Around December 20, the captain actually set eyes on his target at its haunt of Château de la Baume. But his dragoons spooked the creature before he or they could take aim.

Duhamel, desperate for victory, and his men, seeking a payout, were furious that their weeks of hunting had come to naught. Those feelings of frustration were shared by those in power, awaiting results, and of course by locals who'd been plagued by both the Beast's predations and the dragoons' disruptions of their lives.

In a letter written later in the month, Duhamel admitted that he was "inconsolable" over the episode. But the end of 1764 would bring not only a continued reign of terror, but a major guilt trip. The Gévaudanais would learn that the arrival of the Beast and its ravages was all their fault.

***

The Last Week of December 1764

"Be seated, Étienne." The Most Reverend Bishop of Mende waved Lafont toward an ornate upholstered backless chair as he thrust his own slippered feet into a foot muff, an elegant wooden case lined with fur positioned beneath his desk. The December winds, forcing their way through the window casings, caused the flames of the cleric's candles to flicker.

"This Beast in my district. It seems impossible to destroy, does it not?"

Lafont coughed. "It is elusive, Your Excellency."

The cleric smiled, holding out a sheaf of papers. Lafont rose to retrieve the documents.

"I want you to read this," said the bishop. "I am issuing this letter on New Year's Eve. It would be profitable for you to know its contents beforehand."

Lafont paused. "Of course, Your Excellency."He settled in his chair and read.

It was a pastoral letter, but the message was not that of a kindly father.

Entitled "Mandement by Gabriel-Florent de Choiseul-Beaupré, Bishop of Mende: The Bishop's Charge to His Congregation/to Order Public Prayers Regarding the Animal (the Man-eater Who Devastates the Gévaudan)," the bishop mentioned the misfortunes of war, irregularity of the weather, and other woes, and then "this extraordinary scourge . . . a ferocious beast."

Referring to St. Augustine (upon whom the Jansenists, a controversial conservative Catholic group the bishop favored, based their beliefs), the bishop informed his flock, "you can easily conclude that your misfortunes can come only from your sins."

As the monster's reign continued, and word of its atrocities spread throughout the country, the leaders of the Gévaudan found themselves running out of options. A forty-hour prayer vigil was ordered, to be held for three weeks in succession, starting on January 6, 1765, Epiphany.

CHAPTER 8

Wolf Month

January 1765

The Anglo-Saxons called January "Wolf Month," the time of year when the predators were most ravenous. The Beast wasted no time in living up to the reputation of its northern brothers, with the January 2 decapitation of a sixteen-year-old youth; when the crime was discovered, the animal absconded with one of the boy's arms.

There would be more than two dozen attacks and ten deaths in the first month of 1765.

January 6, Epiphany, also known as Three Kings Day, or Twelfth Night, is a Christmas-related Church feast. This day commemorates the visit of the Magi—the Three Kings—to see the infant Jesus in Bethlehem.

It was also the day the first forty-hour prayer vigil was to begin, a day upon which the creature slaughtered two females, in Fournel and in Maurines.

Less than a week later, however, the tables were turned when, in Le Villeret, France, the Beast attempted to besiege twelve-year-old Jacques-Andre Portefaix and six of his friends.

***

It was January 12, 1765. Seven children from the parish of Chanaleilles, in Le Villeret, the Gévaudan, France, were watching their families' cattle on a local mountainside.

"Keep your cow away from the bog, Panafleu!" shouted Jacques Portefaix, as he dueled with Jacques Couston and Jean Pic. Portefaix, Couston, and Pic were the same age—twelve. Each wielded a long stick topped with a triangular iron point covered by a sheath.

"Watch it!" said eight-year-old Jean Veyrier, collecting firewood. "You almost hit me."

"It's very cold today," complained Joseph Panafleu, also eight. At Portefaix's bidding, Panafleu guided his cow away from the marshy area nearby. He snuggled up to its thick winter coat and closed his eyes, shivering. The cow flapped its ears.

"Ha!" exclaimed Madeleine Chausse, age nine. Said her friend Jeanne Gueffier, "It's only January, Panafleu. Winter has barely begun."

The cattle, hardy Salers stock, grazed outside year-round. Today they nibbled on snow-dusted grass.

Panafleu stroked the cow's side. He felt the sun come and go on his face as it flashed beneath speeding clouds in the hard blue sky.

The cow snorted. Panafleu opened his eyes.

The big boys were still dueling. Veyrier was stacking his wood. The girls were singing.

And through the leafless trees, Panafleu saw a monster loping up the mountain trail toward them.

Panafleu's jaw dropped. He slid down, onto the snow, clinging to the cow's leg.

The other children laughed.

"What are you doing, Panafleu?"

"Sitting in fresh manure? That will warm you up."

"Or are you after warm milk? That's not where her teats are."

Panafleu did not answer.

Jacques Portefaix ceased dueling. He eyed the little boy and followed his gaze.

A four-footed demon was nearly upon them.

La Bête, Portefaix breathed, staring through his own frosty breath. "La Bête!" he bellowed. He dashed to Joseph and hauled the youngster to his feet. "Everyone! Here! Now!" He pulled the sheath from the end of his pike and made the sign of the cross. "Madeleine! Jeanne! Veyrier, Panafleu, behind! Couston! Pic! With me!"

But *La Bête* had already arrived. She prowled about the little troop, leering.

The Beast of the Gévaudan was the size of a one-year-old calf. Her fur was reddish. She had a black stripe along her back, and a long tail. And fangs.

"She's ugly," Jeanne whispered.

"She smells," added Madeleine.

The Beast salivated.

"Circle!" shouted Portefaix. "Turn with her!" He shoved his companions. "Keep her in front of us."

The cattle stamped their feet and lowed.

"The cows will protect us," Joseph cried. "Hide among them!" He bolted for the herd.

La Bête leapt. In one fluid motion she caught little Panafleu by the throat. Portefaix marveled: *How easy it is for her.*

The children gaped.

"Come on!" Portefaix yelled. As if awakened from some trance, the youngsters moved, thrusting primitive spears. "Harder!" said Portefaix. They stabbed, shrieking. The Beast, disoriented, released Panafleu. But not before she tore away his right cheek.

She devoured it in an instant.

Madeleine dragged Panafleu away and held him.

The Beast's eyes snapped. It rushed again.

The girls screamed.

"Stay together!" shouted Portefaix. "Circle!" The beast lunged into eight-year-old Jean Veyrier, who fell. It drew back, then lunged again, biting him on the lips. The older children advanced. Still La Bête struck, dragging Jean away by his arm.

Couston wailed, "We must get help!"

"No!" roared Portefaix. "We rescue Jean. Or perish with him. Pic, go left! I'll go right! Drive it into the bog. Everyone!" They all followed Portefaix. Even the cattle moved toward the creature, tossing their horns. Distracted, La Bête stumbled into the swamp with Veyrier and struggled in the freezing water.

The children caught up.

"Charge!" commanded Portefaix.

"Monster!" shouted Couston.

"Demon!" said Madeleine.

Yelling for all they were worth, the boys and girls of the parish of Chanaleilles surrounded the famous Beast of the Gévaudan.

"Attack her head, her eyes, her jaws!" advised Portefaix.

They jabbed at the creature over and over again. It seemed like forever, when in fact the entire encounter lasted mere minutes. La Bête was unable to kill or even bite little Jean; she was too busy snapping at the primitive pikes and dodging blows.

Once she seized Portefaix's iron tip and bent it.

Portefaix and company battle the Beast on January 12, 1765. *Bibliothèque nationale de France.*

Finally La Bête dropped Veyrier and drew back. Portefaix scrambled down to help the boy.

La Bête freed herself from the bog, shaking the wet from her fur like a dog. She turned to study her attackers from atop a mound.

"We have her now!" said Portefaix. The seven clenched spears.

But La Bête had had enough of the youngsters of Le Villeret. She darted into the forest.

"She's gone," said Madeleine.

"Children!"

The children wheeled.

An adult had arrived, at last.

***

The courage of seven children rallied king, court, and people, and provided the young hero Portefaix with an all-expenses-paid education and a career in the military. But the triumph was a temporary one.

The Beast immediately resumed its month-long January rampage, even assailing pike-armed men and mauling a twenty-year-old woman, Catherine Boyer, of Lastic, who survived to became *la Balafrée* (the Scarred, or Scarface).

***

Publications in London, Amsterdam, Brussels, Cologne, Boston, and other cities gave coverage to the story of La Bête. Images of the Beast were reproduced on tin plates and ceramic ware. Taxidermy specimen hyenas "of the Gévaudan" were sold in subsequent years as yard accents. The Abbé Pourcher says, "Even the peddlers sang about [the Beast] in public places, with the exaggeration that followed the fashion and served their own interests."

In fact, along with news-making Serbian vampire Arnold Paole and German werewolf Stubbe Peter (more on these to come), the Beast may be considered one of the first media sensations.

The predations of such a mysterious beast, the tragedies it effected, and the difficulties encountered by its hunters captivated audiences far from the "theater of drama," as historian Moriceau terms it. Says scholar Judith Devlin, "Its immense renown was due partly to the work of printers and hawkers of broadsheets, and it quickly became legendary, not only because of the fear inspired by its great size and ferocity, but also because it fitted easily into a well-established imaginative tradition and could be seen as a realization of ill-defined and complex as well as conscious fears." Moriceau has commented on how such coverage, designed to "shock the public," contributed to negative impressions of wolves.

***

On January 27, a startling announcement was made: His Majesty, King Louis XV, would pay six thousand *livres'* reward for the Beast's hide! This was on top of the four thousand offered earlier. A notice with the particulars of the announcement was to be displayed in the towns and cities of the region. Hunters were instructed to register with Lafont prior to their *chasses* (hunts). In England, the London media repeated the announcement in English:

> By the King and Intendant of the province of Languedoc. Notice is given to all persons, that His Majesty, being justly affected by

RELATION

*GE'E'RALE & circonstanciée de tous les Désordres commis par la Bête férece
ravage le Gévaudan & les Pays circonvoisins; avec une Description curieuse, fid
& exacte des Chasses qui ont été faites pour delivrer ces Pays d'un si cruel Anim
le Récit des Combats que différentes personnes soutinrent contre cette Bête fére
l'Aventure du jeune* Portefaix *à la tête de ses Camarades; celle de plusieurs au
Enfans; l'Action merveilleuse & touchante d'une tendre Mere à la vue du dan
qui menaçoit trois de ses Enfans; & les Gratifications que* SA MAJESTE' *l
a fait donner pour récompenser leur bravoure*

TOUT le monde a entendu parler de cette Bête féroce, que l'on croit être une Hyene, qui ra
depuis si long-temps le Gévaudan près Langogne, & tous les Environs. Plusieurs Lettres p
culieres avoient annoncé la destruction de ce cruel Animal, ce qui commençoit à repandre d
tous les esprits une soudaine joie; mais on a appris depuis que ce n'étoit qu'un Loup qui avoit été tué d
le Limousin.

La premiere personne qu'elle attaqua, fut une Femme près de Langogne; mais des Bœufs qui arrive
à tems, la secoururent, & elle n'eut d'ailleurs aucun mal, que ses habits déchirés. Cette Bête est la ter
des Chiens; dès qu'ils la voyent ou la sentent, ils prennent la fuite sans donner un coup de gueule
Taureau seul ou les Bœufs ont acquis le droit de lui tenir tête; dès qu'ils l'apperçoivent, ils lui cou
sus, & ne la quittent point qu'elle n'aye abandonné la place. Plusieurs n'ont conservé leurs jours q
se réfugiant parmi les Troupeaux.

Elle attaqua le 12 de Janvier dernier cinq petits Garçons du Village de Villeret, Paroisse de Chana'ei
Le plus âgé avoit environ onze ans, les autres n'en avoient que sept à huit. Ces enfans gardoient
bétail au haut d'une Montagne. Ils étoient armés chacun d'un bâton au bout duquel ils avoient attach
fer pointu. La Bête vint les surprendre, & se jetta sur un des plus petits. Les autres fondirent sur elle a
intrépidité, & lui firent lâcher prise; mais en quittant elle arracha une partie de la joue droite de c
qu'elle avoit saisi, & se mit à manger devant eux ce lambeau de chair; puis elle retourna à la charge
jetta sur le plus petit de tous, & l'emporta dans sa gueule. L'un deux épouvanté, proposa aux autres
se sauver, pendant qu'elle dévoreroit celui qu'elle venoit d'emporter; mais le plus grand, n
Portefaix, dit qu'il falloit délivrer leur Camarade, ou perir avec lui. Ces Enfans, ranimés par le je
Portefaix, se remirent à poursuivre la Bête qui s'étoit engagée dans un Marais dont la terre étoit mo
& ils la harcellerent avec tant de vigueur, qu'ils parvinrent à lui faire lâcher leur Camarade qui n
qu'une legere égratignure au visage. Comme cette petite Troupe ne cessoit de crier de toutes ses for
un homme parut; ce que voyant l'Animal, il prit la fuite, & tourna ses pas du côté du Marel
dévora un jeune Garçon de quinze ans. Le ROI informé de la bravoure du jeune *Portefaix*, lu
donner 400 liv. de gratification, & 300 liv. pour partager entre les Camarades.

Le 21 elle se jetta sur une jeune Fille qui fut heureusement secourue à tems, & [illegible]
Bête alloit lui faire subir. Le lendemain elle coupa la tête à une femme de [illegible]
saint Chely & saint Alban gagna le Rouergue & l'Auvergne où elle dévora plusieurs personnes. Ses [illegible]

1765 news update: The Beast as depicted on a broadsheet of the time. ***Photo Schwalb. Archives départementales de l'Hérault.***

> the situation of his subjects, now exposed to the ravages of the wild beast which for four months past has infested Vivarais and Gévaudan. And being desirous to stop the progress of such a calamity, has determined to promise a reward of six thousand livres to any person or persons who shall kill this animal. Such as are willing to undertake the pursuit of him may previously apply to the *Sieur* de la Font, sub-deputy to the Intendant of Mendes, who will give them the necessary instructions agreeably to what has been presented by the ministry on the part of his Majesty.

Pourcher tells us that this same day, a "robust" man from Marvejols, hunting "with a well-loaded gun," suddenly realized La Bête was seven paces from him, believed he was going to be its next meal, and, forgetting his rifle, "began to run away crying for help."

CHAPTER 9

Wolf-Stalk

February 1765

Massive hunts resulted in more near-misses for Duhamel, whose relationship with his network of superiors were becoming as frosty as the fastnesses of the Gévaudan.

On the first day of February 1765, the Beast went after an eight-year-old boy in Javols, but his father and their dog put the enemy to rout. Duhamel, however, was not immediately told of this incident, and later imprisoned the father for withholding information.

A complex wolf-stalk involving twenty parishes and thousands of participants in two provinces was slated for the morning of February 16, 1765.

Contingents of nobles, dragoons, peasants, outlanders (Pourcher tells us hunters came from all over central and southern France and from Spain), horses, and dogs gathered in fog and falling snow under a leaden sky, their breath condensing in the cold air.

Their goal: Drive the Beast out of the forest and into the open. Surround it. Destroy it.

***

The aromas of animals, men, and leather mixed with those of fir trees and woodsmoke. The fog and snow muffled the sounds of creaking saddles, jangling bridles, panting dogs, and men's voices: talking somberly, laughing raucously, whistling.

The nobles exchanged wineskins and portions of a flaxen-hued wheat bread, among them Count Morangiès, one of his brothers, and a Count d'Apcher of Besques, France, accompanied by his excited teenage son, the Marquis d'Apcher.

Huddled beaters shivered, backs to the wind, blankets and cloaks around their shoulders, tricorn hats tied under their chins. They gnawed on hunks of coarse black bread and warmed their lower halves around fires lit here or there, keeping their weapons—pikes, tree limbs, garden cultivators, pitchforks, whatever might be employed to both beat the bushes and defend themselves against the Beast—beside them.

Lafont scanned the gloomy horizon, patting his mount anxiously. He checked his bridle and saddle, the reins, the girth strap. The sub-delegate turned up one of the shoulder capes of his woolen topcoat and held it around his neck.

Duhamel rode into view, his skittish horse trying to anticipate the demands its impatient rider would make. The captain reined in the animal with one hand, the other protecting a sheaf of papers inside his coat.

"Here," he said to the beaters. "Copies of a sketch of the Beast, from an interview I conducted with a witness in December."

Jean (John) Chastel, a local farmer and tavernkeeper, took a copy and shared the image with his sons, Pierre and Antoine.

"A decent likeness," he commented.

Chastel's mount, a bay mare, rubbed her head against her master's arm.

"Steady, girl." He reached in a pocket for a piece of the dark bread and held it out flat in his palm. The mare took it greedily.

Trocelier, the priest of Aumont, asked for another copy of the sketch as his pony pawed the snow-covered ground, seeking the grass beneath. The curate dreaded these confounded hunts, knowing his steed would seek to scrape its rider's legs against any fence post, wall, or tree trunk they passed, in hopes of dislodging him.

The dogs began to bay, sensing their forthcoming release.

"Take care. Let us have no accidents!" Lafont called out. "Let's locate this Beast once and for all. Spring will be here before we realize it!"

"Hah! When?" A peasant laughed. "Lafont, you think only of planting and farming and the economy."

"Know that His Excellency, our bishop, prays for us," the sub-delegate responded, as if focused elsewhere.

Duhamel interrupted. This was his moment. "This Beast lays waste to the countryside, attacks and kills herd boys, girls, women, and men," he shouted, his horse tossing its head. "We must cooperate to destroy it. Think of the rewards we will share when we bag this animal! Men from all over Europe will wish that they had been here with us on this day!"

"I dare say the king the most!" said the Earl of Saint-Paul, a colonel of advanced years.

"Count Morangiès, take command," Duhamel said.

Morangiès, in a familiar role, that of field marshal, ordered the dogs set loose.

Baying in excitement, the dogs ran ahead joyfully, noses deployed, seeking their target in the mists beyond.

The peasants advanced to the woods before them, and began whooping, shouting, and beating their implements against the trees and underbrush, creating the din intended to rouse the Beast from its lair.

Hunters swung themselves up and astride their mounts. The horses nickered, adjusting to the weight of men and equipment.

They were off.

***

The Beast would be observed in Prunières that morning, and hunters from that community trailed it to the river Truyère. Residents of nearby Le Malzieu had been instructed to guard the opposite bank, but, in protest of Duhamel's pushy ways, the townsfolk shirked their duty. (King Louis XV later ordered a reprimand of their officials.) And so La Bête paddled across the river and loped away. The Prunières party followed, braving the benumbing water and tracking the animal in the snow until it disappeared into a stand of timber. Others from Le Malzieu sighted it later, fired upon it, and even hit it. Once more the creature got up, fled, and evaded its pursuers.

Two days later, a stunned parishioner from Le Malzieu beheld the Beast on the move, a human head in its jaws. It had just slain twelve-year-old Marie-Jeanne Rousset. Its gruesome spoils were recovered by outraged neighbors. The poor girl's body was used by Duhamel as bait with no result, and she was at last buried. Hunts continued over the next two days, but they too were fruitless.

More than three hundred miles from the dark winter wilderness of the Gévaudan, in Versailles, ablaze with candles, it had apparently been understood for some time that it was time for Duhamel to go.

CHAPTER 10

"An Old Norman Gentleman Who Has Grown Gray in the Pursuit of Wolves"

Duhamel's relations with locals continued to cool, as the Beast set upon twenty peasants in February 1765, killing five. The dedicated yet unlucky captain was eventually replaced by Jean-Charles d'Enneval, a virtuoso wolf hunter from the province of Normandy, more than two hundred miles to the north.

D'Enneval, who was said to have destroyed twelve hundred wolves, had been recommended by Laverdy, the king's controller-general. D'Enneval would have the aid of his son Jean-François after the latter's release from the military as a captain of the Alençon, France, recruits regiment.

The father/son team estimated that it would take them a couple of weeks to bag the Beast.

***

Young d'Enneval wrote to the Bishop of Mende, describing their plans, and letting him know they would bring "six hunting dogs, perfect for the wolf, and specialized for this purpose. . . . With this help and our [two] huntsmen plus thirty good shots chosen from the district, we hope to succeed."

Young d'Enneval also added that if another party managed to kill La Bête, the animal was to be brought to the Normans in order that they might identify its species. "A surgeon has been appointed to open her up on the spot. . . ." D'Enneval, son, also petitioned Saint-Priest to direct Lafont to advance them thirty *louis*, gold coins.

The d'Ennevals arrived while Duhamel was still on the ground and, though the captain of the Clermont-Prince unit was technically still in charge, there were conflicts. These were refereed by Lafont, who asked his brother Trophime to keep tabs on the Normans, headquartered in Saint-Alban. The bickering did not help the hunters with their main objective: locating the Beast. It killed five more people over the course of more than a dozen attacks in February.

Pourcher, from his research, was convinced Duhamel did all he could, every day he could, "to deceive and surprise La Bête . . . [what he took upon himself] is today very difficult to appreciate."

Artificial Women and Little-Girl Lambs

Well-intentioned people—and those hoping for reward money—proposed a wide-ranging assortment of ideas and contrivances for the capture of La Bête.

A Mr. Joas de Papoux wrote to officials in February of 1765 to suggest the counterfeiting of women. "To this end, seeing that the monster is ravenous for females, it is only necessary to place in the places where it appears artificial females, composed of the most subtle poison and expose them on flexible posts on the various roads to invite the cursed animal to show its unbridled fury and swallow its own end." Three expanded pig bladders, seasoned with poison, would make up a "woman's" head and breasts. A painted face would be affixed.

Monsieur de Papoux wrote again in ten weeks with another plan, this one involving twenty-five "intrepid" men dressed in assorted animal skins and feathers, with headgear trimmed in feathers and small knife edges. Everything should be coated in honey and fragrant with musk. Then, the hunters should combine twelve ounces of human fat (from a Christian) with viper's blood (if available) [the asp viper is found throughout much of France], and distribute to the parties in boxes. The men should be armed with Urson pistols and three square bullets, "bitten by the teeth of a woman or girl," then joined with pieces of iron and also covered in fat, plus hunting knives and iron claws, also greased. They should patrol three by three in silence in a large triangle. "A single one of them could be the vanquisher of the cruel Bête."

Another plan proposed by a Monsieur Herbert of Vernières, France, was to dress a sheep like a little girl, fasten a bonnet on its head, and tie it out. "Note that it is best to arrange that the sheep is upright and of about the same size as a child." Children fashioned from straw could be placed by the sheep. Marksmen were to lie in wait nearby. He also suggested having children cavort before another contingent of hidden marksmen. Says Herbert in a letter to Monsieur de Montluc, sub-delegate of Saint-Flour, "The whole universe must be touched by so many massacres so often repeated."

A curate from Reims, who thought the Beast was a tiger-cat from Mexico, directed officials to grease the backs of veal calves with poison and surround them with traps, luring the Beast to its doom.

A Lieutenant-Colonel Duparquet advised that the Beast's hunters should switch to steel musket balls since the Beast, rumored to be covered in scales, was impervious to lead. Monsieur Lespinasse de Mongibaud proposed an "infallible wooden machine" on a twenty-five-foot track to take the creature alive for the king. A model of a child would be inside as bait, while, in a tree nearby, someone would "cry and lament all day and even more at night" to attract the Beast.

CHAPTER 11

"Courage, Hunters of France"

March 1765

The king re-announced his reward in March 1765 as the d'Ennevals situated themselves, awaited their dogs, which arrived on March 9, and petitioned for Duhamel's dismissal. La Bête, meanwhile, was busy with more ravages—twenty-three attacks in March—and was responsible for the deaths of two more women and six more children.

But mid-month, the Beast would famously clash with another force of nature: the *femme* Jouve.

March 13, 1765

Jeanne, the *femme* (woman or wife) Jouve, spouse of tenant farmer Pierre, was in the garden beside their house in La Bessière, France, parish of Saint-Alban, with three of her six children.

Jeanne's daughter was holding her youngest child, a baby boy, and singing to him. Her six-year-old son, meanwhile, was playing with a stick, poking it into the receding snow and mud beneath in the shade of the garden wall.

The late-winter sun felt good on Jeanne's face, and the fresh air was invigorating, but a glance at the forest beyond confirmed: The trees were not yet ready to leaf out. Spring was still a long way away.

The six-year-old bent down to pat the mud with a small hand. Jeanne sighed. "No, no."

An unexpected breeze made her shiver. The slender *mère* drew her shawl around her. "It's too cold to stay out, children. Let's go inside." She reached down, taking the stick from the boy.

Then, from the corner of her eye, she saw a stone falling from the wall. And something else. An animal plummeting from the top. A brute. A monster! It was like a wolf, but not a wolf, large, reddish. Its coat was scarred, diseased.

Jeanne froze, gripping her shawl.

The brute landed, splattering snow and mud, lashing its tail, appraising the stunned mother and her brood. "La Bête," Jeanne whispered. She began to shudder. "In our garden."

Our Lady, protect us!

And then it pounced.

Jeanne watched in horror as it struck her daughter, grabbing an arm. The impact caused the girl and her baby brother to fall to the ground. Her daughter cried out, but managed to hold onto the babe.

Jeanne fell upon the Beast, flailing it with her son's little stick. "Let them go!" she screamed. The stick broke. The Beast growled and clawed at Jeanne's arms and head, ripping out tufts of hair. She fought back, punching it. "Let them go!" Her daughter gave it a kick. The Beast roared, slamming all three against the wall. Jeanne's face scraped against rough stone. Her daughter shrieked. The baby cried. Weeping herself in pain and fear and anger, the mother shielded the pair with her body.

"Mama!"

Jeanne groaned. *Her son! Her six-year-old boy!* The Beast whirled to face the child who'd been left alone, lunged forward, wrapped its jaws around its new quarry . . . and shook.

Something within Jeanne snapped. "Take the baby to the house!" she screamed at her daughter. As the girl darted off, Jeanne rose, hands curled to fists, and scrambled, slipping on snow and mud, to the Beast. She shoved it over, freeing her son. *There.*

But the Beast got to its feet instantly and went for the boy again.

"Mama!"

"I am here!" shouted Jeanne. This time she leapt upon the monster's back. *Anything to distract it.* Pulling its head backward to her chest, she screamed, "Leave us alone!" The Beast collapsed. Jeanne tumbled off, grasping for her son. The Beast snarled, breathing in her face. *The smell.* Woman and Bête were eye to eye, panting. *Its eyes are as fiery as they say,* Jeanne thought, as if from somewhere far away.

Without warning, the Beast swiped at her again. "Oh!' cried Jeanne, clapping her hands to her head, feeling warm, sticky blood. La Bête took her son again, and this time, leapt up and over the wall, carrying the youngster away.

No.

Shaking, Jeanne got to her feet once more. She picked up the fallen stone. And went after them.

She ran around to the gate as quickly as she could and left the garden. Beast and boy were ahead. The Beast was strong, but the weight of the boy slowed its progress. Heart pounding, Jeanne rushed and, unbelievably, caught up with them.

And then she grabbed the creature's tail. (Some accounts said she grabbed a foot, some that she "seized La Bête in the place she judged to be the most sensitive.")

The Beast dropped the boy and gave a cry, spinning toward Jeanne. She let go of its tail and smacked it on the head with the stone. *Take that.*

The Beast, mad with pain, clawed her once more. Jeanne faltered.

Retrieving its prey, the creature made for a hole in a hedge before them, evidently striving for the open fields beyond.

Jeanne pushed herself again, this time grasping for her son's feet, dragging along the ground. *I can't reach him.* Her six-year-old was silent now.

"Help! Help!" Jeanne cried in despair.

"Mother!"

Jeanne started. Her two older sons appeared; they'd been moving the family's flock of sheep. And there was their dog. Weak now, the *femme* pointed to the departing beast. "La Bête! Your brother!"

The dog was already making for the Beast, barking furiously. It threw La Bête to the ground. The six-year-old fell to one side. Enraged, the Beast twirled and body-slammed the dog, throwing it head over heels several yards.

Jeanne's older son rushed to his mother. The other son, brandishing a spear, joined the dog in combat and stabbed the Beast in its haunches.

The Beast bailed, streaking away. The blood-soaked Jeanne flung her stone after it and went to her injured son.

Her courage and example were lauded throughout France, but despite best efforts, her six-year-old son died of massive wounds three days later. The king awarded her three hundred *livres* for her bravery. Trophime Lafont, brother of Étienne, would deliver the reward to the grieving Jeanne on April 25.

***

As with Portefaix, the skirmish with the *femme* Jouve failed to slow the Beast down. It actually killed and half-devoured a boy that very night. At dawn the next morning, it showed up almost at the doorstep of a woman of Estival; she shouted for everyone to "see La Bête," and they did before the creature made a getaway.

While waiting for their dogs, which were transported separately from the Normans, the d'Ennevals squandered advance money and fumed about Duhamel. In a March 9 letter to Ballainvilliers, intendant of the province of Auvergne, the elder d'Enneval states, "The dragoons go on hunts in their own districts. That gives me a lot of trouble because I have no control over them. I will do all I can."

The d'Ennevals and Duhamel both wrote to Count Moncan to complain about each other.

On March 19, Lafont penned a lengthy missive, about thirty-seven hundred words, to the governor regarding the situation. The letter also mentions the subdelegate's receiving communication about Portefaix's reward, three hundred *livres*, with an additional three hundred *livres* to be divided among the brave twelve-year-old's friends.

Lafont discussed the d'Ennevals' request for thirty *louis* and a meeting with them in which they expressed their conviction that, if they hunted with Duhamel, and, if the father/son team killed La Bête first, the dragoons would shoot the Beast after them and refuse to relinquish it to the hunters from Normandy. Lafont stressed cooperation was needed, but the d'Ennevals would not budge. They expected Count Moncan to order Duhamel to cease hunting; if the count did not, they would write to the court.

Lafont then met with Duhamel, who claimed young d'Enneval told him he had orders to fire him, but would not show these papers to the dragoon captain. Duhamel said he would continue hunting until he received word personally to cease. Lafont wrote that Duhamel was "a gallant person and listens to reason. Everyone praises his behavior in the face of the d'Ennevals."

Still, the next day, the d'Ennevals brought Lafont a list of demands along with a letter from Controller-General Laverdy to the Governor of Alençon. They would commence operation in districts between the Gévaudan and the Auvergne, and asked Lafont to communicate to those communities that individuals should assist them, that they let the Normans know right away if La Bête attacks, and that they be provided with two horses in each parish.

Lafont pressed upon the Normans that the hunt was open to anyone and that he had already issued several permits to locals and outsiders. He was also under orders to send the Beast's remains to his superior in Montpellier, who would forward the carcass to Versailles. D'Enneval said he had later orders and would show them to Lafont. Lafont wrote later that he did his best to produce agreement between the captain and the Normans, "but the thing was not possible."

The subdelegate noted that the elder d'Enneval now seemed a bit flustered and said he could not promise his dogs could find the creature. "I think he . . . did not expect to find so many mountains, woods, swamps, and so much snow, nor that La Bête covered so much territory."

Young d'Enneval, dining with Lafont, showed him a document that appeared to be signed by the king, but would not allow the subdelegate to read it.

The dogs arrived at last, but some said they'd been brought to the area days before and hidden. Lafont shrugged. There would have been no hunting the week before. "The weather was as cruel as it could be and a large amount of snow fell."

He advised Duhamel to hunt away from the d'Ennevals, and told his superior that under the circumstances, the Sunday and feast day hunts had been postponed.

Meanwhile the Beast was enjoying carte blanche, devouring children day after day.

And now we see where Lafont was going: "All these horrors are preparing us for even bigger ones, because there is much to fear if this Bête is not destroyed before the month of May, that is to say before the grain begins to come up."

By the end of the month the d'Ennevals had begun their own hunts, but they'd also gained a fuller appreciation for what they'd gotten themselves into, even keeping their valuable dogs from pursuing the Beast when questionable conditions prevailed.

***

Carrying on ancient oral traditions of spreading news and stories, eighteenth-century poems and ballads or laments (writings that commemorate a calamity) were featured on broadsheets and in news accounts, often accompanied by images of the Beast.

Here are two examples:

Courage hunters of France,
Depart for the Gévaudan,
Go by a fast coach,
Don't lose a minute.
In hunting the Beast

Who ravages the countryside.
He's eaten up so many folk,
The Beast of the Gévaudan,
that he's grown round, like a ball,
The Beast of the Gévaudan.

CHAPTER 12

"An Unfortunate Time"

Representatives from the various Estates of the Gévaudan met for their annual meeting with the bishop of Mende on March 26, 1765. Normally they met to discuss the economical and spiritual health of the region. This year's discussions would understandably focus on the Beast.

Lafont presented an action plan, which included arming the peasantry (cautiously), hiring poachers, guarding livestock in common areas, and allowing Count Morangiès to coordinate contingents of guards in locales frequented by the Beast. He was disappointed to receive little initial support for his plans, and forwarded the proposals to Saint-Priest. Ultimately, however, the authorities allowed the d'Ennevals their opportunity to hunt at large. The father and son from Normandy asked for the speedy reporting of attacks and for bodies to be left in place until they arrived.

April 1765

The Beast butchered several children during Holy Week, the days leading up to Easter. A total of six perished in April, out of seventeen attacks. The d'Ennevals hunted, but with no success, stymied by hail and snow.

A large hunt involving twenty communities was held on April 21, which to Lafont turned out to be a surprisingly similar strategy to that of Duhamel. The result: a saber-armed teenager chanced upon the Beast, but it ran off as he shouted for help. A wolf-stalk on the twenty-third disbanded after the Beast was seen elsewhere. A small she-wolf was killed. The month ended with more inclement weather and another hunt made up of participants from fifty-six parishes. Again, it was a nonsuccess.

May 1765

Four country people were killed in May, all female, ranging in age from thirteen to forty-five.

Some wondered if there was more than one manslayer out there because of the distance between some of the more than twenty attacks on men, women, teens, and children. Multiple attacks occurred on several days, yet in different locations.

On the evening of May 1, the Beast was seen and fired upon on by three brothers named La Chaumette at their home in Saint-Alban parish. After spying the creature from a window, one brother alerted the others; they seized their weapons and went after it. Two brothers were able to hit the animal, and it fell both times, but ultimately got to its feet and eluded them in the brushwood. The brothers immediately sent word to the d'Ennevals, but the Normans did not come until the next day. The brothers concurred with other witnesses that the Beast was a wolf of a different color, large and striped. And they were convinced it would be found dead.

But the Normans found nothing.

More hunts were held, wolves were spotted, fired upon, mostly missed. The d'Ennevals were losing credibility rapidly. One of their dogs, which had gone MIA, returned with a damaged collar, indicating a brawl with the Beast. Men from multiple communities assembled for an additional hunt on Ascension Thursday (observed forty days after Easter, this holy day commemorates Jesus's ascent to heaven) and the following Sunday, during which a woman—in the very neighborhood of the hunt itself—was decapitated. The Normans had her remains poisoned and set out as bait, again with no results.

As chronicler Pourcher comments, "It has to be admitted that this was indeed an unfortunate time!"

***

The Beast's reign served many enterprising souls, even as it satisfied its own appetites. It provided local, national, and international media with exciting content that sold papers, broadsheets, and merchandise. It continues to do so today. If one searches French

"An exact representation of the FURIOUS WILD BEAST, which has so long ravaged the Gévaudan," "From a drawing sent in April 1765 to the Intendant of Alençon." (Artist I. Bayly) *The London Magazine, vol. xxxiv, May 1765.*

bookshops and bookselling websites, one finds dozens of books, novels, and graphic novels devoted to fictitious and historical accounts of what happened between 1764 and 1767.

The Beast also provided material for humor, thanks to misunderstandings of what the hunts for this creature truly entailed. A spoof account published in London wrote that the Beast, after having bested thousands of Frenchmen simply by wagging its tail, breaking wind, and so forth, was vanquished by an angry mother cat after it ate one of her kittens, a yarn that did not go over well with the French.

The lead story of *London Magazine: Or, Gentleman's Monthly Intelligencer*, May 1765, was entitled "Ravages of the Wild Beast in

France," "With an exact representation of the FURIOUS WILD BEAST, which has so long ravaged the Gévaudan." Said the publication,

> Altho' we have taken care not to stuff our Magazine with the many accounts we have had of the ravages committed among the people of the South of France by a wild beast, to which they have not as yet given any proper name; yet as we have in this month given a representation of that voracious creature, we think it necessary to give at least one of the most remarkable accounts that have been communicated to the publick by the foreign news-papers . . .

This was a preface to the story of Portefaix and his companions that appeared in the *Paris Gazette*. After relating the account, the *Magazine* added, "Capt. Duhamel of the dragoons is in pursuit of [the Beast], who has caused several of his men to dress themselves in women's apparel, and to accompany the children that keep cattle."

News stories about the Beast and other creatures provided an outlet from the everyday, especially for those for whom reality was one hardship after another. People were and are fascinated by unusual animals, whether in an eighteenth-century menagerie or on the twenty-first-century World Wide Web. Printers and newshawkers of that time took advantage of this curiosity by making accounts of the Beast's activities and those of its victims and hunters widely available. Scholar Judith Devlin tells us that the story of the Beast, along with that of other creatures, such as Mérénas, the Amphibious Animal of Algeria of the mid-1800s, a creature which was said to have consumed French soldiers on the North African coast, were re-run again and again by publishers and printers.

Imagine: The peasantry had no television, no Internet, no movies, no magazines, and so on. If we were to attempt to live as they did, it would be as if we lived in conditions of a natural or man-made disaster: no power, no phones, no news. The local church, with its modest sculptures and other artworks, depicting religious subjects, provided one of the few cultural diversions for countryfolk. Images and figurines of saints and national heroes were also sold by peddlers to those who could afford them.

A Dickens of a Beast

Charles Dickens, nearly one hundred years later, made use of accounts of the Beast's life and times in an 1858 issue of his own publication, *Household Words*.

"The way in which such a beast ought to have been dealt with," says Dickens, "is very plainly stated in a letter addressed by an English foxhunter (who had read the royal [French] proclamation with great disgust) to the printer of the magazine in which an English version of the document was published:

> 'Is it to be imagined, Mr. Printer,' he says, "that the fiercest animal that ever traversed the wilds of Africa, would have been suffered in this nation for six whole months, to fatten upon the young boys and virgins of a country, throwing meanwhile the remaining ones into the most distressful consternation for the fate of their women and children, when a scarcity of provision might bring it to their turn to maintain him? No, sir, in England, not less superior to France in the achievements of the camp, than in the manly exercises of the field, if he had lived six weeks only, it would have been merely *ex gratiâ*, for the sake, perhaps, of hunting him a second or third time. . . .

Dickens continues, "The king [of France] . . . directed that he [the Beast] should be embalmed, and stuffed with straw! He was in that condition returned to Monsieur de Beauterne [meaning royal gunbearer François Antoine], who kept him till the Revolution came, and amongst other institutions swept away the terror of the Cévennes. . . ."

Dickens' own opinion of the Beast:

> He was, doubtless, a terrible creature to behold, but if he at all resembled the portrait of him which was sent in April, seventeen hundred and sixty-five, to the Intendant of Alençon, (in case he should happen to pass that way—some three hundred miles off), he must have been a creature rather to kill you with laughter than with his teeth and claws. I have the engraving from the original picture before me at the moment, and it bears this inscription: *'Figure de la*

> *Best féroce quo l'on a nommé l'hyène, qui a dévoré plus que quatre-vingt personnes dans le Gévaudan.'* The animal, is, in truth, a most ridiculous monster . . . Indeed one that Trinculo [of Shakespeare's *Tempest*] would have jeered at as 'a very weak monster,—a most poor credulous monster,—a puppy-headed monster,—a most scurvy monster.' Indeed the jester could hardly have hit upon any phrase of absurdity whereby to load him with contempt, as he stands, passant gardant [a heraldic term meaning having one paw raised in the air] . . . his curly tail trailing on the ground, with ponderous head and cropped ears,—with his mouth filled with enormous teeth, wide open, as if he were catching flies; with his small sleepy eyes, and with the most good-natured expression on his foolish face.

CHAPTER 13

The Royal Gunbearer

June 1765

There were fewer attacks in June 1765, only about a dozen (which still was an average of four per week!). Nonetheless, the Beast took the lives of four people: three children (one may have been a young teen) and a forty-five-year-old woman, with two decapitations. Three deaths occurred within two days, June 20 and 21. The Beast roved the areas of Auvers-Nozeyrolles, Saugues, Le Malzieu, and Venteuges, France.

On June 1, 1765, the Beast "devoured a nine- to ten-year-old boy . . . in Auvergne, bordering the Gévaudan," says Pourcher. "A young sister of this boy, who was with him, took flight to save herself and hid in a nearby wood. As she had not reappeared, it was assumed she had been devoured like her brother. Her parents found her three days later, hidden in some rocks. She had completely lost her mind."

French functionaries deemed it time for the d'Ennevals to step back and allow a third hunter to take over: King Louis XV's own trusted gunbearer—among his duties was that of loading the ball and powder of the king's rifle—and lieutenant of the hunt, seventy-one-year-old François Antoine, a knight of the Royal and Military Order of Saint Louis. He was joined by his son, Robert-François Antoine de Beauterne, a company of royal gamekeepers sent by princes from court, and other assistants.

After a two-week journey to the Gévaudan vicinity from court, François Antoine (who was an acquaintance of the senior d'Enneval) hunted with the father and son on June 23. He also met with Lafont, noting requirements, setting ground rules, offering rewards for wolves killed, with greater monies for the Beast.

It had been one year since the death of the first official victim, Jeanne Boulet, of Les Hubacs.

July 1765

With an arsenal that included harpoon-like poles with barbed iron points, François Antoine took over, but like the hunters before him, he would face his share of setbacks, including rain and heavy fog that hampered his initial efforts from late June into the second week of July.

Two people would lose their lives to the Beast in July 1765: On July 4, a woman in her fifties or sixties, of the parish of Lorcières was fatally assaulted; on the evening of the twenty-second, a nine-year-old boy from Auvers disappeared.

The Beast attacked a number of people in July, including a mail carrier and two nuns. Two herdboys escaped harm by scrambling up a tree, prompting the thwarted Beast to destroy the little shelter in which they slept at night. The creature then threw itself at the tree, but withdrew at the sight of an approaching horseman.

François Antoine observed two sets of wolf tracks (one very large) after the first death, and the Beast was spotted on the move over the next days and weeks, but easily outmaneuvered the hunters from court.

The gunbearer again came across large paw prints at the location of the second death, that of the nine-year-old boy, which occurred on July 22. He ordered his hunters to beat the woods nearby, but their numbers were not adequate to the task.

On the twenty-seventh, the Beast seized four-year-old Pierre Roussel (a future great-uncle of Abbé Pierre Pourcher), and carried him more than five hundred yards before dropping the boy. Unfortunately, a gullywasher destroyed all traces of the animal before the gunbearer could get there.

Determined to locate his target, François Antoine ordered a large hunt for Sunday, July 28, but once more, Mother Nature was uncooperative, sending cloudbursts and, incredibly, summer sleet.

August 1765

August brought more bad weather, more bad luck, eight attacks, and one death, that of a sixteen-year-old girl from La Besseyre-Saint-Mary.

But one feisty young woman took on the Beast with her pike and sent it packing.

On August 11, 1765, mid- to late morning, a young woman named Marie-Jeanne Valet, nineteen or twenty years old, a servant of the curate, or clergyman, of the parish of Paulhac, and her sister Thérèse, sixteen or seventeen, were crossing the river Desges on their way to the community's tithe farm. (Local peasants contributed a tithe, or one-tenth, of their output for the support of the local church and cleric; it was kept in a tithe barn.)

The Beast, lurking in the underbrush along the river banks, spotted the girls and flung itself at Marie-Jeanne.

Luckily, the sensible young woman had brought along a spear, "a stick with a bayonet sharp on both sides about half a foot long and an inch and a half wide."

She used it.

Marie-Jeanne Valet impaled the Beast with her weapon, actually knocking it down, all the while yelling for help, along with her sister. According to the accounts and letters presented by Pourcher, La Bête retreated, "cried out very loudly and held her paw in front of the wound," then "threw herself in the river, where she rolled over several times" before disappearing.

Later, when questioned by authorities, the girls—their testimony translated into French by Trophime Lafont—described the Beast as being the size of a large farm dog. It was gray with a white chest and black back, they said. Its front was bigger than its rear. It had a big flat head and big teeth.

The authorities examined Marie-Jeanne's spear and noted that the shaft of the weapon was coated in two to three inches of blood. The intrepid Jeanne-Marie was an "Amazon," according to the local press. Royal gunbearer François Antoine, impressed with her bravery and composure, called her a second Maid of Orleans—Joan of Arc.

The girls, meanwhile, being uneducated, were unable to sign the statements documenting their experience.

Marie-Jeanne Valet now has a sculpture commemorating her valor in a windswept churchyard in Auvers, France. The sculpture is by French artist Philippe Kaeppelin (1918–2011), who also created an altar for the Mende Cathedral.

August 16 brought with it another pivotal episode in the chronicles of the Beast, an ill-fated encounter between two of François

This dramatic sculpture by Philippe Kaeppelin represents the confrontation of young Marie-Jeanne Valet with the Beast on August 11, 1765. *Photo Schwalb.*

Antoine's royal gamekeepers and members of the Chastel family—father Jean Chastel, farmer and tavernkeeper, and two of his sons, Pierre and Antoine—at the forest of Mont Chauvet.

On August 16 at the forest of Mont Chauvet, the gamekeepers of royalty asked the boys from La Besseyre-Saint-Mary if the area before them could be navigated safely on horseback.

The Chastels said yes, likely knowing the area referred to was actually a bog.

The first royal horseman's mount became mired in the morass, panicked, and jettisoned its rider, much to the amusement of the Chastels.

The incident ended badly, at gunpoint, and with the Chastels thrown in jail until François Antoine's departure in November.

Despite the misadventure, other locals were impressed with François Antoine if not the other envoys from court. During his stay, the gentleman requested that Catholic masses be said in support of the communities and he contributed personally to church charities.

Touched by the poverty and hard lot of the peasants of the Gévaudan, François Antoine proposed a fireworks display to celebrate the feast day of Saint Louis, which occurs on August 25. (Louis IX [1214–1270], reformer and Crusader, was the only king of France to become a saint.)

At first worried they might be taxed for this event, the peasants relaxed after assurances this would not be so. Some brought forth foodstuffs and even wine they kept hidden from tax collectors to share with the man sent to help them by a far-away king.

Using fireworks he'd set aside to use in flushing the Beast from the forest, François Antoine and his assistants presented a grand spectacle. The loud and colorful pyrotechnics (which until the Revolution demonstrated the power of the crown) awed the countryfolk.

As a subject and servant of Louis XV himself, here on a mission he knew he was expected to wrap up very, very soon, François Antoine felt an affinity for these souls.

"We will destroy this Beast!" he shouted at the end of the entertainment.

Most of the *paysans* could not understand his French, but smiled and nodded, the kaleidoscope of fleeting lighting effects lingering in their minds and explosions echoing in their ears.

The cause of the show, the Beast, had also observed it from not so far away, more curious than frightened.

Days later, on August 28, François Antoine's nephew, a man named Rinchard, who was a gamekeeper and horse wrangler for the Duke of Orléans, killed a big wolf in the Bois Noir (the Black Woods).

As nearly one year ago, when a similar wolf was killed on September 20, 1764, the question again on everyone's mind: Had the Beast been destroyed at last?

September 1765

The deaths of two twelve-year-old girls, one on September 8, one on September 13, proved that the Beast's offensive was not over.

A string of attacks took place during the first half of the month, including one in which the Beast attacked a man who'd fired upon it, a first.

When a pack of wolves, including an immense male, was reported in the vicinity of the Abbey of Chazes, a nunnery near the river Allier, the the lords of venery moved in.

And François Antoine would find he was in for the hunt of his life.

CHAPTER 14

Chazes

On September 20, François Antoine and his men reconnoitered in the Abbey forest called the woods of Pommier (apple trees)—in which the wolves were observed.

The royal gunbearer came upon a number of animal trails in the Pommier Woods. While examining the tracks he found at a convergence of several paths, he happened to look up.

A donkey? Here?

No.

A wolf.

Fifty steps away and closing in.

It was monstrous.

Mon dieu, breathed the knight of Saint Louis.

He scrambled for his gun and took aim.

François Antoine used a large-caliber long-barreled *carardière,* (a duck-hunting shotgun), loaded with five charges of strong powder (twenty grams, we are told) and thirty-three buckshot pellets ranging from four and a half to eight millimeters in diameter.

He fired.

And stumbled back two paces—the gun kicked like a mule.

Wildly he recovered and peered through the gunsmoke.

The load had hit home. It looked to have gone through the wolf's right eye and into its right side. *Hurrah!*

But . . .

Impossible!

The wolf got to its feet.

And charged.

Tight-lipped, Antoine forced himself to focus.

No time to reload!

My knife! He felt for it at his side.

The gap narrowed.

François Antoine's mind raced.

Beat and stun it with the gun. Then use the knife.

The wolf was ten steps away.

He brought up the gun.

BAM!

What? Who?

"Uncle!"

Rinchard! Thank the Lord!

Antoine's nephew, gamekeeper of the Duke of Orléans, had positioned himself behind the Beast and fired.

Nephew! Did he succeed? The white smoke blinded Antoine, who expected the Beast to be upon him at any moment. He clasped the barrel of his gun. It burned.

"Uncle!"

Then he saw.

The wolf had fallen again, but, true to the stories the peasants told, it was rising once more.

How could this be?

"Your knife!" shouted Rinchard.

But there was no need.

The wolf staggered off in a different direction, running crazily for twenty yards, fell, and died.

The delighted hunting party contacted the local surgeon, who was to do a complete autopsy. The king was determined to know exactly what this animal was.

"Then," said François Antoine, "it is expected at court."

***

King and court were pleased with François Antoine's feat, but back in the Gévaudan, there was controversy. Shouldn't Rinchard be credited since he actually fired the shot that killed the Beast? Was the animal truly the Beast? Meanwhile, the Chazes wolf was prepped for its close-up in Versailles, to be accompanied by François Antoine's son, Robert-François Antoine de Beauterne. As this Beast had technically been destroyed in Auvergne, not the Gévaudan, it would make a brief stop, not in Mende, but in Clermont-Ferrand, France, and the headquarters of Auvergne intendant Simon-Charles Ballainvilliers The gunbearer himself remained in the Chazes area to hunt down the rest of the pack.

On the first day of October 1765, François Antoine's wolf was presented at the court of the King Louis XV in Versailles.

Visiting at the time was a prolific letter writer, Horace Walpole, Earl of Orford, England, whose missives are tremendously valued by historians for their depictions of eighteenth-century life. According to an October 3, 1765, letter from Walpole to John Chute, Esquire:

> In the Queen's antechamber we foreigners and the foreign ministers were shown the famous beast of the Gévaudan, just arrived, and covered with a cloth, which two *chasseurs* [pageboys] lifted up. It is an absolute wolf, but uncommonly large, and the expression of agony and fierceness remains strongly imprinted on its dead jaws.

(Walpole had had a pet spaniel seized by a wolf while crossing the Alps twenty-six years before.)

In another letter, also written on October 3, to the Right Honorable Lady Hervey, Walpole wrote,

> Fortune bestowed on me a much more curious sight than a set of princes; the wild beast of the Gévaudan, which is killed, and actually is in the Queen's antechamber. It is a thought less than a leviathan, and the beast in the Revelations, and has not half so many wings, and yes, and talons, as I believe they have, or will have some time or other; this being possessed but of two eyes, four feet, and no wings at all. It is as fine a wolf as a commissary in the late war, except, notwithstanding all the stories, that it has not devoured near so many persons. In short, Madam, now it is dead and come, a wolf it certainly was, and not more above the common size than Mrs. Cavendish [according to Smith, "a famously portly woman of English society"] is. It has left a dowager and four young princes.

Back in the Gévaudan, during October, François Antoine tracked down and destroyed the Beast's mate and pups.

November 1765

The gunbearer left the Gévaudan for good on November 3. The Chastels were released from prison shortly thereafter. The Gévaudanais enjoyed some much-deserved peace as winter set in once more. There was also a falling off of the official conversation regarding La Bête du Gévaudan, which means less documentation of the story to come.

Another Version

Noted Scottish scholar and folklorist Andrew Lang devoted several pages to the Beast in "Stories about Wolves" in his 1896 *Animal Story Book*. "There have been instances, but fortunately few, of wolves with a perfect craving for human flesh," he begins. "Such was the notorious Bête (or beast) du Gévaudan." Lang tells his readers that the Beast was six feet long, and that it "was attacked from first to last by between *two and three hundred thousand* [sic] hunters, probably not all at once." He further comments, "With half a dozen wolves, each equal to 200,000 men, a country could afford to do without an army. But the wolf of Gévaudan was no common wolf. He never married, having no leisure, fortunately for the human race."

Lang describes some of the Beast's most famous qualities: the creature's escaping the pursuit of experienced huntsmen by "disappearing as if he had been turned into smoke," how "bullets had rebounded off him, flattened and harmless," how it possessed "a pair of fiery eyes," "that it was no ordinary wolf . . . but the Fiend himself in beast shape."

The folklorist also relates an alternative version of the Beast's story. In it, "The young Countess de Mercoire, an orphan, and châtelaine [lady of the manor] of one of the finest estates of the district, offered her hand and fortune in marriage to whoever should rid the country of the scourge. This inspired the young Count Léonce de Varinas, who, though no sportsman by nature, was so deeply in love with the Countess that he determined to gain the reward or perish in the attempt. Assisted by a small band of well-trained hunters, and by two formidable dogs, a bloodhound and a mastiff, he began a systematic attack on the wolf."

One can guess the ending from the image reproduced here. Lang concludes, "It was not long before the Countess and the gallant champion were married; and, as the wolf left no family, the country was at peace. Are you not rather sorry for the poor wolf?"

December 1765

Seventy-two days after the Chazes wolf met its end, little Vidal Tourneyre, six or seven years old, was taken by an animal while with

THE DEATH OF THE FAMOUS WOLF OF GÉVAUDAN

An illustration of La Bête's demise by H. J. Ford for the 1896 edition of *The Animal Story Book,* edited by Andrew Lang. *Dover Publications, Inc., 2002 edition.*

his family's livestock. Teenager Jean Couret, nearby, charged after the predator and stabbed it with his spear until it released the herdboy.

Three more attacks occurred that last month of the year, one on December 10; another about seventy-two hours later; then, on December 21, another, with a decapitation of an eleven-year-old girl from Lorcières. Two days later, a thirteen-year-old girl from Julianges was killed. Pourcher tells us she was consumed "with such voracity that, according to one document, they could only find her two hands, and, according to another, the two hands, the two legs, and some remnants of her clothes. Either way, so much of her was eaten that the Prior of Julianges considered the remains were insufficient for a burial service to be carried out."

In faraway Versailles, the case was officially closed and king and court had moved on. Indeed, the court was in mourning for the king's son, Louis, who had passed away of consumption in December 1765. He was thirty-six. (Horace Walpole had written back in October that, on the same day he took in the sight of the Beast at Versailles, he saw the Dauphin [the title of the eldest son of the king of France], who looked "ghastly," and he thought the young man would live only three months more.) Louis XV's grandson, also named Louis, then only eleven, would become heir to the throne.

***

One year after the Bishop of Mende's pastoral letter, and after learning that a Beast-like creature had returned to the Gévaudan, Laverdy prepared a report to be communicated to the distant provinces regarding methods of poisoning to help them in the self-management of nuisance wolves. Saint-Priest would write Laverdy on December 30, 1765, to affirm that he did receive the report.

In the Gévaudan, locals and officials came to realize that the state had miscalculated what would be required.

An outspoken area priest, Jean-Baptiste Ollier, wrote many letters trying to convince authorities that the Beast was not just a wolf, and not the animal François Antoine had destroyed, but a monster of some kind that was still at large. The lack of response to his missives only served to frustrate the cleric.

Getting rid of the Beast would have to be a do-it-yourself project.

CHAPTER 15

"A Short Truce"

1766

"Chastel, tell me again: What happened when you and your sons ran into the gamekeepers from court?"

The Marquis d'Apcher had been sixteen "at the apparition" of the Beast nearly two years before, and had been among those on the great hunt of February 16, 1765. Still, he demanded to review each chapter of the story with his favorite old stager, Jean Chastel.

Now that the Beast had returned, or perhaps had never been killed in the first place, the enthusiastic young aristocrat aimed to bask in the glory of its destruction once and for all.

Meanwhile, Lafont and the other local authorities had to be prudent about what was communicated with the court in Versailles regarding wolves. To say the Beast was back was to offend the king himself.

And so small and informal groups of locals, spurred on by the marquis, went hunting on their own.

Sources vary with regard to the number of attacks in 1766. As mentioned, there was much less formal documentation of such incidents now that the court-approved Beast had been killed the previous September. In any case, a February 1766 letter speculates on whether the Beast was an animal killed in 1765, or whether it was "another of the same nature. Either way, the peace of the Gévaudan has proved to be only a short truce."

It seems between sixteen and twenty-two people were set upon during the first half of 1766, and in March and April, three children: an eight-year-old boy, an eight-year-old girl, and a six-year-old girl. On May 31, the Beast took a ten-year-old herdboy named Pierre Teyssèdre. Pierre's older brother Jean had been wounded by an animal the previous September.

In a somewhat lighter account from March 1766, Jean-Pierre Pourcher, who would become the great-grandfather of Beast historian Abbé Pierre Pourcher, is said to have been journeying in the vicinity with a fellow named Antony after a fair when the Beast came

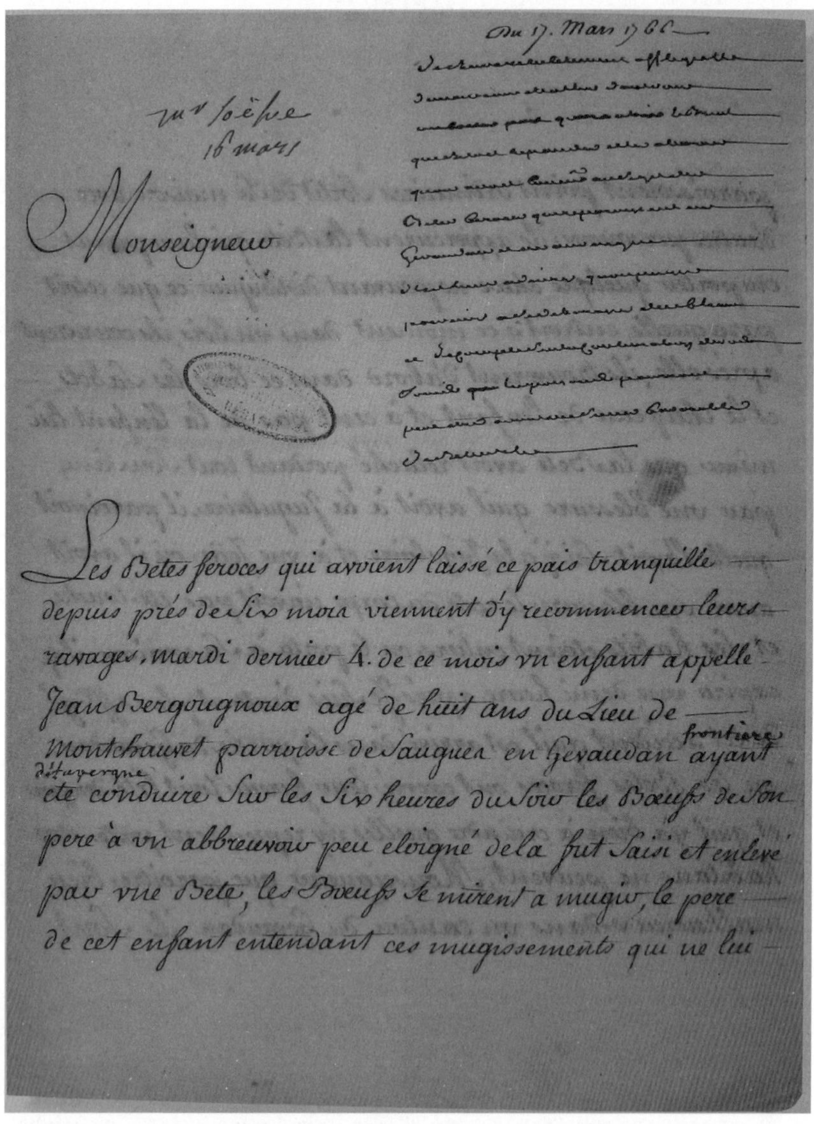

Du 17. Mars 1766

Mr l'évêque
16 mars

Monseigneur

Les Betes feroces qui avoient laissé ce païs tranquille depuis prés de Six mois viennent d'y recommencer leurs ravages, mardi dernier 4. de ce mois un enfant appellé Jean Bergougnoux agé de huit ans du Lieu de Montchauvet parroisse de Sauguez en Gevaudan frontiere d'auvergne ayant eté conduire Sur les Six heures du Soir les Boeufs de Son pere à un abbreuvoir peu eloigné de la fut Saisi et enlevé par une Bete, les Boeufs se mirent a mugir, le pere de cet enfant entendant ces mugissements qui ne lui

A March 1766 letter from intendant Étienne Lafont describing the death of eight-year-old Jean Bergougnoux, "seized and carried off" while tending cattle. *Photo Schwalb. Archives départementales de l'Hérault.*

upon him. Pourcher insisted his companion was responding to a necessitous call of nature at the time. The creature left after being

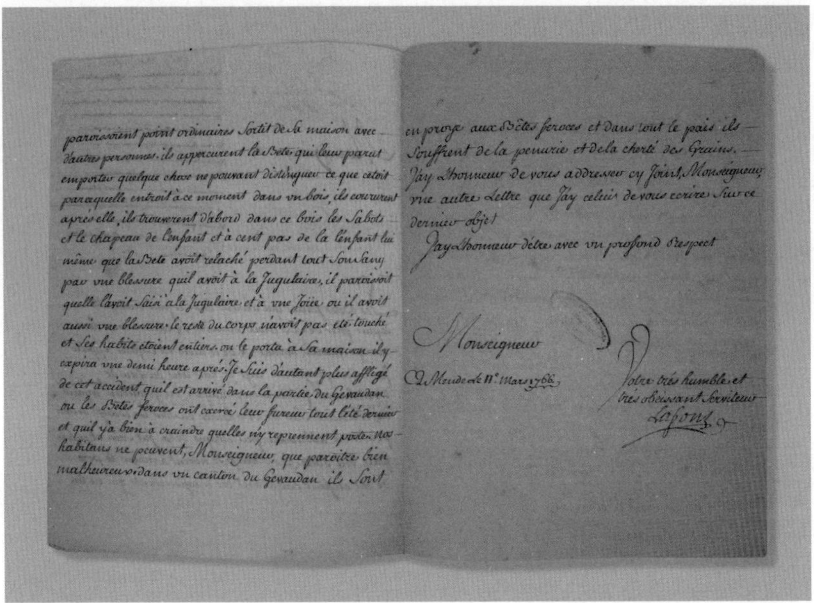
paroissoient point ordinaires sortit de sa maison avec
d'autres personnes. ils apperceurent la Bete qui leur parut
emporter quelque chose ne pouvant distinguer ce que c'etoit
par laquelle entroit à ce moment dans un bois, ils coururent
aprés elle, ils trouverent d'abord dans ce bois les Sabots
et le chapeau de l'enfant et à cent pas de la l'enfant lui
même que la Bete avoit relaché perdant tout son sang
par une blessure qu'il avoit à la Jugulaire, il paroissoit
qu'elle l'avoit saisi à la Jugulaire et à une Joüe ou il avoit
aussi une blessure. le reste du corps n'avoit pas eté touché
et ses habits etoient entiers. on le porta à sa maison il y
expira une demi heure aprés. Je suis d'autant plus affligé
de cet accident qu'il est arrivé dans la partie du Gevaudan
ou les Betes feroces ont exercé leur fureur tout l'eté dernier
et qu'il y à bien à craindre qu'elles n'y reprennent poste. Nos
habitans ne peuvent, Monseigneur, que paroitre bien
malheureux dans un canton du Gevaudan il sont

en proye aux Betes feroces et dans tout le païs ils
souffrent de la penurie et de la cherté des Grains.
J'ay l'honneur de vous addresser cy joint, Monseigneur,
une autre Lettre que j'ay celui de vous ecrire sur ce
dernier objet

J'ay l'honneur d'etre avec un profond respect

Monseigneur

A Mende le 11e Mars 1766.

Votre trés humble et
trés obeissant serviteur
Lafont

Second and third pages of March 1766 letter from Lafont. ***Photo Schwalb. Archives départementales de l'Hérault.***

smacked with sticks by the two men, but it moved so fast Antony believed he'd been attacked by two beasts.

The Estates of the Gévaudan met once more in March 1766, with, to their chagrin, discussion of the Beast again monopolizing the agenda. Discussion centered around the government's directives and strategies concerning wolf poisoning.

The Beast slowed its predations during the latter half of 1766, with, according to sources, between about ten and twenty attacks over the six-month period, and from four to eleven deaths.

August 1766

The summer sun washed over the Massif Central. Granite peaks and limestone plateaus baked beneath the crystalline sky. The wind moved through the grasses in which a flock of goats grazed. Their mistress, a fourteen-year-old girl from Auvers, France, lay in the grass watching the clouds. She stroked her youngest charge's head. The baby goat butted her hand and twitched its tail.

Then it stopped.

"What?" asked the girl, sitting up. The little creature was gazing at something behind her.

A family member, come to check on her?

A boy from the village, up to no good?

She turned.

A strange animal was sprinting toward her. The girl stood up, staring, her hand on the little goat's head.

A dog? *Too big.*

A wolf? *In the day?*

Her heart began to pound.

The animal was strange—scrawny, bony, with a rough coat and a long tail. It leered at her with a snaggletooth grin.

And ran faster.

La Bête, she gasped. The Beast.

The shepherdess scrambled to a rock outcropping nearby, where there was a small cave in which she played while the goats grazed. She flung herself through the small opening into the cool darkness.

Snarling, the Beast rushed in behind her. Pebbles scattered, striking the girl. The Beast thrust a misshapen muzzle within the opening, snapping its jaws. She felt its hot breath.

The smell. She clapped her hands to her face and shrank back.

Outside, the Beast paced. The baby goat bleated. There was a pause. The girl's heart pounded. The Beast seized the kid in its jaws and shook. The little goat cried out piteously for its mistress.

"My baby!" shouted the girl. "Let him alone!" Without thinking, she lunged from the cave. "Get away, you devil!" she exclaimed, hurling a stone. The Beast dropped the goat.

Then—according to the 1889 chronicle of Abbé Pierre Pourcher—the Beast, "quick as lightning, jumped on the girl and ate her almost completely."

And so Madeleine Paschal, a fourteen-year-old shepherdess from Auvers, became the sixty-sixth victim of the Beast of the Gévaudan.

***

A twelve-year-old boy was killed on September 12 in Paulhac, another on November 1: "Jean Pierre Ollier of La Soucheyre, aged about twelve years, was devoured . . . by La Bête Féroce, which is eating everybody . . ."

The Beast seemed to be on hiatus from November 2, 1766, until March 2, 1767, as far as records show. But then it returned for what would be a final killing spree.

CHAPTER 16

Ténazeyre

From March 2 through the end of May 1767, about three months, thirteen people lost their lives, an average of about one death per week, including seven children, five teenagers, and a forty-eight-year-old woman. Many were around the parishes of Saugues, La Besseyre-Saint-Mary, Grèzes, and Auvers. Two females were killed on May 5. There were possibly as many as thirty attacks altogether during this period.

June 1767

Tradition holds that, in the face of these new predations, the terror-fraught peasantry came together for support at community gatherings and pilgrimages to sacred sites of the Virgin Mary: Nôtre-Dame d'Estours near Saugues, and Nôtre-Dame Beaulieu, "lovely place," near Paulhac. Throngs of Gévaudanais came out, praying for deliverance from this latest onslaught.

Pilgrim Jean Chastel famously had his blunderbuss (the word comes from the Dutch for "thunder-box")—a short-range gun loaded with shot, slugs, nails, etc., to cover a wide area—and his ammunition—cast from "leaden medals of the Virgin of the type affixed to the brim of one's hat"—blessed by the priest.

Many historians say such pilgrimages would have been unlikely in May and June, as it would have been in the midst of the busy spring agricultural season. However, Judith Devlin says it was common for country people to embark on pilgrimages in which they followed time-honored rituals appropriate to each sacred site, be it church or fountain. These pilgrimages were not made for spiritual salvation, but rather to bring about solutions to various real-life problems, from finding husbands to keeping livestock safe from wolves.

From June 1 through June 17, there were yet more attacks, perhaps half a dozen. Nine-year-old Catherine Chautard of Le Malzieu was killed on June 12. On June 18, Jeanne Bastide of Desges, nineteen years old, perished.

The wave of new attacks compelled the Marquis d'Apcher, now twenty years old, to renewed action. It was close to midnight on June 18, soon after the most recent fatal assault, when the young nobleman, on impulse, managed to convince twelve locals to accompany him on a hunt, among them Jean Chastel and three of his sons.

Under the light of a pallid half moon, the group and their dogs hastened to the vicinity of the crime, searching the dense forest far into the night.

Finally, the exasperated marquis stopped his mount on the banks of a stream and dismounted, allowing the horse to drink. The elder Chastel followed suit.

"The Beast has eluded us once more!" The marquis said in despair.

Chastel looked up above the trees. He studied the stars thoughtfully.

"Let's try the Ténazeyre woods, Marquis," he said quietly. "Perhaps we've driven him there."

It was nearly four o'clock on the morning of June 19 when the thirteen arrived at Ténazeyre, on the lower slopes of Mont Mouchet—where, one hundred seventy-seven years later, during World War II, French countrymen would fight a different kind of evil.

Among the silent, resin-scented pines, the weary hunters regrouped, resuming their efforts in a rolling pre-dawn fog so dense that their dogs, scrutinizing it, growled from deep within their throats as if it were a living thing.

On all minds was the ever-persistent question: Would this new day be the day?

***

Jean Chastel had moved away from the others, who were now crashing through the underbrush some distance from him, startling wildlife, searching for the enemy.

The dawn had come and gone and he had not yet paid his respects to Our Lady.

He stopped at the Sogne (marsh) d'Auvers, placed his gun against a tree, and retrieved his spectacles and prayer book from his pockets.

The sun, still cloaked in a misty gauze, shone down through the trees.

Chastel prayed.

The wind muttered among the pines.

A twig snapped.

Chastel calmly looked up from his book. There, through the pines, was one of the marquis's dogs coming toward him, in hot pursuit of—

—the Beast.

"In a spirit of piety and confidence," Chastel finished his prayers and slipped his book and spectacles into a waistcoat pocket.

The monster turned, to the dog's surprise, and lunged at the canine, snapping, savagely biting its nose and face. The dog howled, blood running into its eyes.

Chastel took up his gun.

The Beast proceeded on its course, moving fast, winding through the trees.

Then it saw Chastel.

It slid to a stop.

Chastel did not move.

Man and menace faced one another.

Chastel ticked off all the characteristics of the Beast: the immense size, the odd coloring, the blazing orbs.

Like a wolf and yet not a wolf.

He fired.

BAM! The shot echoed through the woods of Ténazeyre.

It was good.

The medals of Our Lady hit home.

The shot severed the animal's trachea. The Beast shuddered, as if something possessed it. It stumbled, got up, stumbled again.

Chastel waited as the chalky gunsmoke cleared.

The Beast fell.

It did not get up again.

Sides heaving, fighting for its breath, it focused on Chastel with a savage look.

And then the hunter watched as the embers of its eyes faded and went out at last.

"Beast," said Chastel softly, "thou will eat no more."
A griffon vulture, *Gyps fulvus*, circling above, gave a raspy cry.

***

"Jean! Are you well?"
D'Apcher materialized in the mist.
Chastel said, "Marquis, our prayers have been answered."

Epilogue

After the Ténazeyre creature was killed by Chastel, its remains were taken to d'Apcher's château and, as with the Beast of Chazes, thoroughly examined by local surgeons, in this case Boulanger, father and son, with the results confirmed by Roch-Étienne Marin, royal notary.

Nearly two centuries later, a document confirming Chastel's deed was found in the National Archives of France. He received a modest reward.

Legend has it Chastel is said to have taken the Beast's remains to Versailles, accompanied by a d'Apcher servant named Gilbert who, after their by-then malodorous offering was rebuffed by the king, interred it somewhere on the palace grounds. However, many believe this anecdote to be a part of tradition. Louis XV may have been hunting at his summer residence, Compiègne, north of Paris, at this time of the year.

In any case, three years and six days after the first herdgirl, Jeanne Boulet, was laid to rest in Les Hubacs, a July 7, 1767, communication authorized by notary Marin stated, "The monster of the Gévaudan is no longer . . . tranquility reigns in the country . . . Children which were contained within their homes so long lead their cattle to pasture safely, and men of mature age leave them these tasks to resume those more substantial and more fruitful."

***

The Bishop of Mende, coincidentally, passed away that very day.

Afterword

Paris, early 1900s

Paul Le Blanc, a visitor to Paris, wandered its *Jardin des Plantes*, the National Museum of Natural History, taking in its exhibits of plants, minerals, and fossils. Founded in 1626, the Jardin was originally *Jardin du Roi*, the King's Garden.

But where were the remains of *La Bête*?

He proceeded to the main desk. The lone administrator seemed extremely busy.

Inexplicably, Le Blanc's heart began to race.

The administrator barely glanced at him, rustling papers. *"Oui?"* ("Yes?")

Le Blanc took a breath. "I am inquiring," he said, "about a creature killed by one Monsieur François Antoine in 1765." He referred to his *carnet*, or notebook. "It was originally exhibited in the *Jardin du Roi*."

"Oui."

"Is it . . . here?" Le Blanc blurted.

The administrator rolled his eyes. "That specimen? *Non*. We disposed of it not long ago."

"Disposed of it?" Le Blanc exclaimed.

Other visitors stared.

"*Monsieur*, please," said the administrator.

"But," Le Blanc sputtered. "It was *La Bête Féroce!*"

"Non." The administrator sniffed. "It was a hairless remnant *rustique* from another time. Destroyed according to the policies of the museum." He arched an eyebrow, returning to his papers. "Why would someone of this century ever want to see such a thing?"

Part 2
The Hunt for Truth

CHAPTER 17

Hypotheses

Whence this creature came no one knew; as to what he was like no two persons could agree; but the terror inspired by his presence was universal.

—Charles Dickens

The 2001 French film *Le Pacte des loups* (*Brotherhood of the Wolf*), directed by Christophe Gans, is a lush kaleidoscope of entertaining elements, from exotic armored attack beasts with fangs of steel, to an investigative French naturalist and his friend, a Native American martial arts expert, to religion, revolution, secret societies, and much more, all set against a "gloriously atmospheric" (according to the late film critic Roger Ebert) backdrop. And, as Ebert pointed out in his January 2002 review, it's based on a true story.

The real deal is no less intriguing. What or who was responsible for the attacks in the Gévaudan? Since the time of the Beast, many unusual suspects have been considered culpable for the approximately two hundred attacks that took place between 1764 and 1767. Besides a wolf or wolves, historians, researchers, and novelists have speculated about a hyena, a bear, a primate, a lion, wolf-dog hybrids, animals thought to have been extinct, a werewolf, a mad human trainer of attack animals, a new species, and the Marquis de Sade.

Through the years, and especially during the twentieth century, French books, novels, dramas, periodicals, websites, films, television programs, comics, and graphic novels have presented the story of the Beast, along with various hypotheses as to the events of 1764, 1765, 1766, and 1767.

Conjectures

There are a number of camps: One believes wolves are blameless, as, generally speaking, in our modern world, *Canis lupus* is a reserved and cautious animal, as far as humans go. Therefore, lovers of the wolf credit the theory that the culprit, if an animal, had to have been a hyena or other exotic animal, or possibly some sort of hybrid animal.

In 1911, Doctor Paul Puech, a professor of the University Montpellier's medical faculty, proposed in a paper that there were three possible culprits. First, wolves. Second, cruel jokesters who may have been responsible for some of the Beast's more fabulous behavior, such as peering through the window of the home of one of its young victims, even as preparations were underway for the child's funeral. Third, a maniac who, dressed in wolfskin, preyed upon children using the Beast's attacks to cover up his own perversions. Perhaps he used one or more dogs outfitted in suits of armor of tough boarskin to expedite his evil actions. In responding to Puech, Richard Thompson points out that wolf attacks at the time were not unusual, and generally the natives were prepared to stave off such predators with staffs, pikes, and whatever else was available. What was uncommon were mortalities, "especially on the scale experienced in the Gévaudan."

The Dogs of War

French writers Abel Chevalley and Henry Pourrat of the 1930s and 1940s, respectively, among others, introduced now-popular ideas that have been modified and reinforced so that they are often taken to be historical fact. There are those who support the ideas put forth by Chevalley and Pourrat, that the animal was an armored attack dog or another creature trained by Antoine Chastel. Chevalley held that Count Morangiès was in league with Antoine; Pourrat that Antoine acted alone, and that his father, Jean Chastel, eventually ended the affair by putting down the animal himself.

Some believe the Beast was covered in boarskin in order to deflect eighteenth-century musket balls. Boarskin was also proposed by Raymond Francis Dubois and supported by zoologist Louis Michel, not only for its level of protection, but because it would present the dorsal stripe for which the Beast was famed. Dogs have been used, and are used, as formidable agents of war in military organizations since ancient times, often outfitted with various types of armor and spiked collars to protect their throats. Today, the US military's highly trained dogs of war wear bulletproof armor, protective footwear, "doggles" (canine goggles), and other equipment, depending on the circumstances of each mission.

***

The horrors of the Gévaudan included sixteen known decapitations. Researcher Phil Barnson, of the site www.labetedugevaudan.com, states that after speaking with French rural historian Jean-Marc Moriceau in 2012 and studying the semantics of the documentation related to the beheadings, a human may or may not have been responsible for half of them; the other eight appear to have been carried out by an animal. But, he adds, this does not contribute to the theory of a sadistic killer, or another very disturbing theory: that the murderer may have been collecting victims' heads. It simply indicates that these incidents were subject to individual interpretation, and the wording used by those whose responsibility it was to create the record succeeded in amplifying the awe and dread of the Beast. He also tells us that of the many attacks in which witnesses were present, their reports spoke of an animal, not a human. Others believe the Beast could have been a disguised and disturbed member of Paris's *beau monde*, getting his "kicks" by coming to the Gévaudan to kill children of the rural highlands.

Count Morangiès of Saint-Alban, son of the most influential nobleman of the area, is also suspected of carrying on a duplicitous existence: on one hand actively partaking in the *chasses* (hunts) for the Beast in the Gévaudan; on the other, frequenting Versailles and Paris on mysterious business, perhaps related to his many debts, or perhaps as a playboy. Derek Brockis, English translator of the Abbé Pierre Pourcher's seminal account of La Bête, describes Morangiès as a "powerful local nobleman. Independent abrasive attitude. Suspicious character." Writer Roger Oulion considered Morangiès to be at the helm of a gang of malefactors carrying out evildoings in the Gévaudan.

The Marquis de Sade (1740–1814) was even suggested as a potential culprit in the 1962 booklet by Mademoiselle Marguerite

Aribaud-Farrère, mentioned in our Foreword, but the time of the Beast prefaced the activities for which he is notorious; in August 1767, he was married and a new father.

A 2014 novel by French senator Gérard Roche entitled *Gévaudan: The Novel of the Beast* approaches the story by focusing on one rural family and on what life was like in the Gévaudan. The author says he explored several theories in the course of his writing, including that of the Beast being a result of a collective psychosis after a harsh winter, or wolves that devoured cadavers left behind after the Seven Years' War, or that the Beast was an experimental hybrid.

Religious Turbulence

Was the Beast an instrument of the seemingly never-ending conflicts between religions? The diocese of Mende became an ecclesiastical, or church, principality in the fourteenth century, when its bishop also became the Gévaudan's count after negotiating with the king the lands each would rule separately and together. In other words, in his diocese, the bishop of Mende was on equal footing with the king. The bishop at the time of the Beast was Gabriel-Florent de Choiseul-Beaupré. (His cousin, Étienne François Duc de Choiseul, was a prime minister in King Louis XV's administration.) The bishop held that the Beast was a scourge of God in his famous *mandement* of 1764, as did nineteenth-century Beast chronicler Abbé Pierre Pourcher.

Seventy-nine years before the Beast's appearance, Louis XIV revoked the Edict of Nantes (which had been intended to bring some civil accord between religious factions). The revocation meant that French Protestants who refused to convert to Catholicism were "invited" to leave the country. The Camisards, as mentioned in our introduction, revolted in the early 1700s. The wild mountains of the Beast became a haven for fugitive Protestants. Two centuries later, in the 1920s, the author of the book *Undiscovered France* came across homes near Florac with large white crosses painted above their doors. This, she was told, signified that the household was made up of Catholics who would not associate with those of the *religion réformée*. The two faiths "existed side by side in sort of an armed truce."

Richard Thompson points out, however, if the Beast was used in this way, "Catholics got the worst of it, as all of the hundred-odd victims of the Beast were Catholics and there is no record of a series of retaliatory murders in Protestant districts south of the Margeride." French anthropologist and folklorist Véronique Campion-Vincent mentions another hypothesis sometimes proffered: A Protestant was "settling his scores with the Catholic inhabitants."

In the mid-eighteenth century, the Jesuit order, the Society of Jesus, was in conflict with the Jansenists, a growing faction of Catholic conservatives opposed to the faith in favor at the time, including the concept of "easy grace," whereby one's salvation could be acquired by such means as indulgences, written statements offering amnesty from punishment for one's sins. The Jesuits quelled the Jansenist movement for a time, but their own approval ratings were dropping due to various offences, such as favoring papal supremacy over Bourbon paternalism (the king, or father of the country, Louis XV, was a member of the Bourbon dynasty), and even for possible involvement in an assassination attempt upon the king. The Society was exiled from France by Louis XV in March 1764; by 1767, the priestly order was nullified by Pope Clement XIV. Back in Mende, Bishop Choiseul-Beaupré was known to be forbearing of Jansenism and even to have inclinations toward it. His December 31, 1764, *mandement* included reference to St. Augustine, the teachings of whom are the basis for Jansenism. Could that mean that the Jesuits, seeking reprisal, might have somehow been behind the Beast?

Further, according to tradition, in the days of the early Christians, Saint Severian was the first bishop of Mende, and his feast day was celebrated yearly on January 25. But in the eighteenth century, says Pourcher, Mende's bishop Choiseul-Beaupré, in exchange for support for a roadway project with which to boost the local economy, was asked by his cousin, the king's secretary of state, to supplant the old church breviary, or calendar (a book of church services, prayers, feast days, and so on, for each day of the church year) with a new one that omitted Saint Severian's feast. It was opined that this irreverent action had provoked God to set the Beast loose on the diocese.

In 1858, Charles Dickens, writing in his publication *Household Words*, states, "It was generally supposed that the wild beast of the Gévaudan was an allegory . . . for, in the *Gentleman's Magazine* of

February, eighteen hundred and sixty-five, we read: 'By the wild beast is meant the heretics; by the children killed are intimated the converts that are frequently made by them to the protestant faith; and by the dragoons sent out against the wild beast, the violent attacks of the clergy are signified, who are always persecuting the protestants with the utmost rigor.'"

Finally, during the hunts for the Beast, Duhamel and other hunters actually used a number of the victims' cadavers as bait, hoping the Beast would return to its kill in each instance. Locals wondered: Could the gruesome presence of these bodies strewn about augur the time of the Apocalypse, as foretold by the Scriptures?

Pourcher and the Deception of François Antoine

One hundred twenty-four years after François Antoine and Rinchard killed the large animal at Chazes, the Abbé Pierre Pourcher published his famous chronicle of the Beast, and in it, accuses the king's gunbearer of trickery. He holds that François Antoine, once situated in the Gévaudan, realized that he was facing something unique. But he sought fortune and fame as a great and speedy deliverer of the region, and thus tricked king and court by killing and displaying a mere wolf, albeit a sizable one. But where was La Bête, the true monster? Pourcher writes that the Beast "disappeared from the scene and remained hidden during all Antoine's hunts at Chazes," Further, the Abbé believed François Antoine could somehow foresee the victory that would be achieved by Jean Chastel two years later, and so the gunbearer abused Chastel and his sons, throwing them into jail until his own departure from the region in November 1765. "[The Chastels'] innocent joke [luring a royal gamekeeper into a bog] perhaps created enemies for them at Court and from competitors who were jealous of losing the glory of killing La Bête and conscious of the Chastels' superior hunting skills . . . And so, Antoine succeeded in imposing his will with an audacity which would not be acceptable today." Doubters of François Antoine also said he actually killed a domesticated wolf brought in from the royal hunting complex. Others, such as Monsieur Ollier, a cleric of Lorcières, France, wrote many letters insisting the Beast was not dead because it was not a wolf.

The Inscrutable Chastels

Some of the many facets of the tale of the Beast of the Gévaudan relate to the Chastel family of La Besseyre-Saint-Mary. Patriarch Jean Chastel, according to the story, slew a second man-eating Beast on June 19, 1767, with a gun and ammunition blessed the day before during a pilgrimage at the church of Nôtre Dame de Beaulieu. This was after a previous pilgrimage to Our Lady of Estours. La Bête appeared before Chastel at Sogne d'Auvers as he prayed to the Virgin Mary, devotional book in hand. Chastel saw the Beast, but, as he was a good Catholic, he took the time to finish his prayers. The Beast, meanwhile, waited patiently. The hunter put his book and spectacles away, raised his gun, and killed the marauder.

Some have purported that Antoine Chastel, son of Jean, procured a Beast for fellow suspect Count Morangiès. Many wonder if the Beast could have been a hyena, a creature Antoine acquired during his time on the Mediterranean island of Minorca, of the Balearic Islands off the east coast of Spain. Others wonder if "lone wolf" Antoine kept a menagerie, which included a hyena. Beast buffs note that attacks mysteriously stopped in the autumn of 1765 when the Chastels were imprisoned by the royal gunbearer. Father Jean Chastel put a stop to the madness in June 1767, when he killed the creature. (The animal, we are reminded, would have recognized Jean as being part of its human "pack" with master Antoine Chastel, which explains why it would have sat patiently before the elder Chastel.)

There is evidence that there was a living hyena among the animals of the King's Garden, and a taxidermic hyena specimen in the King's Cabinet (the foundation of the collection for the present-day National Museum of Natural History in Paris). The latter may have come from the Gévaudan, but there is no evidence this animal had anything to do with the killings. More on this to come.

Antoine, it is said, made his way to the Mediterranean Sea years before, and was shanghaied by pirates. He was supposedly castrated and put to work as a menagerie keeper on Minorca, where he may have met Count Morangiès. He later returned to the Gévaudan, where he became a solitary forest warden, residing atop Mont Mouchet with his dogs. Some say he also had wolves as companions. Barnson tells us, however, that according to records,

Antoine Chastel was married and actually had a number of children.

Jean Chastel, like the elder d'Enneval and François Antoine, was a veteran hunter. He was born in 1708, and so would have been in his late fifties at the time of the Beast. He is said to have been an excellent marksman. The father of five or six children with his wife, Anne, Jean was a farmer, hunter, and operated a bar. And contrariwise to his being a reverent Catholic, he was also thought to be a sorcerer, or a *meneur de loups* (a wolf leader). A nickname for him was *le fils de la masque* (son of a witch). (Barnson adds that the expression *porter la masque*—to bring bad luck—is still in use today.) The Chastels were even been said to have been part of an occult group.

There was a case in Marvejols, France, in 1762, in which a clan named Rodier—father, mother, and two sons—was charged with employing wolves to intimidate and rob passersby. The parents were hanged and the older son was sent to the galleys (prison ships powered by sails and the labor of slave or convict oarsmen). Perhaps the account of the Rodier family was the kernel of this concept. Some wolf leaders were said to set their trained animals on sheep belonging to enemies.

Cannibal Soldiers?

Another theorist, André Aubazac, proposes that the gruesome acts of the first Beast were carried out by humans, transients working on road projects and soldiers returning from the Seven Years' War (which ended in 1763, the year prior to the Beast's first appearance) who may have had to become cannibalistic in order to survive during the conflicts. Aubazac believes the second Beast's crimes resulted from a Chastel family feud.

Thinking Like a Conspiracy Theorist

The *Wall Street Journal* column "Mind & Matter," by Robert M. Sapolsky, touched on the topic of conspiracy theorists in the newspaper's November 9 and 10, 2013, editions. Citing studies of online discussions about 9/11 and about the death of Princess Diana, the column states that nonbelievers of various theories are more frequently persistent in spending time discussing real proof for their view. Cabalists are seen to concentrate on dismissing accepted notions and may take up theories that are actually inconsistent with one another. Sapolsky references philosopher Paul Thagard as writing about how such theories do help meet "our need for explanations that provide coherence to our view of the world." He adds that doubting authorized information may in fact direct one to the authentic.

Political Issues

The reign of King Louis XV was marked by costly wars, humbling losses of international territory, religious and political disputes, and continuing issues such as the famine pact, in which the public suspected the nobility of hoarding grain in order to raise prices. Born in 1710, Louis was fifty-four years old at the time of the Beast's first appearance. He'd been crowned nearly half a century before, at the age of five (though the French Regent was in charge until Louis turned thirteen). Afterward, he ruled with his first minister, Cardinal Fleury, until the Cardinal's death in 1743, at which time Louis took sole control of the throne. Historians paint a picture of Louis XV as a monarch who seemed uninterested in his duties. The king frequently withdrew from court to go hunting. His many mistresses scandalized his subjects. But the ravages of a monster in a far-flung district of his kingdom piqued his interest; he was said to be fascinated by the accounts and ordered its remains be brought back for his personal collection. As the Beast's attacks continued, the king's advisors saw that involvement in the plight of the people of the Gévaudan might boost public opinion and help distract from its problems. In February 1765, as Duhamel and his dragoons and local hunters continued to miss the mark, it was proclaimed that the concerned king would offer a startling six thousand *livres* (pounds) for the destruction of the Beast. This was in addition to a number of other rewards, for a total of ten thousand *livres*, an incredible sum. The public eye was certainly focused on the Gévaudan as a result.

More on Those Attacked

The Beast sometimes killed one or two people per month, one or more per week, or one or more within the course of twenty-four hours. Beast Number One was responsible for eighty deaths (Barnson), fifty-nine deaths (Moriceau), or fifty-six deaths (Abbé François Fabre, a cleric/historian who published his own Beast chronicle at the beginning of the twentieth century). Beast Number Two was responsible for twenty-four deaths (Barnson, Moriceau, Fabre).

Researcher Phil Barnson tabulates more than two hundred attacks altogether. Barnson's figures comprise individuals attacked or menaced themselves, those attacked as part of a group, and individuals attacked more than once. Barnson indicates a number of men in this number, more than a quarter of those attacks. The ages of those attacked range from babies and a three-year-old girl to a sixty-eight-year-old woman. The majority are children and teens, individuals less than twenty years old. Women were the second largest group attacked.

The consensus is that not all the attacks and deaths are accounted for. There is a remarkable amount of information available in the French archives about the case of the Gévaudan, but gaps in the record remain. Barnson tells us, for example, that in about sixteen killings, the victims' genders are not known.

Those left behind may not have wished to share their family's misfortune with authorities who might want to use a loved one's body as bait. Or because the Beast was depicted as a scourge of God, a death might bring dishonor.

Some discrepancies may be due to the fact that the testimonies of those who experienced or witnessed attacks and those who observed the Beast's movements would require translation into the official *langue d'oïl*, the French spoken in the north. It is possible or probable that some information was mistranslated, contributing to discrepancies. Some accounts of deaths may be duplicates.

In any case, as Father Pourcher comments, "Peasants do not write diaries."

CHAPTER 18

Modus Operandi

Singular cunning and inconceivable agility.
—From an account from the meeting of the Estates of Mende, March 1765

Here, based on the various accounts, we offer a basic "profile" of the chimerical Beast and its more iconic qualities and patterns of behavior. How was the Beast described? How extensive was its range? What types of wounds did it inflict? Contenders for the Beast are more closely examined in sections to come.

General Impressions

What would someone in the 1760s *see* if the Beast lunged into their line of vision? In reality, many victims likely heard only "a twig snap," per researcher Derek Brockis, or nothing at all, perhaps only a flash of reddish fur from the corner of an eye. Many would have had their nostrils assaulted by something truly foul before being forced to the ground and plunged into pain, shock, and darkness.

Time and again, we read that the Beast was "like a wolf, but not a wolf." And we read that the people of the Gévaudan *knew* wolves. Phil Barnson reports that the more than one hundred witnesses said they observed some kind of *animal*.

To further follow in the tracks of such an animal or animals, which specialized in killing people, we might formulate intriguing questions, such as: What did the creature(s) look like? What might it have resembled? A new species or something known? Hybrid animal, mutant, or giant wolf? How was it described by those who saw it eye to eye? Let us consider some of these inquiries.

Here is an English translation of the description of the creature that appeared in the *Gazette de France*, the official state newspaper:

> A very strange wild beast has lately appeared in the neighborhood of Langogne and the forest of Mercoire which has occasioned great commotion. . . . Those who have seen him say he is much higher than a wolf, low before, and his feet are armed with talons. His hair is reddish, his head large, and the muzzle of it is shaped like that of a greyhound; his ears are small and straight; his breast is wide, and of a grey color; his back streaked with black; and his mouth, which is large, is provided with a set of teeth so very sharp that they have taken off several heads as clean as a razor could have done. He is of amazing swiftness; but, when he aims at his prey, he crouches so close to the ground that he hardly appears to be bigger than a large fox; and at the distance of some one or two *toises* [a unit of measurement of Old France; one *toise* is nearly six and one-half feet long], he rises upon his hind legs and springs upon his prey, seizing it by the neck or throat. He is afraid of oxen, which he runs away from.

An additional quality ascribed to the Beast is singular strength. It was able to travel vast distances at a rapid clip, decapitate victims, and carry young children for surprising distances. It was flexible; media accounts alleged it could bend from head to tail. The Beast was, of course, anthropophagous (a man-eater). It was malodorous. At the beginning of its tenure, it seemed to be a lone animal. Later, it was observed with another, smaller wolf, which in turn was seen with pups.

Size

The Beast was big. Historian Jay Smith states that François Antoine at first thought the Chazes wolf was a donkey. Donkeys' height may vary, from about thirty to about sixty inches, as measured at the withers or shoulders. (Robert Louis Stevenson said his Cévennes donkey, Modestine, was small, the size of a dog.) People frequently said La Bête was the size of a yearling calf. Calves' height varies by breed, from about forty-four to fifty inches at the shoulders. The ancient Salers cattle of the Massif Central are among the larger breeds. The average wolf measures about thirty-two inches high. A hyena stands a little shorter.

Coat

The coat of the Beast was described as reddish gray, sometimes the color of roasted coffee. It was also described as coarse. Its tail was bushy and long. Its head and legs were short-haired and said to be the color of deer. The Beast possessed a black dorsal (of or on the back) stripe. It had a white, heart-shaped mark on its chest.

Eyes

We are told that the Beast's eyes sparkled. In a lament cited by Pourcher, the Beast's "flashing eyes with redoubtable glare, are two glowing coals." More than one hundred years later, in an article on the Beast, Charles Dickens commented, "His eyes sparkled so with fire, that it was hardly possible (for a regiment of dragoons) to bear his look."

Jean Chastel's Beast's (La Ténazeyre Canid) eyes were "cinnabar red." Barnson suggests this may have been the result of *petechiae*, trauma-induced bursting of blood vessels, caused by the shot that ripped the animal's throat and broke its shoulder.

Odor

La Bête's odor was often mentioned in accounts. Pourcher's account states that the hunters hoped their dogs would be "attracted by her bad odor." Dickens spoke of a report stating that the stench of the Beast, when it was said to have "vaulted" into and out of a horse-drawn carriage, "was past description."

Aspect

Pourcher's account tells us the Beast exhibited "singular cunning and inconceivable agility." As described in our report of the doomed shepherdess Madeleine Paschal, the predator did not hesitate to harm a herder's livestock to get to its human prey. According to one account, La Bête allegedly buried a sheep alive to lure its caretaker out in the open. Regarding documented predatory mobility, Jane Goodall says the wolf, as well as the jackal, is "capable of lightning movements—they can thus nip and get away before the larger animal has chance of retaliating."

A Primate?

Clergyman Trocelier of Aumont, France, a hunt facilitator and Beast witness, discussed the belief of some that the animal might be a type of monkey due to the creature's ability to move on its hind legs, especially in water. But Trocelier concluded this was not probable after studying the creature's tracks and body.

Tracks

Royal gunbearer François Antoine, a venerable hunter of many decades, determined La Bête's paw prints were the tracks of a large wolf. Yet, contrariwise, Pourcher's account states that "La Bête did not stop approaching the villages and hamlets during the night, this was known from her tracks, which were said to be different from wolves." Later in the story, it is mentioned that the tracks were abnormal, as if they might have been made by an injured animal. Perhaps La Bête (like many of the American "super wolves" discussed later in this book) had been caught in a trap and lost part of a foot in escaping it. Brockis tells us Pourcher thought it might be a deformed animal, though one sent by God to correct the Gévaudanais.

Behavior Toward Firearms

The animals known as La Bête seemed to learn over time that men with rifles were to be avoided.

Respect for Cattle

A number of those attacked were surrounded and protected by the cattle they tended. The ancient Salers breed of cattle of the Massif Central are known to be actively defiant of predators when it comes to their offspring. Similarly, Goodall tells of a confrontation between a wildebeest cow and a hyena stalking the bovid's calf. The cow "charged, bowling [the hyena] over." A minute later it pitched both predator (and prey) "some four feet up into the air." The cow even pinned the hyena down with her horns. Though the wildebeest mother managed to severely injure one of the predator's front paws, the hyena won in the end, seizing the calf, itself now wounded, by the neck. Says Goodall, "It seems that, like wild dogs and wolves, hyenas are prepared to risk kicks from large prey, but are afraid of teeth and horns if the quarry turns to face them."

Locality

La Bête seemed at home both in remote wild habitats and human environments. The Beast was seen in fields, pastures, along roadways, in villages, and in household gardens. Pourcher reported that a February 1765 letter from Mende stated, "La Bête Féroce, emboldened by the long immunity she has enjoyed, is not at all frightened to show herself in the most frequented places, at the edge of woods, in the hamlets, in the villages and on the most beaten tracks."

Range

The Beast ranged a large territory. A review of the maps of the region published by historians, as well as the one in this book, shows that the Beast covered an area approximately sixty miles long by fifty miles wide. The attacks started in Les Hubacs and continued to the northwest, a movement believed to be caused in part by the frequent hunts. This extent of movement, however, is not unusual with regard to wolf behavior. For example, wolf specialist L. David Mech reported that wolves in Alaska traveled from six to forty-five miles between kills.

Injuries Inflicted

The damage the Beast visited upon it victims was horrific. Heads were separated from bodies. Limbs were torn away. The creature came from behind or from the side, going after the face and neck. There were sixteen decapitations, with instances of heads and/or bodies going missing. Wolves' jaws are capable of fifteen hundred pounds of pressure per square inch.

Evisceration

The Beast by all accounts fancied hearts and livers, as well as blood, intestines, and soft parts. Goodall speaks of disembowelment as being a typical way that hyenas, wolves, and wild dogs consume their prey. "Wild dogs, like domestic hunting dogs, wolves, and hyenas, are quick and efficient killers. They attack their prey where the skin is thinnest and thus quickly reach the internal organs and dispatch the victim." Goodall states that hyenas even eat bits of each other during a feeding frenzy. Squeamish readers might gain a bit of comfort from Goodall's statement that perhaps this is the quickest way to go.

Victims

It is generally held that the Beast's victims were primarily children and women. However, Barnson, in tallying the attacks of the Beast, notes that more than a quarter of those exposed to the creature—via actual physical attacks, belonging to a group under attack, or simply being menaced by La Bête—were men.

Aberrant Behavior

The Beast's behavior often seemed to be highly irregular, especially when compared to that of wolves. As stated earlier, it allegedly was observed walking and wading on its hind legs. It fell when shot, yet was able to rise again and escape on a number of occasions, resulting in a belief that perhaps it was some sort of armored creature.

How else could it withstand the musket balls of its hunters? Boarskin, once used to protect dogs used in battle, is a material cited as a possible covering for the Beast.

It also supposedly looked into the windows of peasants' home, watching a mother feeding her child, or a victim's funeral preparations, and so on.

Time of Year

Most canids (members of the family Canidae—dogs, wolves, coyotes, jackals, and foxes), and for that matter hyenas, are nocturnal hunters. The Beast had no set schedule. "'This animal,'" it was said, 'prowls the evening and the morning.'"

Time of Day

Most canids and, for that matter, hyenas, which are carnivores, are nocturnal hunters. Our Beast had no set schedule. "'This animal,' it was said, 'prowls evenings and mornings.'"

Lone Attacks

The Beast's behavior was also aberrant in that the creature was, for the most part, observed on its own. Wolves generally hunt prey in a pack, displaying highly efficient cooperation. Other wolves were seen in the company of the Beast, and François Antoine killed a she-wolf and cubs associated with the Chazes wolf, but there seems to be no record of wolf pack behavior.

Vocalizations

The Beast was said to "cry out" when it was hit with a bullet. The Beast was also expressive; it was said it could make noises like a human in trouble. It was also said to have "hissed" at cattle when bovines sought to protect their young caregivers.

Victims' Garments

Victims' clothing was often found in shreds, yet bizarrely, were sometimes said to be found placed neatly beside the body. In a side note, naturalist C. H. D. Clarke mentions Canadian naturalist Ernest Thompson Seton's painting *Awaited in Vain*, completed when Seton was an art student in France. The painting depicts a Frenchman being devoured by wolves a short distance from his cottage. Clarke states the work was not well received. In one critique, fellow Canadian Dr. William Brodie, says Clarke, "drew attention to the neatness with which the wolves had piled the defunct's clothing," very similar to accounts of La Bête.

***

It is now time to shift our attention to werewolves.

CHAPTER 19

Werewolves of France

Night after night . . . I have given ear to this perturbing concert of the wind among the woods; but whether it was a difference in the trees, or the lie of the ground, or because I was myself outside and in the midst of it, the fact remains that the wind sang to a different tune among these woods of Gévaudan.

—*Robert Louis Stevenson*

The "woods of Gévaudan" provide an ideal setting for werewolfery. Scholar Judith Devlin, in *The Superstitious Mind*, cites physician Louis-Florentin Calmeil, writing in 1870, that lycanthropy—a condition in which troubled persons believe they are wolves—is particularly found in "remote, half-savage mountainous and afforested areas" and among those with extremely isolated occupations, such as herders or woodsmen.

In this section, we change course toward fabulous and legendary pathways, prowling the realm of the werewolf, especially in France, in relation to the Beast. As we will see, there are surprising circumstances and elements from folkways and French writer George Sand's "great dark night of the primitive" which resonate with accounts of La Bête and support the idea of the Beast's identification as a werewolf—of one type or another.

Westerners are familiar with stories about humans who transform, in what is usually depicted as an agonizing process, into supernatural wolves, particularly when the moon is full and wolfbane abloom, after having been bitten by a werewolf. But these conventions are fairly recent.

The ways of lycans have shifted through time, from ancient myths and monstrous medieval crimes, to spiritual disputes and superstitions, to medical case histories, and, of course, popular entertainment. In early medieval times, many werewolves, such as "Bisclavret" of the twelfth-century lay (narrative poem) by Marie de France, were innocent humans trapped by others (often disloyal wives) in bestial form. Later, lycanthropy was held as a form of sorcery; werewolves were witches.

Shape-shifting creatures around the world are known by many names: *loup-garou* in French; in Spanish *lobishome, lobisome,* or *lobizon*. Petronius's *Satyricon* presents a story of a *versipellis* (turnskin) at the time of the Roman Emperor Nero. Native American culture speaks of skinwalkers. In Britain and Ireland and in the New World, too, stories are told of Black Shuck and other phantom black dogs, creatures that share attributes with the Beast.

The word lycanthropy itself has multiple meanings: One is that it is a form of mental illness in which a person believes he or she is a wolf, as mentioned earlier. The word is also defined as a belief in werewolves, and a conviction that people can become wolves.

Dr. Calmeil enumerated a threefold manifestation of the first definition, in which individuals believe themselves wolves. First there were despondent persons convinced they were helplessly bedeviled, alleging that they had wreaked hurt and havoc after dark, at times in the company of wolves; second, troubled, frenetic persons who took to nighttime roaming; third, dangerous persons who were unable to control themselves, believing they were wolves, attacking humans and animals, uttering wailing cries as they went about on hands and knees.

The medical definition of lycanthropy comes from the words *insania lupina* (wolves furie). Records of instances of this condition are available from days long past. More than a millennia ago, Paul of Aegina, a physician in Alexandria, Egypt, noted the types of symptoms familiar to contemporary mental health professionals: Subjects frequent graveyards or wilderness areas, howling and moving about on their hands and legs in imitation of a wolf. Devlin states that Calmeil considered poisoning a possible factor. Ergot (*Claviceps purpurea)*, a fungus known to prompt hallucinations and hysteria, is thought to be a cause. The fungus forms on grain and cereal plants, especially rye, a staple used in making flour for centuries. And for the peasantry, there was no life without bread.

A *New York Times* piece by Moises Velasquez-Manoff discusses medical cases in which celiac disease, the autoimmune condition caused by a reaction to gluten proteins found in grains such as wheat, barley, and rye, may in some instances affect the brain as well as the gut, causing "seizures, hallucinations, psychotic breaks, and even, in one published case, what looked like regressive autism." Could there be a connection between celiac disease and lycanthropy?

Scholar Charlotte Otten tells us that the word "werewolf" was actually in use about five hundred years before "lycanthrope." The first documented use of "werewolf" shows up in the Ecclesiastical Ordinances of King Cnut (eleventh-century ruler of England, Denmark, and Norway), translated as "Therefore must the shepherds be very watchful and diligently crying out, who have to shield the people against the spoiler, such are bishops and mass-priests, who are to preserve and defend their spiritual flocks with wise instructions, that the madly audacious were-wolf do not too widely devastate, nor bit too many of the spiritual flock." Otten cites the significance of the employment of the word "werewolf" instead of "wolf," suggesting that Satan, the traditional "wolf" of scriptural texts, is employing men to work evil in the sheepfold.

Becoming a Werewolf

Scholars, saints, and the superstitious have perpetually advanced hypotheses about *therianthropy*, translation between humans and beasts. There seem to be a number of ways; one of the best-known paths to wolfhood in contemporary entertainment is simply to have been bitten by another werewolf and to wait for the next full moon. In medieval times, one used various unguents or enchanted belts obtained from a witch or a mysterious Man of the Forest. Sometimes a seventh son would become a werewolf. Fallen angels were also likely candidates.

The controversial twelfth-century compilation of writings, *De spiritu et anima*, once attributed to Saint Augustine, stated that the spells of sorceresses and the devil's power would do the trick, and a man under these influences "to himself seems to be a quadruped," but it is a false notion, an illusion, as in reality such a transformation is not possible: "The Devil creates no new nature."

One medievalism held that excommunicated persons became werewolves for a time; in Normandy, France, they shifted for either three or seven years; in the Vendée, for seven years; there, the offender was also required to haunt unlucky locales. "In Basse-Bretagne, any person who had not been shriven [gone to confession] for ten years nor used holy water could become a werewolf. This belief was still current in the middle of the eighteenth century."

Further, some traditions hold that a lycan may also be a vampire, or may become one when it expires. A side note: Through Elliott O'Donnell, we learn that Louis XV, king of France at the time of the Beast, was also interested in vampires. According to *Chamber's Edinburgh Journal*, the king, like many Europeans, was fascinated by reports such as that of Serbian "vampyre" Arnold Paul (also spelled "Paole"), said to come back from the grave and terrorize neighbors, and requested information about the case from his minister in Vienna. Paul Barber notes the word *vampire* entered English in 1734 (the king would have been twenty-four) and that reports of vampirism created another early news sensation.

Continental Canids

Incidents of "disturber-brutes" *(London Magazine)* have been chronicled for centuries in Europe. Possibly the best known up until the Beast of the Gévaudan was that of German werewolf Stubbe Peter, who allegedly committed horrific crimes for twenty-five years in the late 1500s. He killed his son, was guilty of incest, and attempted to murder and then dine upon his in-laws. His diabolical activities, trial, horrific torture (it was said he welcomed any agony in order to save his soul), and death were graphically depicted on a pamphlet widely disseminated as "a warning to anyone who might be contemplating an alliance with the devil." Stubbe Peter's eyes, like the Beast's, were said to be "great and large" and "in the night sparkled like brands of fire."

Werewolves in France: "An Epidemic of Sorcery"

A twentieth-century researcher and collector of paranormal tales, Elliott O'Donnell flatly states: "In no country has the werewolf flourished as in France. . . . As far back as the sixth century we hear of them infesting the woods and valleys of Brittany and Burgundy, the Landes, and the mountainous regions of the Côte d'Or, and the Cévennes." (This last is in the vicinity of our Beast's neighborhood.) Montague Summers concurs that werewolfery was going on in Gaul (the ancient Roman territory comprising France, Belgium, and portions of Italy, Germany, Switzerland, and the Netherlands) far back in antiquity: "Shape-shifting . . . was part and parcel of the wizard lore of the Druids . . ." He notes that Breton warlocks don wolfskins, à la our Gévaudanais *meneur de loups* (wolf lord), discussed later, or "assume the shape of wolves" to attend wicked gatherings.

Some of the most notorious French lycanthropes lived in the sixteenth century, when "the rank foul weeds of werewolfery flourished exceedingly." We detail two well-documented cases in our section on serial killers. Here we will review several other notable cases, details of which illustrate the wide range of werewolf motivations and permutations.

According to the *Compendium Maleficarum*, a woman of Thiaucourt, in northeastern France, "addicted to these evil practices [witchcraft, sorcery, and so on]," felt she had been cheated in a bargain she'd made with a local herdsman. In consequence, the flim-flammed *femme* went lupine and stormed his sheepfold. The herder in turn took up his axe and slashed her leg. She retreated, he followed, and found her, woman-formed, bandaging the limb with shreds of clothing. With this proof she confessed, and atoned "at the stake."

In 1521, in Poligny, France, "a leash [in hunting, a set of three dogs] of witches," Pierre Burgot, Michel Verdun, and a third, Philibert Montot, were put to death for crimes committed as werewolves, including killing and eating children. Like our Beast, Burgot and Verdun might only leave a child's arm uneaten, or, with "keen white teeth," tear out the throat of a girl. "They loved to lap up the warm flowing blood." They also confessed to mating with she-wolves.

In Auvergne, part of the realm of La Bête, there is an account dating from 1558 of a wolf woman who lived near Apchon. According to the story, a nobleman came upon a hunter acquaintance in pursuit of game, and asked for a portion of the spoils. Soon after, a wolf attacked the huntsman; as they wrestled, he retrieved his knife, and cut off a paw. The animal ran away, and the hunter put the paw in his game bag. He made for the nobleman's château, related what had happened, and reached for the foot. But it had transformed into a woman's hand,

and the hand wore a gold ring the aristocrat knew belonged to his wife. The nobleman confronted his spouse, who'd become suddenly unwell. She admitted she'd lost a hand, conceded to her wolfish ways, and consequently went to the stake soon after. The telltale wound that gives away the wolf has become a classic lycan plot twist.

In Burgundy, France, supreme judge Henry Boguet documented the many trials over which he presided in the late 1500s, says Summers, during the time of his region's "epidemic of sorcery—as it may not unfairly be termed," in his book, *Discours des Soricers.* Cases include that of a female lycan, Perrenette Gandillon—"a huge wolf without a tail" who, upon being killed, returned to the form of a woman—and her brother and nephew, Pierre and George, respectively, who admitted that all three had used unguents and in wolf form had devoured many children. Summers says the judge paints a picture of the Gandillon men as "having lost wellnigh any resemblance to humanity, loping on all fours . . . [having] foul horny nails, unpared and sharp as talons, keen white teeth, matted hair, and [like La Bête] red gleaming eyes."

In nineteenth-century Paris, one Sergeant Bertrand, who claimed he did so against his own will, disinterred and disfeatured newly buried cadavers, so much so that one writer deemed him a "human hyena."

As in reports of the Beast of the Gévaudan, other werewolves were said to have neatly disrobed their victims. Otten cites an example: "The clothes of the children which they have killed and eaten have been found in the fields quite whole and without a single tear; so that there was every appearance of the children having been undressed by human hands."

Wolf Masters

George Sand (a pseudonym for writer Armadine-Aurore-Lucille Dudevant, née Dupin) recounts eerie and entertaining folktales from the region of central France in her nineteenth-century *Légendes rustiques.* One finds stories of spectral laundresses, Huguenot-destroyed and haunted furniture, and more, among them stories of werewolves and *meneurs de loups*, wolf masters or lords. Sometimes these last are considered *loups-garous*, or werewolves, themselves.

The Wolf-Charmer* (1881) by John la Farge (1835–1910). *HIP/Art Resource, NY.

In tales told by country grandmothers (such as her own who lived in Berry, France), says Sand, there are two types of wolf leaders. First, the wolf masters of long ago: evil warlocks who became wolves themselves to prey upon and eat children. As the generations passed, these attributes shifted. Wolf lords were no longer child-devouring sorcerers, but venerable, wolf-whispering woodsmen or gamekeepers, possessing arcane knowledge with which they charmed *Canis lupus*.

Sand also includes personal accounts from her then present-day France countryside, of two acquaintances who claimed to see "an old forester" gesturing oddly near a crossroads. The pair then watched as thirteen wolves appeared and behaved as dogs, listening to the ranger's talk and allowing him to pet them. Then wolves and man vanished into the trees. Sand says other acquaintances happened one night to be in the forest of Châteauroux when they observed a pack of agitated wolves outside a woodcutter's cottage. The woodsman opened the door, came outside, and moved about the animals, talking in an unfamiliar language. The lupines left, apparently reassured.

In the highlands of Morvan, France, at the northern tip of the Massif Central, fiddlers were considered wolf leaders, says Sand, their music a result of a pact with Satan. In the Black Valley, a church bell ringer was reportedly ensorcelled by a *musette*, a set of country bag-pipes, playing an unearthly tune by themselves in the middle of nowhere. The bell ringer, Julien, was found there by his priest a day or two later, playing "the devil's own song" on the pipes and leading three hundred wolves. The priest convinced him to come away and play at church for his flock, but Satan's song was heard even there, no matter what Julien tried to play. It was only when the priest lifted the communion host and recited the words of consecration that the bagpipes ruptured, releasing a sound like "the soul of the devil."

In the present-day region of the attacks of the Gévaudan, casual conversation with locals reveals that many are convinced the Beast was a *loup-garou*, werewolf, or *meneur de loups*, a wolf leader, but not in the supernatural sense of which Sand speaks. Contemporary natives believe our notorious wolf lord of the 1760s was a sadistic nobleman outfitted in wolfskin, who'd trained a dog or wolf to do his bidding and assist in attacks on solitary young shepherds and shepherdesses. There is a striking sculpture representing this version of the story in the town of Le Malzieu (see photo in this book's color insert). Here the menacing *loup-garou* clutches a claw-like implement (perhaps a handheld garden cultivator of old?) in one hand as he slinks toward his prey.

O'Donnell deems this kind of werewolfery as "sham lycanthropy" as it is not traditional human-into-wolf transformation. He cites "rationalists" who attribute this behavior to two types of people. First, troubled persons who, convinced they *are* man-eating animals, slay children and women, as they are most defenseless. Second, persons who are not mentally ill, but who resort to "vulgar trickery," using wolves, legends of werewolves, and fear and dread of the same, to carry out and/or cover up murders or cannibalism. "Rumors (most probably started by the murderers themselves) speedily get in circulation that the mangled and half-eaten remains of the villagers are attributable to creatures, half human and half wolf, that have been seen gliding about certain places after dark." He describes African leopard cults where "human vampires" prey upon travelers and others, slaying them and—very much like the Gévaudan Beast—removing choice pieces. They further disfigure the remains with a leopard's claw or nails, and withdraw to a secluded refuge, where, like La Bête, they "successfully defy capture."

Sand discusses werewolf variations from the stories of her childhood: *Lubins* are mild-mannered moonstruck creatures, the custom of which is to loiter at ramparts and graveyard walls, yowling and chattering in strange tongues. They are giddy and usually bashful. "If someone comes to pass," says Sand, "they run away crying: 'Robert died, Robert is dead!'" (This is perhaps referring to a medieval legend of Robert, a Norman knight who was born a child of the devil; he overcame his wicked ways and died a hermitic saint.) In a footnote, Sand states the *lubin* is "a very good fellow" and a guardian of workmen.

But if a creature resembling a *lubin* breaches the cemetery to unearth and feed upon the graveyard's occupants, it is classified as a *lupin*, as in "lycanthrope" or "werewolf."

Sand relates a *lupin* story involving a hunchback tailor who walked by a graveyard wall one night and observed a company of "spirits" in the form of "black dogs or wolves." When the spirits caught sight of the tailor, they became stock-still, studying him "with eyes that shone like fiery blood" and mouths agape, exhaling "nasty bad breath." (Both qualities of La Bête.) Sand says perhaps the tailor's deformity did not convey "the effect of a Christian." Meanwhile, the frightened tailor dared not hold his nose so as not to slight the wolf-dogs. The *lupins* seemed pleased at this and began to talk and wag their tails, and the tailor exited the scene unharmed. Once home, the tailor shared his story with (insensitive) neighbors who scoffed, remarking that with his appearance, he could scare the devil himself. The next night, much to his dismay, the hunchback found he had to pass the cemetery again; he

An image of werewolves by Maurice Sand from *Légendes rustiques* by George Sand. *Bibliotheque des Arts Decoratifs, Paris, France Archives Charmet/Bridgeman Images.*

fervently hoped the previous evening's incidents were simply a bad dream. Alas, there were the lupins, lollygagging by the wall once more. The tailor, affected by wine he'd had with a client a bit earlier, decided to whistle, thinking it would amuse them. It did not. Instead it brought one, then several, after him. They came close and "sniffed at the location where dogs are wont to sniff each other to see if they should be enemies or companions." The alarmed tailor kept walking, but the lupins circled to his front, prohibiting his progress, apparently standing on two legs, reeking and rabid-like, baring yellow canine teeth. The hunchback pleaded for release but the lupins roared threateningly. Then the hunchback promised to bring them a sheep the next day. At this, they fell silent and reverted to all fours. The tailor ran home and dove into bed, where he stayed for more than a week. The local priest visited, chiding him for offering the creatures a sheep. The fleeced lupins, meanwhile, wanting revenge but not daring to come close to a priest, commenced a shock-and-awe campaign from afar, freakishly throwing their voices outside the tailor's house and casting their shadows upon its walls. The other villagers were terrified and the priest could do nothing. Finally, the tailor worked up the nerve to set a trap.

He tied a sheep to his door, admonished the neighbors to arm themselves with "bullets blessed well," and told the *curé* to hide, *goupillon* (holy-water sprinkler) on hand. The tailor then tempted the sheep with grass, making the animal bleat. The *lupins* found this irresistible, left their wall, and drew closer, where they were "well received." Betwixt holy fire and holy water, they fled. Only one was killed, an aging female, who, upon taking a bullet in her heart, cried out in a human voice, "The moon is dead!" Her head and legs were removed and displayed on the cemetery gate. The *lupins* never returned.

What Else Is in the Woods?

The Beast was not the only creature to haunt the French countryside. Peasants were also concerned about immense serpents and basilisks, even into the early 1900s. A "red man" of the Ardennes was said to lure children into the woods. Though rare, sometimes an abandoned child might dwell there, too, such as Victor of Aveyron, found in 1800. In 1731, a girl was discovered living wild near Châlons-sur-Marne, France; she'd killed another child. Historian Graham Robb tells us that in 1774 in southwestern France, a hairy, unclothed man, believed to have been an extant Neanderthal, was seen gleefully dispersing herds of sheep.

A phantom dog, or "beast-revenant," was said to reside in a village of Normandy, France, province of the d'Ennevals. The pet of an enigmatic sojourner, it was killed by a local farmer. The owner inquired about the animal at the farm and was told the dog died naturally. The owner's reply: "If you are right, you will know." George Sand quotes her source as remarking that the tale expresses the concept that the animal possessed a soul, because "it shares with humans the ability to appear after his death."

A *Grand'bête*, "Great Beast," visited Sand's grandmother's farm from time to time. Like a "dog the size of a heifer," it was also called "the white dog" and "the devil's cow," among other descriptors, and was said to have wandered the countryside since time immemorial. It, like La Bête, had "eyes of fire," and, as in the Gévaudan, the country people tried to ward it off with pitchforks, sticks, and blessed bullets. Once it was expected to appear during a storm; as a child Sand witnessed her family's frenzied preparation. She and her brother were ensconced between beds. Prayers were said to small portraits that had over the years been purchased from peddlers (their subjects were assumed to be saints, though Sand says they were more likely prominent generals). Doors were braced shut. Animals became agitated. According to Sand, however, the Great Beast harmed no one and reportedly exited at any sign of trouble. But because it was a supernatural entity, the country people were truly beside themselves at its advent. Says Sand, "the attack of a hungry pack of wolves was less terrifying than the possibility of a visit from the ghost." In this instance, the Grand Beast never came to call; instead, Sand's tutor arrived in the rain to take her and her brother home.

In British and Irish traditions, spectral black dogs make frequent appearances. They are believed to foretell a death. Sometimes they guard humans against misfortune. Editor and writer Bob Trubshaw says they are "part animal, part specter, part fiend." Again there are parallels to the Beast: Black dogs are said to be as large as a calf or a donkey, have glowing eyes, and "smell like death." As a boy, Charles Dickens was frightened by his nurse Mercy's tales of black dogs. Writer Crispin Andrews notes that Arthur Conan Doyle's Sherlock Holmes tale, "The Hound of the Baskervilles," features a kind of canid master, the character Jack Stapleton, who trains a mastiff to hunt Sir Henry Baskerville, covering it with phosphorus to achieve its ghostly nocturnal glow.

In North America, the Navajo people believed in skinwalkers, persons transformed into werewolves that committed diverse heinous acts. Stanley Young of the US Biological Survey offers a twentieth-century account, that of the Phantom Wolf of Big Salt Wash, Colorado, one of a tribe of famous wolves exterminated by hunters of the US government's Biological Survey in support of stockmen in the late 1800s and early 1900s. Hunter W. J. Nearing was said to have pursued the Phantom Wolf from 1921 to 1923. In Young's story, a local sheepherder from Mexico claimed the Phantom was a *lobo de las animas*, or spirit wolf, a werewolf possessed by an evil spirit. At one point Young claims Nearing was able to get off a shot and was convinced he'd killed the animal, only to find it had vanished, leaving a pool of blood, an incident that spooked him. When he captured the wolf later, he found the scar from that bullet.

The Werewolf in Culture

Stories about wolves and werewolves have frightened and entertained us forever. From the ancient myths and stories mentioned earlier, to the classic 1941 film, *The Wolf-man*, featuring actor Lon Chaney, Jr., to the contemporary explosion of books, television shows, and movies incorporating or featuring werewolf characters. The most popular entertainment based on La Bête seems to be Christophe Gans's 2001 film, *Le Pacte des loups (Brotherhood of the Wolf)*. Unlike vampire mythology, which returns again and again to Bram Stoker's 1897 novel *Dracula* as its wellhead, werewolves seems to be missing that one iconic tale. Still, the werewolf has shadowed scriveners throughout history, and influences of the story of the Beast are found in many tales published after the eighteenth century.

The short story "The Wolf" by Guy de Maupassant was published in 1889, one hundred twenty-five years after the first appearance of the Beast, and is set in France in that year, 1764. It tells of two brothers who are passionate about hunting; as the story begins, they are pursuing "a colossal wolf" that has eaten children, deprived a woman of her arms, "strangled" dogs, and audaciously invaded farm properties "to come snuffling under the doors."

"A Story of a Weir-Wolf" was published in a periodical entitled *Hogg's Weekly Instructor* in 1846; in it a father and daughter of Auvergne, in the country of the Beast, are rescued at the last from suspicions of evildoing and a sentence of the stake.

Alexandre Dumas, author of *The Three Musketeers* and *The Count of Monte Cristo*, wrote a tale entitled *Le Meneur de loups*, or *The Wolf Leader*, in 1857. The story itself is set in the late 1700s and describes a pact of revenge between the protagonist, a shoemaker, and an immense wolf that walks about on its hind legs.

Dracula character Jonathan Harker, in Bram Stoker's 1914 short story "Dracula's Guest," encounters a wolf which is described by soldiers as, "A wolf—and yet not a wolf! . . . No use trying for it without a sacred bullet." Professor and writer Bourgault du Coudray connects Stoker's prose with influences by Baring-Gould.

The Wolves of Paris by Daniel P. Mannix, based on a true story of a pack of wolves that lay siege to Paris during the fifteenth century, reverberates with influences of the story of the Beast, down to the royal *louvetier* (wolf hunter) Boisselier quoting Jean Chastel in saying, "Beast, you will kill no more."

A French Werewolf in Kent, England

Stories of werewolves have been fare for popular magazines since the 1800s. The July 1838 edition of a British publication, *Court Magazine, Monthly Critic, Lady's Magazine, and Museum. A Family Journal of Original Tales, Reviews of Literature, the Fine Arts, Music, Drama, Fashions, &c. &c. Under the Distinguished Patronage of Her Royal Highness the Duchess of Kent,* includes a tale entitled "Hugues, the Wer-wolf: A Kentish Legend of the Middle Ages," presented by writer Sutherland Menzies, with an introduction to werewolves preceding the story. In the tale, a clan by the name of Hugues, "(or Wulfric, as they were commonly called by the Saxon inhabitants of that district)," whose ancestors came from Normandy, France, live a meager existence in the formerly forested tracts around Ashford, Kent, in southeastern England, at the time of "our second Henry" (Henry II, 1133–1189). The Hugueses/ Wulfrics are known by their neighbors "as belonging to the accursed race of wer-wolves" but their habitation is protected by archaic woodland law.

The family is ostracized by the community, though to all outward appearances, they fail to live up to their lycanthropic reputation. Still, they are accused of nefarious behavior, witchcraft, and being culpable for many sorrows: untimely deaths, accidents, fires, and incidents of starving real-world winter wolves digging up the deceased in the graveyard.

Starving themselves, the Wulfrics become very ill, and give up the ghost in quick succession: father, mother, and daughters. Hugues, the son, is the only survivor. Desperate for food, he seeks employment in Ashford, to no avail; however, he begins to attract the attention of local females, owing to his pitiable circumstances and his looks. It turns out Hugues is a hunk: "one . . . could not have failed to admire the savage beauty of his head . . . crowned with a profusion of waving hair, and set upon shoulders whose robust and harmonious proportions were discoverable through the tattered attire investing them." Further, "the tone of his naturally soft voice accorded admirably with the purity in which he spoke his ancestral language—the Norman French."

Hugues beseeches the Virgin Mary to end his sufferings. He wishes he *could* become a wer-wolf, not to kill his neighbors, but to torment those who drove his family to isolation and death, and to perhaps find carrion to eat. Shortly after, while scrabbling for fuel to throw on his fading fire, Hugues discovers a long-forgotten chest, which turns out to contain "the complete disguise of a wer-wolf:—a dyed sheepskin, with gloves in the forms of paws, a tail, a mask with an elongated muzzle . . . furnished with formidable rows of yellow horse-teeth." (Note, however, that the chest lacked the usually requisite lycan ointment.) Hugues is at first horrified by his find, then recalls wild tales recounted by his grandfather years before, as "his mother wept silently."

Menzies offers a striking description of Hugues's subsequent transformation, employing classic symptoms of the lycanthrope:

> Hunger and despair conjointly carried him away: he saw objects no longer save through a bloody prism: he felt his very teeth on edge with an avidity for biting: he experienced inconceivable desire to run: he set himself to howl as though he had practiced wer-wolfery all his life, and began thoroughly to invest himself with the guise and attributes of his novel vocation. A more startling change could scarcely have been wrought in him, had that so horribly grotesque metamorphosis really been the effect of enchantment; aided, too, as it was, by the fever which generated a temporary insanity in his frenzied brain.

Hugues becomes "a confirmed wer-wolf," but unlike other French lycanthropes, he does not undertake to roam the countryside, eviscerating women and children. Instead, he extorts choice cuts of meat from the local butcher and seeks the company of the butcher's niece, Branda, who in turn acquires feelings for Hugues.

The furious butcher seeks the advice of the local "oracle," a parish grave-digger and sacristan (caretaker of church accoutrements). The information he presents recalls the Gévaudan Beast's seeming invincibility save for a sword: "Slay a wer-wolf thou canst not, for his hide is proof against spear or arrow, though vulnerable to the edge of a cutting weapon of steel. . . ." Foreboding words, but the story has an upbeat conclusion.

The Power of Silver and Sacred Bullets

Philip of Macedon (382–336 BC) learned from the Oracle of Delphi, Greece, "With silver weapons you may conquer the world." Why is this? What is it about silver that associates it with the power with which to take on *loups-garous*?

Silver is a precious metal with many unique properties and associations. Webster's defines it as "a white ductile very malleable metallic element that is capable of a high degree of polish, is chiefly monovalent in compounds [resistant to toxic organisms], and has the highest thermal and electric conductivity of any substance." The ancients kept milk and other beverages and fluids fresh in vessels of silver.

Hunter Jean Chastel was said to kill the second Beast of Gévaudan with ammunition made from silver medals depicting the Virgin Mary and blessed by the local priest.

Contrariwise, folklorist Andrew Lang, in relating his own account of the wolf of the Gévaudan, said that perhaps the Beast was immune to the power of silver: "Others alleged that when he [the Beast] had been shot, like the great Dundee [John Graham, the Viscount Dundee, a Jacobite highlander who, some say, was impervious to lead ammunition through a pact with the devil], with a silver bullet (a well-known charm against sorcery) at such close quarter that it appeared impossible he should not be mortally wounded, in a day or two some fresh horror would announce that the creature was still uninjured."

The story "The Wolf" by Guy de Maupassant, mentioned earlier, includes the idea of having one's ammunition consecrated: The younger brother asks, "Perhaps we should have our bullets blessed by our cousin, the bishop . . ."

Devlin refers to a case in the Vendée, France, in which a sorceress, in the guise of a wolf, made daily calls on a country laborer, who was advised to shoot it with "blessed bullets." He did so, and the wolf transformed into the sorceress—who was also an ex-girlfriend. (Devlin explains that the incident, validated the farmhand's breaking off relations with the wolf-girl; she was in the wrong by stalking him and by taking beastly form.)

Worthy French Werewolves

Investigator Elliott O'Donnell informs us that not all the werewolves of France were wicked. "Many were exceedingly virtuous, and owed their metamorphosis to the vengeance of witch or wizard." At least two saved human lives: the first, an abbot (the superior of a monastery), and the second, a reformed hunter of Huguenots (French Protestants). In the first tale, *The Case of the Abbot Gilbert, of the Arc Monastery, on the Banks of the Loire River*, the Abbot was on his way home when he dozed off and tumbled from his horse after making merry at a village fair. He was about to be attacked by wildcats, when he was saved by a werewolf, who fought off the felines. Despite the Abbot's protestations, the lycan insisted on accompanying him back to the monastery. The next morning the monks were astonished to find that the werewolf in its natural state was "a stern and awesome dignitary of the Church," who rebuked Abbot Gilbert for his behavior at the fair.

In the latter account, *The Case of Roland Bertin*, a ship's commander named André Bonivon was attacking Huguenot communities along the banks of France's river Rhône when his vessel ran aground in a storm. Bonivon fell overboard into a whirlpool, but was hauled ashore by a werewolf (much to his consternation), led to a home in a nearby town, fed, and locked in for the evening. In the morning, the werewolf released him as it revealed itself as Roland Bertin, a Huguenot minister, whose wife had been killed by Bonivon's men the night before. The minister told the astonished Bonivon a local woman named Mère Grénier was responsible for his lycanthropic state; in reality, he was a man who loved life and could not kill. Said he to Bonivon, "Assassin, I have spared you. Spare others." André did.

Memory and Story

It is important to keep in mind that memories are not infallible. Scholar and author Jonathan Gottschall relates how in 1995, psychologist Elizabeth Loftus was able to plant a fabricated childhood remembrance—that of being separated from parents at a shopping mall—within the minds of a quarter of the undergraduates with whom she was working. The students even tendered extra embellishments, amplifying the false incident. Gottschall explains too that we may reconstruct events in order to give ourselves the starring role: "We misremember the past in a way that allows us to maintain protagonist status in the stories of our own lives." Patients undergoing psychotherapy, who feel their lives are off balance, find sharing their experiences may aid in the process of scripting new personal narratives, providing "a story they can live with."

French rustics in the nineteenth century and earlier frequently made use of traditional elements of the supernatural in their recountings of interactions with others. Many of these accounts germinated from hostilities and grudges held against neighbors or authorities. Through a story, a *paysan* might allege that the farmer next door was observed in the form of a werewolf or warlock. Such a narrative, with footings in traditions of occult coding, seemed more credible than owning up to one's enmity toward the neighbor, and spared one from publicly admitting their animosity. Thus story became safehold. One of Devlin's examples is the Beast account of Bégou, who claimed he came upon a hairy Antoine Chastel washing in a moonlit brook; the startled Antoine attacked his onlooker wolf-formed. Bégou's audience may well have concurred that the "shifty" son of Jean Chastel was a *loup-garou.*

Stories were also told "to excuse the narrator's shortcomings," or to "explain and vindicate one's behavior" (echoes of Gottschall, above). For example, Devlin relates a tale of southwestern France, in which a youth from Asasp fancied a girl from Lurbe. When attempting to call on his intended with a companion, the girl was discovered in the form of a goat. After she was caught and translated herself into a young lady again, she was released in more ways than one: The engagement was off.

Werewolves = Man-Eating Wolves?

We learn through Montague Summers that some authorities, such as George Turberville, author of *The Noble Art of Venerie or Hunting*, published in 1575 and 1611 and recalling a 1400 *Booke of Huntynge*, hold that, "Some Wolues . . . kill children and men sometimes: and then they neuer feede nor pray vpon any thing afterwards . . . Such Wolues are called War-wolves, because a man had neede to beware of them." Richard Thompson says the French *loup-garou* (translated as "wolf-werewolf") also simply implies a wolf that is anthropophagus; that is, a man-eater, and this meaning was a familiar one at the time of the Beast.

Sabine Baring-Gould reproduces a sermon about "were-wolves" given by Doctor Johann Geiler von Keysersperg to his congregation in Strasbourg on the third Sunday in Lent in 1508. The doctor commences with the question, "What shall we say about were-wolves?" and states that they can be also called *ber-wöllffs* (bear-wolves), or *wer-wöllffs*, and they eat men and children for seven reasons (several of which support the theory presented in this book). The first reason is simple hunger, especially in winter when prey may be scarce. The second is savageness; this is why they eat children, again in winter and when they have offspring to feed. The doctor cites a proverb, "He who seeks a wolf at Candlemas, a peasant on Shrove Tuesday, and a parson in Lent is a man of pluck." He also notes that wolves of colder climes are smaller and more savage. The third reason is age; the maturing wolf can no longer run as fast as its prey; also, it may be what twentieth-century US government Biological Survey hunters four centuries later called a "gummer" (an old wolf with poor teeth) and so it prefers the easier-to-catch-and-eat human. Next is experience. *Canis lupus* finds human flesh sweet and addictive. "So he acts like old topers [drunkards], who, when they know the best wine, will not be put off with inferior quality." The fifth reason is ignorance. Mad dogs bite randomly, and, per von Keyserberg, the wolf is a "mad and inconsiderate" dog. Sixth is the devil, who may become an animal. The doctor also mentions lycanthropy and "a man who had the phantasy that he himself was a wolf. And afterwards he was found lying in the wood, and he was dead out of sheer hunger." The seventh reason is God, and to this the bishop of Mende might well subscribe: "For God will sometimes punish certain lands and villages with wolves . . ." Says Baring-Gould, "It will be seen from this extraordinary sermon that Dr. Johann Geiler von Keysersperg did not regard werewolves in any other light than natural wolves filled with a lust for human flesh; and he puts aside altogether the view that they are men in a state of metamorphosis."

Heinrich Kraemer's 1487 *Malleus Maleficarum*, "Hammer of Witches," also considered lupine predations as not irregular when wolves are famished. However, *Canis lupus* could be "possessed," used by sorcerers or demons to carry out fiendish acts, or to rebuke sinners for their transgressions. It also held that men could commit crimes under the conviction that they have become beasts, especially under occult influences, but human beings could not transmute into wolves.

Werewolf Sorcerers

Another type of werewolf was what was held to be a warlock who ranged nocturnal byroads of rural France materialized as a wolf. Devlin states that rustics might report an encounter with such a being, but claim the sorcerer as a local with which they were feuding. Such traditions "reflected not only people's appreciation of the dangers of their environment and their ignorance of nature, but also a tendency to exaggerate the fearful—both to divert and admonish listeners." Graham Robb notes that stories of werewolves "reflected real fears" related to lupine encroachments in developed areas; wolf invasions were related to environmental causes, such as unsparing hibernal conditions and the felling of timber, reducing animal habitats.

According to Montague Summers and other sources, "The countryfolk in the Gévaudan district were well assured that the monster was a warlock, who had shifted his shape, and that it was useless to attempt to catch him." There is one instance of a boy stating he saw buttons on the underside of La Bête, indicating that it was "a werewolf (in a waistcoat)." Pourcher states that indeed the Beast was considered a werewolf or demon that "could charm firearms." One farmer, a well-to-do and much-respected man, deposed before a magistrate that on one occasion when he had encountered the Beast after it had made a prodigious bound through the air, he heard it murmur: *"Convenez que, pour un vieillard de quatre-vingt-dix ans, ce n'est pas mal sauter.* (Admit it, for an old man of ninety years, that was not a bad leap.)"

Richard Thompson tells us that English writer and Earl of Orford Horace Walpole commented on this anecdote in January 1765, likening the Beast to London's Cock Lane Ghost, a performing spirit also known as "Scratching Fanny," which had been the talk of the town a few years before. Said Walpole, "Compare the two cases and then tell me that we live in an enlightened century."

The Beast of Gévaudan: A Werewolf?

Yes, if one is referring to historical sources that defined man-eating wolves as werewolves. And the Beast is also a werewolf of *viva voce*, by word of mouth. The legends of La Bête, as Devlin points out, can be enfolded within a long tradition of purposeful storytelling. The Beast's eyes, odor, and ability to move on its hind legs are all attributes of the traditional French country werewolf. Devlin quotes an area *seigneur*'s letter in relating other qualities ascribed to the Beast by locals: "It talks, takes tobacco, becomes invisible, boasts in the evening about its exploits of the day, goes to the sabbath, does penance for its sins."

But this was storytelling not intended to explain or identify the creature. Instead, country yarns related to werewolves and the Beast served their yarnspinners in helping them deal with real circumstances, perhaps providing some relief from the apprehension of succumbing to its predations, having a loved one fall prey, enduring the authorities' ceaseless and fruitless hunts, withstanding untrustworthy and disruptive interlopers, and, using the Beast in traditional fashion, to implicate a disliked neighbor.

CHAPTER 20

Man-Beasts and Serial Killers

There he uttered howling noises, and his attempts to speak were all in vain. His clothes became changed into bristling hairs, his arms to legs, and he became a wolf.

—*Ovid, Lycaon*

The eighteenth-century French countryside at night: total darkness, as if the world were caught within a great vial of ink. There was no light save that of the moon and stars along desolate byways that connected isolated villages. The flicker of a torch now and then or the glow of a fire beneath the threshold of a humble home might serve as a reference for those daring to brave the impenetrable black. And something or someone seemed to be watching from the edges of the intricate forests.

By conjuring up such an eerie scenario, we can imagine how travelers could fall victim to a gamut of misdeeds by vagrants and others in the middle of nowhere. And, as discussed in our section on serial killers, there was most definitely a criminal element in the French countryside. Phil Barnson says, "We are not yet in Chicago, but close." Outlaws, military deserters, the unfortunates, and drifters could make life perilous. It was not so different more than one hundred years later, when serial killer Joseph Vacher murdered eleven and possibly twenty-five or more mostly young people (at least more than twice the number killed by London's Jack the Ripper in 1888), many guarding livestock, in rural southern France from 1894 to 1897.

A homeless person might beg for bread to stave off hunger for one more day. A highwayman might knock a rider off his mount and make off with horse and possessions. Others may have sought to satisfy carnal or bloodthirsty desires. The motivations for such acts were greatly varied, possibly including disrupted, impoverished, or traumatic childhoods. During the attacks in the Gévaudan, witnesses spied haunting figures within the forests' shadows, human, yet clad in fur and animal skins. Could they have been men possessed? Bloodthirsty criminals using the crisis of the Beast to conceal heinous acts? Aristocrats with twisted tastes, demanding horrible favors? Victims of hallucinogenic nightmares? Malnourished peasants, army deserters, abandoned children, or the mentally ill? Perhaps their presence reveals the unshackling of primal instincts under the most wretched of conditions.

Marauders and Intruders: Human Beasts?

It has been claimed that some or all of the killings of the Gévaudan may have been perpetrated by humans, not by mysterious beasts. It is easy to imagine how evildoers might exploit such a situation. To confuse the population, to intimidate authorities, and to achieve the illusion of supernatural status, these blackguards seemed to transform into something other than human. To achieve this metamorphosis, they may have used animal fur or skins, parts of animals, or exotic amulets.

An ancient phenomenon that has been extensively studied and archaeologically verified, our desire to be on equal footing with the formidable wild beasts we once hunted—and which hunted us—is as old as humanity itself.

Before detailing the cases and sightings of bestial humans related to deaths in the Gévaudan, let us recall examples of our long-time fascination with man-beasts.

Scholar Anne Clark reminds us that there have been accounts of man-beast hybrids since the remote ages: the famous sphinx, harpies—in the Greek *harpyiai* (snatchers)—mermaids, mermen, centaurs, and so on. Men might associate with animals so much so that they identify themselves with them, or are identified with them (e.g., modern sports teams and their fans). The ancient geographer Isidore reported that Thessalonian warriors were so in harmony with their horses they gave the impression that man and mount were one creature.

New World colonists viewed Native Americans as being very much like wolves. The French actually began referring to various tribes as *loups* (French for wolves). Those resisting Christianity were believed bewitched by *ce loup infernal*. A number of North American peoples seemed to have lived side by side with *Canis lupus*. Some groups believed they were descended from wolves. Biologist and historian Bruce Hampton says a Pawnee group known as the Skidi were considered so lupine in their ways that a Bureau of American Ethnology report stated that other indigenous peoples claimed the Skidi were able to see as a wolf, "two looks away," and to possess the auditory capability, like a wolf, to hear clouds move overhead.

The inclusion of (depending on the biblical translation) satyrs or men-goats or "hairy ones" of Isaiah 34:14 in the Old Testament—a passage sometimes referred to in conjunction with werewolves—may, Clark says, result from a slip of wording acquired in translation or from a desire to amplify the forlorn atmospherics of the passage: "And demons and monsters shall meet, and the hairy ones shall cry out one to another, there hath the lamia lain down, and found rest for herself" (Douay-Rheims Version). Clark notes that the Hebrew phrase for "hairy ones" is translated as "Devil" in Revelations. The word "lamia" is associated with Lilith, folkloric female vampire and first wife of Adam before Eve.

Classic myths describe the gods changing men into beasts, such as the goddess Artemis changing the hunter Actaeon into a stag after he came upon her bathing; he was then destroyed by his own hounds. An outraged Zeus transformed Lycaon (the name comes from the Greek word for wolf: *lykos*), ruler of Arcadia, into a wolf when the mortal served the deity human flesh as a test of his divinity. Such myths, say Otten, serve as warnings not to indulge in bestial appetites. In other stories, beast-like creatures become men, such as Saint Christopher, sometimes said to have been a cynocephalus, or dog-headed being, who, upon angelic intervention and conversion, relinquished his animalic side.

Writer Richard Bernheimer examines a curious phenomenon of the Middle Ages: the wild man. This hale, hearty, and hairy fellow, usually unclothed, is depicted, like a medieval Kilroy, in all sorts of works of art, illuminated manuscripts, and architecture dating from feudal times. Wild men (who, Bernheimer says, perhaps represent our primitive side) preferred forests to civilization and subsisted as hunter-gatherers. Armed with hefty cudgels, these mighty wildings were ready to take on all comers: humans, dragons, or other wild men. They had dominion over animals, reigning as beast-tyrants, bullying bears and boars with muscle and mace; strong-arming stags and unicorns to serve as their mounts. And like the French country *meneur de loups* (wolf master), the wild man might have a pack of *Canis lupus* companions. Also, as do some lycanthropes, he went about on all fours, and (very werewolf-like) a wonder-working animal skin might be the key to his fortitude. Wild women lived in the forest, too, and sometimes wild parents attempted to switch their offspring with those of unsuspecting human passersby.

It was debated whether or not the wild man was human, and what of his spiritual status? He could not speak and so likely could not know God. "Wild" was equated with insanity, making his forest home a fitting refuge for fugitives of all sorts. Another vein of tradition painted the wild man as an über-naturalist and sylvan guardian, having knowledge of the properties of plants, sharing his arboreal expertise with humans for gain or good will. In mountainous Europe, especially in the Alps, the wild man was identified as a cannibalistic demon giant who preyed on unchristened children. He might also helm the Wild Hunt of myth, coursing nighttime skies and rural byways with a squad of phantoms, slaying all in their path.

Sometimes a human became a wild man after a personal tragedy, as did Geoffrey of Monmouth's twelfth-century character, Merlinus Caledonicus, when his brothers were killed in war. Or one might go wild if rejected in love. Wild men might be captured, as was the hermit Saint John Chrysostom, who so resembled a beast that his captors believed him to be an "unheard-of animal crawling on the ground." As with lycanthropy, wildness might be temporary. Some wild men, once domesticated, made excellent knights. Innocent of (as Robert Louis Stevenson calls it) "the Bastille of civilization" and its own madnesses, wild men were honorable and without guile. Bernheimer notes that in later feudal times, it "became fashionable to identify oneself with savage things . . . and thus to repudiate the very principle of hieratic order upon which medieval society was founded."

In the seventeenth century, a popular book entitled *Historie of Foure-footed Beastes* by Edward Topsell catalogued varmints real and fabulous. One anthropophagous man-beast, the *manticore* or *mantichoras* (man-eater), was a hairy, Simba-sized creature native to India; it had three rows of teeth. Clark comments that Topsell's woodcut depiction "seems in some extraordinary way to anticipate the typical Edwardian face."

***

Perhaps one of the most famous ancient instances in which man combines his identity with that of an animalistic one is that of the "Sorcerer, Shaman, or Warlock" in the Trois Frères cave, in Ariege, France. This Upper Paleolithic site, about fifteen thousand years old, is remarkable for its beautiful cave paintings—depicting bison, deer, horses, and more—attributed to Cro-Magnon man. For some researchers, the anthropomorphic figure represented here, which is possibly conducting a ritual dance or incantation, comprises human body parts (genitalia, legs, and a beard) and animal attributes (a wolf tail, deer horns, and bear paws). This shaman, which could play varying roles—magician, herbalist, shape-shifter, "doctor," or medium—between the world of the living and that of the spirits, is also clothed in fur-covered ceremonial dress.

The figure could have multiple meanings: Perhaps the shaman seeks to conduct a ritual dance to promote hunting, or perhaps he worships a lord of animals. He may be trying to communicate with the spirits or with Mother Nature. What is clear is that the figure represented is using parts of animals in order to try and meld with them, acquiring their characteristics to achieve an enhanced connection to the natural world, trying to understand it in a more profound way.

In Trois Frères we also find the Bison Man, a hybrid playing, in a bipedal stance, what looks to be a musical instrument. Is he a transforming shaman or animal spirit?

This short journey through the world of prehistoric anthropomorphic representations combined with animal forms cannot end without mentioning the lion man or lion woman, from the Hohlenstein-Stadel cave, Germany. The thirty-centimeter (nearly a foot) tall figure is carved from a mammoth tusk and dates from about thirty thousand years ago. The small sculpture leaves no doubt: A bipedal and erect human body, provided with arms close to the torso, has a lion's head without hair. This exquisite carving is executed with great detail. For many researchers it may represent

Bison Man, left, and the "Lord of the Animals" shaman found at Trois Frères, French Paleolithic cave.

a witch wearing a "mask" shaped like the head of a lion. Perhaps our ancestors sought to take on the characteristics of dreaded wild animals, such as the terrible cave lion of the past. Hence the use of tanned leather skins and other ornaments made from animals killed in death-defying real-life hunts.

It is curious, as more than one paleontologist has pointed out, that these early human artists chose to depict only the strongest and fiercest animal opponents. Later Paleolithic bestiary representations include less savage animals: horses, bison, deer, reindeer, wild goats, etc. The phase in which the prehistoric environment was rife with fearsome animals shifts into an era in which man gained more dominance over nature.

So far we have seen anthropomorphic lions, biped deer, and human bison; an alleged connection between mind, body, and nature; and the possession of animal attributes that would allow us to become them in order to understand, venerate, and be inspired by them—something that could make us stronger.

A perfect example of this archaic process is found in the ways of Nordic and Germanic Berserkers. These ancient warriors formed a

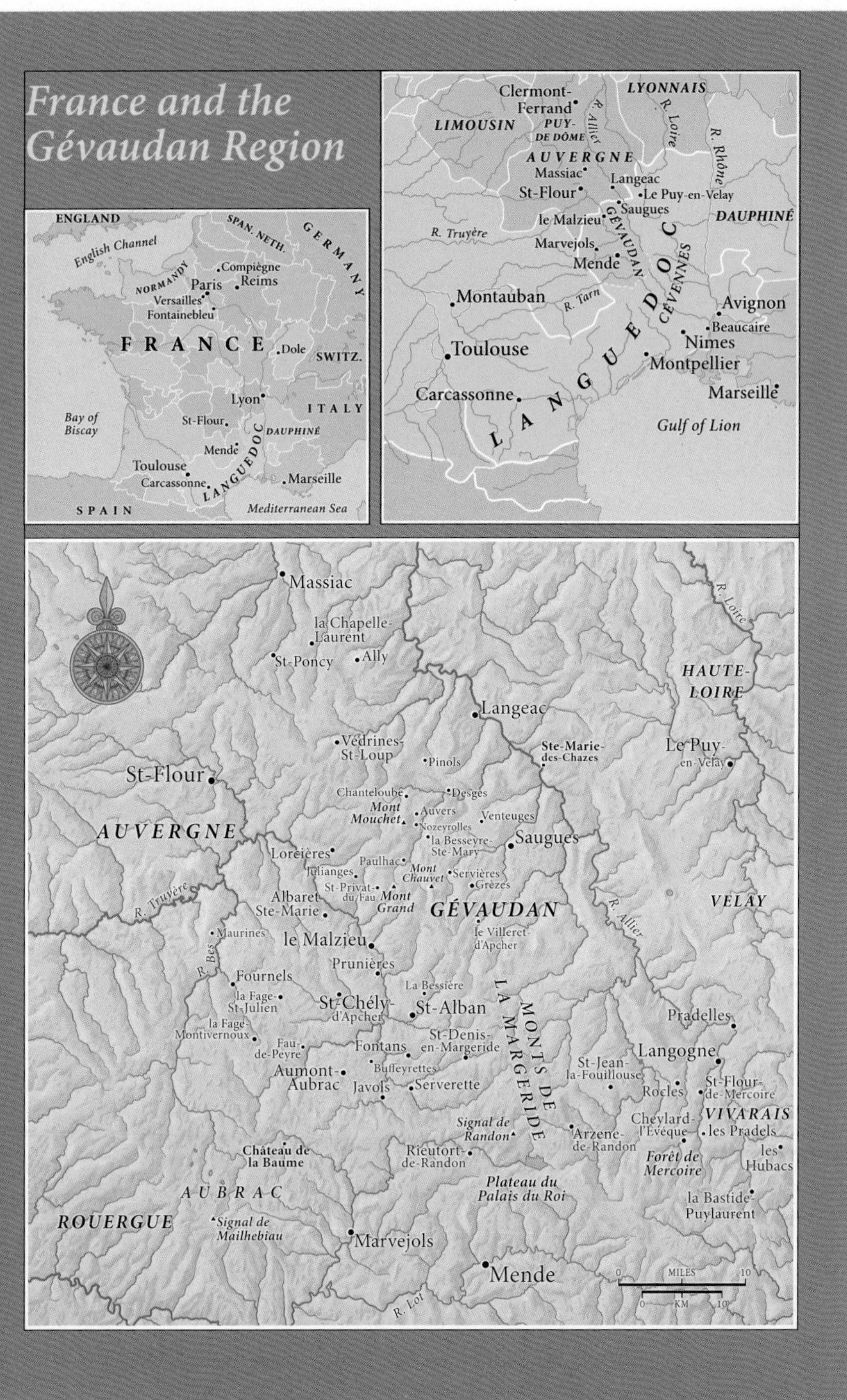

Maps of France and the Gévaudan. ***Cartography by David Lindroth Inc.***

The landscape of the Beast. *Photo Schwalb.*

"Depiction of the ferocious Beast believed to be a hyena." A woman is attacked by the Beast. "The king, being informed of the havoc, sent Captain Duhamel and his dragoons, and offered a reward." *Bibliothèque nationale de France.*

Depiction of the international commercial fair in Beaucaire, France, by Paul André Basset (1750–1785). Could a hyena have escaped from a menagerie here? *Bibliothèque des Arts Decoratifs, Paris, France/Bridgeman Images.*

King Louis XV Hunting in the Forest of Saint-Germain, painted by Jean-Baptiste Oudry (1686–1755). The king, an avid hunter, was known to bag 200 or more game animals on a shoot. Artist Oudry is seen in the lower right-hand corner. *Musée des Augustins, Toulouse, France/Bridgeman Images.*

The Beast eluded its pursuers more than once in the woods on the grounds of Château de la Baume. ***Photo Ancalagon (Own work) [GFDL (http://www.gnu.org/copyleft/fdl.html)]***

Interior, cathedral of Mende, France, from which Gabriel Florent de Choiseul Beaupré, the bishop of Mende, declared the Beast a "scourge of God." ***Photo Schwalb.***

The femme Jouve attempts to save her son. ***Patrick Aventurier/ Gamma-Rapho Collection/Getty Images.***

Close-up of the sculpture in Auvers, France, depicting the battle between Marie-Jeanne Valet and the Beast on August 11, 1765. ***Photo Schwalb.***

The ancient Chapel of St. Mary of Chazes, sited above the river Allier. *Photo Schwalb.*

The "Chazes Wolf" is presented to King Louis XV (at left) and his court in Versailles on October 1, 1765. *Bibliothèque nationale de France.*

Foreboding Mont Mouchet, France, nearly 5,000 feet high. Antoine Chastel was said to have lived here among wolves. It is also the vicinity of the site where his father Jean Chastel destroyed the second Beast in June 1767. *Photo Schwalb.*

One can view the monument honoring Jean Chastel for killing the Beast of the Gévaudan along the D30 roadway in La Besseyre-Saint-Mary, France. *Photo Schwalb.*

A menacing *loup-garou* or *meneur de loups*, dressed in wolf skin, accompanied by an attack dog in protective covering, advances toward a lone shepherdess. This sculpture group, in the town of Le Malzieu, depicts one of the hypotheses regarding the Beast's identity. *Photo Schwalb.*

Children defend themselves from the Beast. Sculpture group in Le Malzieu, France. *Photo Schwalb.*

An abstract sculpture of the Beast menaces Marvejols, France.
Photo Schwalb.

Silver Bête medallions dot the streets throughout Saugues, France.
Photo Schwalb.

A giant wooden sculpture of La Bête overlooks the town of Saugues, France. *Photo Schwalb.*

Stonehenge-like megalith or *menhir* in Cham des Bondons in the Cévennes, south of Mende, France. *Photo Schwalb.*

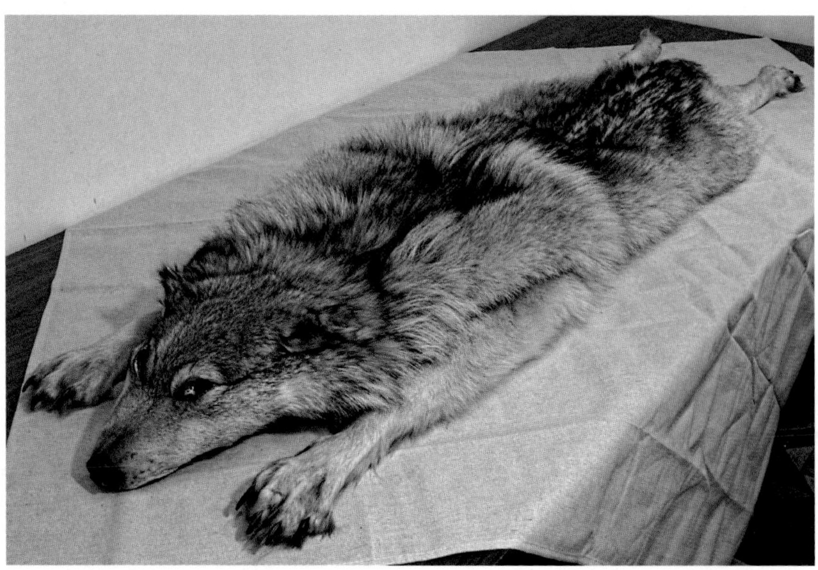

Skin of a Canis specimen identified as a hybrid bred and raised in captivity, acquired by the American Museum of Natural History in 1936. *Photo Schwalb. American Museum of Natural History.*

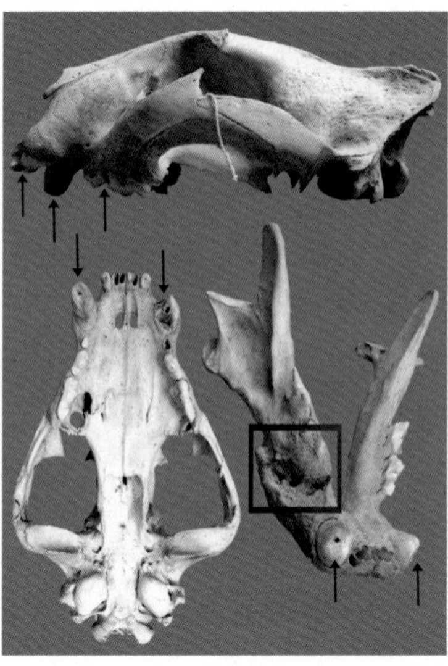

Skull and jaws of an Indian man-eating tiger *(Panthera tigris)* dating from 1933. Note the worn canines (arrows) and broken/healed jaw (box). *Manabu Sakamoto, Bristol Museums, Galleries, & Archives, Bristol, UK.*

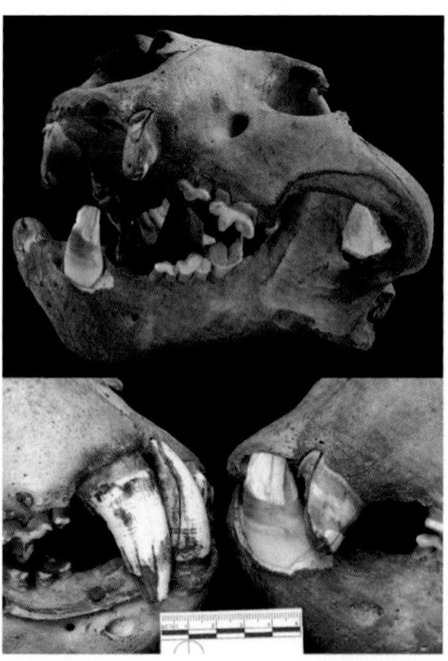

Another skull of a man-eating tiger (top). Note the round and reduced canines (bottom right) in comparison to a normal specimen (bottom left) also showing considerable use (chipped and rounded tips). *Paolo Viscardi, Horniman Museum & Gardens, London, UK.*

A mounted striped hyena *(Hyaena hyaena)*. Hall of evolution, National Museum of Natural History, Paris, France. *Photo G. Sánchez Romero.*

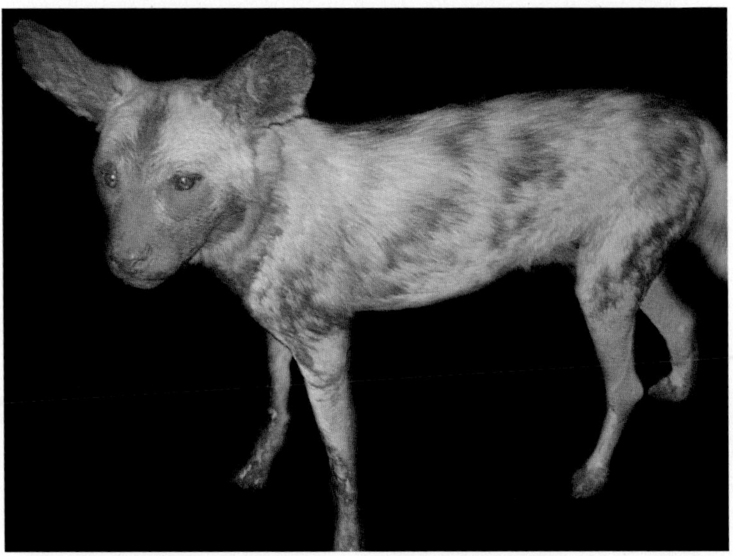

An African wild dog *(Lycaon pictus)*. Hall of evolution, National Museum of Natural History, Paris, France. *Photo G. Sánchez Romero.*

A medieval hunting scene, entitled "Hunting a Wild Cat," depicting a nobleman spearing a spotted big cat (probably a leopard). From *Le livre de la chasse (The Book of the Hunt)* by Gaston Phoebus (1331–1391). *Bibliothèque nationale de France.*

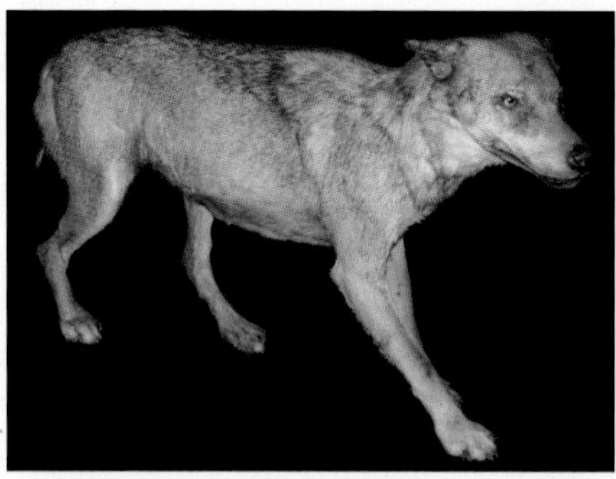

The Chaingy Beast, Museum of Orléans, France. Total length (without tail): 117 cm. Shoulder height: 60 cm. Height at top of the head: 69 cm. ***Photo and measurements by Michel Binon.***

Eischoll Wolf: (VS) HN 128. Also known as the "Valais Monster." Museum entry date: November 11, 1947. Collector: Wildlife, Game, and Fish Service, 1951 Sion. ***Prepared by: Geneva Museum. Copyright: Musées cantonaux, Sion; Heinz Preisig, Sion.***

Reckingen Wolf: HN 98-52. An Italian wolf shot in the Conches Valley (Haut-Valais), Switzerland. Museum entry date: November 23, 1999. Collector: Wildlife, Game, and Fish Service, 1951 Sion. ***Prepared by: Périsset Aloïs, La Léchaire 23, 1618 Châtel-St-Denis. Copyright: Musées cantonaux, Sion, Heinz Preisig, Sion.***

Fresh track (white circle), measuring approximately 10 cm x 10 cm, from the Rhone, France, big cat identified as a black jaguar *(Panthera onca)*. October 2009. *Photo Le Républicain Lorrain, France.*

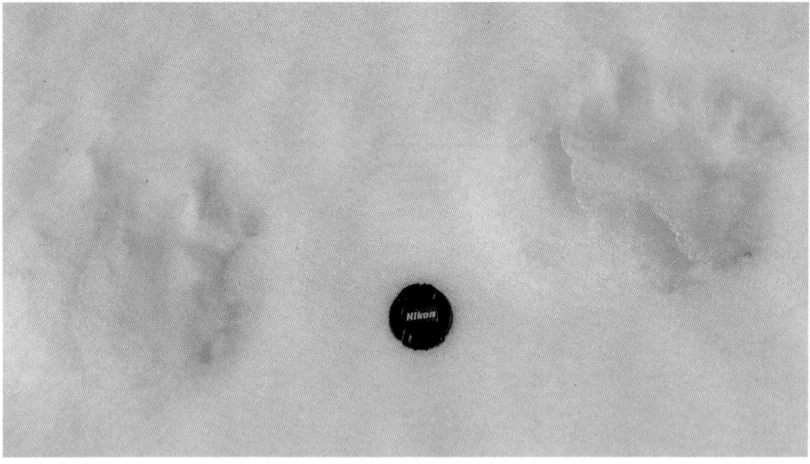

Unusual large tracks photographed near Chullo Peak, Sierra Nevada (Almería, Andalucía, southern Spain), probably belonging to a big cat or large carnivore. April 2012. *Photo Manuel Limón.*

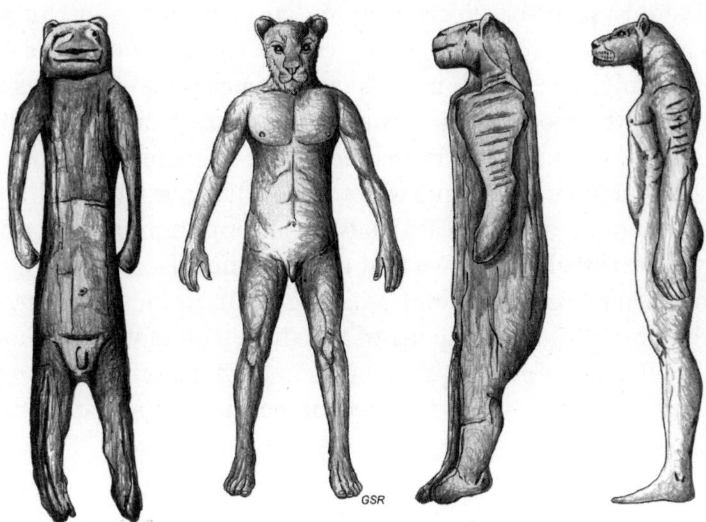

The "human-lion" carved in a mammoth tusk and a possible reconstruction of what the artist had in mind.

kind of professional army, possibly the earliest in history. Dressed in animal skins, usually bears' and wolves' hides (worn on the torso and around the waist; the animals' tanned heads were used as rudimentary helmet motifs), they fought in brutal and bloody ways. And they were accomplished hunters. Apparently those who hunted bears had to wear, during certain ceremonies and festivals, the head and fur of the animals killed. They were also believed to drink the blood of the animal to acquire the carnivores' strength and fierceness, all for victory in combat. The bear figure or spirit provided the warrior with brute force and power, important for individual and face-to-face combat.

The wolf, on the other hand, hunts in packs, inspiring communal planning and split-second execution, also useful in the battlefield. Therefore, both species were esteemed for their intelligence and strength, crucial qualities for every warrior. There has been much discussion as to how the Berserkers reached such a degree of combat effectiveness and downright cruelty. It has been speculated that they received special training (almost certainly true), and maybe fighting under magic spells, or even "altering" their body with drugs and potions. The warrior ingested hallucinogenic mushrooms, plant-based concoctions, etc., and, Hyde- or Hulk-like, switched on a new physiognomy (where clues about one's inner qualities might be found in one's outer appearance): His eyes were injected with blood, his hair bristled like that of an angry wolf, his rage grew exponentially; he seemed even to increase in size. Possession, madness, pre-combat autosuggestion, or chemical alteration? Recent studies indicate that the latter option probably never happened. Tests have shown that reaction time decreases under the influence of powerful alkaloids, making it almost impossible to handle the heavy Viking weapons of the time. Therefore it is thought that the Berserker's brutal state was something more psychological, not having yet discovered the mechanism triggering such fury and violence.

***

In the eighteenth century, in the case of the Beast of the Gévaudan, strange individuals, reminiscent of the brutal Berserkers and others, were spotted on more than one occasion. Derek Brockis, prominent British researcher, presents two disturbing episodes in which "human beasts" appear on the scene:

> There was the mysterious case of the three women of Pompeyrac, going to church near the wood of Favart, when a dark man offered to escort them through the wood. They refused, but before leaving, he touched one of them with a fur-covered hand. Dragoons arriving on the scene warned the terrified women not to go into the wood, because La Bête had just been seen there.

Coincidence, observed exaggeration, or magic man-animal influence? Consider the second case cited by Brockis:

> Two women of Escures, also on the way to church, had a similar experience in an area where, unknown to them, La Bête had just been seen by several people. This time they saw that the man accosting them was covered in fur only when his shirt blew open in the wind. It was said at the time that La Bête, instrument of the Devil, was trying to stop them from going to mass.

This time it is clear that the alleged assailant wears some fur under his clothing, perhaps as protection against the elements. The circumstances of these sightings were suspicious and alarming. Brockis comments:

> As with all good monster murder mysteries, there has to be the wicked aristocrat solution. In one case the murderer was supposed to have hidden among the nuns of the Cistercian abbey of Mercoire, which is now a farm. The abbess was thought to have taken contributions for hiding fugitives. Some documents mention a name, Count Vargo or Vargas, as being a werewolf or having other connections with the La Bête story.

A human solution to the La Bête mystery is unacceptable to many students of the subject, but perhaps the person really did exist.

There are other instances where appearances or attacks by La Bête were associated with a human presence, including a famous moonlit sighting by a witness from a cottage near a river. A peasant by the name Pailleyre (nicknamed Bégou) of Pontajou, Venteugues parish, said he came upon a big man bathing in the river near his home (Servières) in the pre-dawn light of the full moon. Surprised, the man jumped out of the water, turned into a Beast, and dashed toward Bégou's house so quickly that Pailleyre scarcely had time to shut himself inside. He was so afraid after this vision, he refused to come out again until the next day. Later, Pailleyre would admit that the beast bather reminded him of Antoine Chastel. French author Pascal Cazottes speculates in his book, *La Bête du Gévaudan*, about the incident:

> Let's ignore the "metamorphosed animal" and ask if Pailleyre actually saw Antoine Chastel bathing in a stream in the moonlight, and if, as some have suggested, the hairy man who caused, twice, extreme restlessness in two women, was none other than Antoine Chastel. He happened to belong to a family of witches, associated, allegedly, to lycanthropy and wolf training. He had also done some traveling, including a trip to North Africa in which, it was said, he had been castrated. Furthermore, apparently, Antoine Chastel suffered from hypertrichosis, as stated before. Hypertrichosis can be sometimes partial. There are known cases involving the face, neck, and shoulders, but not the rest of the body. Conversely, it

> can affect more than one body part, even the whole body but not the face, where it may only show as an overabundance of beard and hair. Affected by hypertrichosis, Antoine Chastel only had to wear a wolf-shaped mask (like those worn on the pagan solstice festivals) to take on the appearance of an animal. My reasoning is a bit farfetched, but in a case in which so many elements are included, intersected, and intertwined, I think nothing should be ruled out.

Other French writers and researchers, such as Xavier Pic, author of *La Bête qui mangeait le monde en pays de Gévaudan et d'Auvergne (The Man-Eating Beast from Gévaudan and Auvergne)* believe that these cases were just folk tales, gossip, small talk, and nonsense, not to be taken into account.

But what if the truth lay somewhere in the middle? A possible scenario brings into play the mysterious figure of the *loup-garou*: literally, a man who changes into an animal, in this case, a wolf. Could someone who was extremely hirsute, Antoine Chastel or another, disguise himself as a wolf-man and use superstitions and folktales to commit some of the horrible crimes attributed to the Beast and link the human figure clad in animal (wolf) skins with the strange sightings discussed above?

Some citizens that author Sánchez had the opportunity to speak with in the Lozère region in 2013 believe this is the case. A striking bronze sculpture group in Le Malzieu, France, a community in which attacks occurred, depicts such a scene, frozen in motion: A sinister man in wolfskin, carrying a hooked metal implement and accompanied by a dog wearing a protective leather coat, stalks a young girl who sits watching her sheep. This sculpture group may represent part of the solution to the mystery of the killings in the Gévaudan. Is its menacing man similar to the figure Pailleyre spied in the river that moonlit dawn in early 1765?

Finally, it is said that two victims attacked by the Beast were found roughly "redressed" after death. Another victim was devoured after their clothing (a shirt and vest) had been removed, seemingly almost carefully, without damage. How could this be achieved by a wild animal? Fact, fiction, or imagination? Or human interference?

***

Real-Life Lycan Serial Killers: Romasanta, a Classic but Little-Known Murderous Wolf-Man of Spain

My first transformation occurred in the mountains of Couso. I met two fierce-looking wolves. Suddenly I fell down, I began to feel convulsions, I wallowed three times uncontrollably and within seconds I myself was a wolf. I spent five days hanging with the other two until I got my body back. The one you see now, your honor. The other two wolves that were with me were also changed to human form. They were from Valencia. One was called Antonio and the other Mr. Genaro. And were also cursed, like me. For a long time I went as a wolf with Mr. Genaro and Antonio. We attacked and we ate several people because we were hungry.

—Manuel Blanco Romasanta, Case Number 1778: Case Against a Wolf-Man, Allariz Courts (Orense, Galicia, northern Spain).

Allariz, Spain, located in Galicia, is home to a number of curious legends, the most impressive being one of real-life werewolves. The *lobisome* (wolf-man) legend begins in the small village of Regueiro, of the council or municipality of Esgos, where Manuel Blanco Romasanta was born on November 18, 1809.

Romasanta became known as a lycanthrope at a young age. He married at twenty-two, but soon became a widower. He took up the trade of street peddling and began to travel. His first victim disappeared in 1843. A policeman from the vicinity (León, Spain) sought to arrest Romasanta for a debt of six hundred *reales* (local currency); instead, he ended up convicted of murder. Romasanta escaped from prison, returned to his hometown, stopped peddling for a time, and tried to go unnoticed.

But he started peddling again and apparently murdering as well. His next victims were two women from a nearby town, who trusted him to guide them to the city of Santander in search of better fortune. Upon his return, Romasanta claimed that both women had found good jobs there and were fine. After, and by chance, he met a priest looking for a maidservant. The younger sister of one of the two victims, who was also looking for work, set out with Romasanta to meet the priest. Romasanta found he was now trusted by locals seeking employment in far-off places. But what he was doing in reality was killing them and selling their clothes and belongings. As time passed, his victims' families became worried, as they received no news from their loved ones. To calm them, Romasanta even began falsifying correspondence from those missing. But people were suspicious.

It ended when two brothers of one of the victims recognized their sister's clothes. An unknown woman was wearing them and said Romasanta sold them to her. Over time, this occurred again. Romasanta was accused and prosecuted, but again escaped, this time to the town of Toledo. There he was found by happenstance by two Galicians who warned the mayor that Romasanta was a wanted fugitive. He was immediately arrested and taken to jail in Allariz.

At the time, his trial captured the attention of the press, and the summary file is kept nowadays in the archive of the Kingdom of Galicia, the only case of a werewolf sentenced to be executed by a national court of justice.

Romasanta confessed to all the murders (there were thirteen in total), claiming he was under the influence of the moon. He stated that he took his victims to discreet places in the Galician forest, where he would tear them up and devour them afterward. In addition he would remove their *unto* (body fat) which he sold profitably in Portugal.

He explained that as a teenager, he'd been affected by a family curse that would transform him unavoidably into a werewolf. When in that state, he lost human consciousness and was dominated by animal instinct, killing his victims and devouring their flesh. In his own words:

> I could remain as a wolf up to eight days in a row, but usually did not exceed two or four. Antonio, however, could do it for ten days and Mr. Genaro fifteen, but usually only between four and five days. With them I killed and devoured several people, although I attacked alone two women called Josefa and Benita, respectively, and their children.

Attempts from his lawyer to get Romasanta acquitted due to lack of evidence connected to the absurdity of his statement ceased when a reconstruction of the murders was performed. Romasanta also revealed precisely where he had killed and eaten several victims. The

Artistic reconstruction of Romasanta by Spanish forensic experts Fernando Serrulla and Marga Sanín.

werewolf trial lasted a year, and at the end, Romasanta was sentenced to be strangled by *garrote vil*, after paying court costs and compensating victims' families.

But the werewolf's luck took a strange turn for the better when the Spanish queen, Isabella II, received a letter from a French hypnotist known as Mr. Philips, also a professor in Electro-Biology (probably French physician Joseph-Pierre Durand de Gros, 1826–1900), who'd followed the trial and called for Romasanta's acquittal. Philips believed Romasanta suffered from the ancient affliction lycanthropy, the mental disorder causing hallucinogenic episodes in which the affected person believes that he is able turn into an animal.

With Philips's influence, Romasanta's condemnation was reduced to life imprisonment. He was said to have died soon after in prison at Allariz. However, we now know he was transferred to another prison, but which one? In 2011, during a "Manuel Blanco

Romasanta Symposium" held in Allariz, Felix Castor and Vicente Castro, researchers from Ourense, Galicia, presented evidence, such as newspaper stories published in *La Iberia a Liberal Journal* and *The Journal for All*, both from Madrid, stating that Romasanta died from stomach cancer in 1863 in a prison in Ceuta, a Spanish city on the North African coast.

But what caused Romasanta to commit so many crimes? The family curse? Insanity? Possession? Or something else? Spanish researcher and writer Luis García Mañá, author of the only Galician werewolf physiognomic reconstruction, based on Romasanta's historical forensic examination, suspects the answer may be in the food. It turns out that Spain in the mid-nineteenth century experienced persistent rainfall, resulting in poor harvests and crop loss due to harmful fungus growth. The Civil Governor of Orense alert-

Historical photograph of another Spanish serial killer, Juan Díaz de Garayo Ruiz de Argandoña (1821–1881), alias Sacamantecas. He would remove victims' body fat to produce a certain "ointment."

ed the public about the risks of food poisoning, specifically referring to rye ergot, *Claviceps purpurea*, a parasitic fungus, and the basis from which lysergic acid diethylamide, LSD or LSD-25, a potent hallucinogenic drug, is synthesized. Mañá concludes that "Romasanta revealed symptoms consistent with the ingestion of hallucinogenic mushrooms and under the influence of ergot could have killed the victims. This theory may be more or less assumed or discussed."

Real-Life Lycan Serial Killers: A Wolf Boy and a Wild Man of France

In this next section we provide short biographies and accompanying data on two famous serial murderers, showing clear connections with Romasanta. The cases referred to are among the most famous of those recorded in France in the sixteenth and seventeenth centuries. Both of these persons confessed to having committed horrible murders while they were transformed as wolves, or while wearing the skins and/or other parts of a wolf. Their cases, too, may be linked to remote rural environments and impoverished backgrounds. Could some of the deaths allegedly perpetrated by the Beast of Gévaudan be connected with a human through the demonstration of psychological characteristics or a similar anatomy to what we are seeing? This may be part of the riddle that we are trying to solve.

The Case of Jean Grenier, French Wolf Boy

Our first case is unique because the phenomenon of transformation associated with wolves and skins smeared with magic potions knows no particular age. Jean Grenier, a real-life French boy, was exposed to this phenomenon from an early age: "When I was 10 or 11 years old," Grenier said, "my neighbor, Duthillaire, introduced me, in the depths of the forest, to a M. de la Forest, a black man, who signed me with his nail, and then gave to me and Duthillaire a salve and a wolf-skin. From that time have I run about the country as a wolf."

For this youth, the "black man," whom he also called "Lord of the forest," was the devil himself, a being who had shackled Grenier with a great and horrifying curse: the ability to transform himself into a fearsome beast, and, in that form, commit terrible crimes. Grenier would later admit that, craving human flesh, especially that of little girls, he had devoured more than thirty children. He openly stated that he searched the countryside until he identified a vulnerable, unattended victim. Then he hid within the shadows of the woods until he attacked and killed the child. Afterward, he would take the body to a remote location and consume the remains. Area officials confirmed the corresponding disappearances of children in many of these locations. Grenier's story is well documented in *The Book of Were-Wolves* by cleric and scholar Sabine Baring-Gould (1834–1924):

> Jean had often told her [Marguerite Poirier] that he had sold himself to the devil, and that he had acquired the power of ranging the country after dusk, and sometimes in broad day in the form of a wolf. He had assured her that he had killed and devoured many dogs, but that he found their flesh less palatable than the flesh of little girls, which he regarded as a supreme delicacy. He had told her that this had been tasted by him not infrequently but he had specified only two instances: in one he had eaten as much as he could, and thrown the rest to a wolf, which had come up during the repast. In the other instance he had bitten to death another little girl, had lapped her blood, and, being in a famished condition at the time, had devoured every portion of her, with the exception of the arms and shoulders.

Eventually, fourteen-year-old Grenier stood trial in June 1603. The court found that the youth was essentially "feral," having experienced throughout his short lifetime abuse, neglect, and malnutrition. Physically, the boy was hairy, had fingernails like talons, seemed oblivious to his surroundings, presented "physical developmental delays and cultural incompetence," and "was incapable of rational thought because of a disorganized brain."

Jean was imprisoned for life at a nearby cloister, where, initially, he behaved as a wild animal. His incarceration did not better his condition: As the years went by, Grenier remained small in size, was inarticulate, seemed muddled in his thinking, was ill at ease or totally withdrawn around people. He continued to insist that he was a werewolf. He died seven years later.

***

After reading this account, questions arise: What could have driven young Grenier to commit such crimes? Witchcraft, diabolical possession, or bestial transformation? Lycanthropy? Terrible hallucinations? A true *loup-garou*? And what about his physical appearance? How could we explain these odd behaviors and features satisfactorily?

To some historians, medical professionals, and researchers, Grenier's strange appearance may have been attributed to a metabolic disorder that causes an unusual illness known as porphyria.

This rare congenital disorder is characterized by extreme sensitivity to light. A subject's exposure to sunlight causes vesicular (blistered) reddening of skin, itching, scarring, and hypertrichosis, or abnormal excessive hair growth, as well as reddish-brown urine, reddish-brown teeth, and ulcers that destroy cartilage and bone, causing the deformation of the nose, ears, eyelids, and fingers through progressive mutilation. Mental aberrations, such as hysteria, manic-depressive psychosis, epilepsy, and delirium, also characterize this condition.

Clinical neurologist L. Illis argues that the physical deformities, in conjunction with psychopathology and nocturnal wandering due to photosensitivity, plus hypertrichosis, could be mistaken as evidence of lycanthropy and vampirism. In ancient times, these symptoms would be accompanied by physical and social mistreatment by community members, who would instinctively explain the subject's appearance in terms of witchcraft, satanic possession, and the like.

The condition seems to include a geographic factor. Many cases occur in Switzerland and Sweden (also known for historic reports of werewolves) in certain districts and valleys.

Should we also include some French regions?

The Wild Man

The case of Gilles Garnier, the "Wild Man of Saint-Bonnot, France" is perhaps even more interesting than the events surrounding young Grenier's case, due to two important factors: Garnier, who also mentioned his wolfish transformations, was an adult, and his attacks occurred at about the same time and in the vicinity in which a great wolf apparently beheaded and mutilated several children.

In this sense the parallels are even more relevant to the events in the Gévaudan: As has been discussed, perhaps an animal and a human beast were responsible for the killings. We believe it is crucial to address and understand this as part of the mystery of the Beast of the Gévaudan, offering the reader explanations from multiple angles.

Before we relate the activities of this alleged murderer-wolf from Lyon, we must pinpoint the location in which he lived: Armanges, near the city of Dole, France, an area harassed by packs of wolves at the time. Summers here are short and winters long, with limited prey. At the time of Garnier, wolves became increasingly bold, approaching villages, towns, and even larger urban areas. The real fear of these threatening animal predators, combined with ancient superstitions and the word "werewolf," caused a furor, especially in small hamlets and among isolated populations. Accounts circulated of an enormous "murderer" wolf terrorizing Armanges, in the vicinity of Dole, near Gilles Garnier's dwelling place, deep in the woods of Saint-Bonnot.

Apparently the canid targeted children; some victims' recovered remains exhibited the terrible marks of a predator's jaws. The year was 1572 and for Garnier, who'd recently settled in the area with his wife, this was bad news. But why? Garnier was apparently ostracized by the community because he had no real occupation, begging to support his family, and living as a "wild hermit" in a hut made of battered tree limbs. Further, like our Wolf Boy, he, too, seemed antisocial and locals reported that he suffered from serious mental or psychological disorders. His strange appearance, as described in the following passage, was also a cause of concern:

> The man, Gilles Garnier, was a somber, ill-looking fellow, who walked in a stooping attitude, and whose pale face, livid complexion, and deep-set eyes under a pair of coarse and bushy brows, which met across the forehead, were sufficient to repel any one from seeking his acquaintance. Gilles seldom spoke, and when he did it was in the broadest patois of his country. His long grey beard and retiring habits procured for him the name of the Hermit of Saint-Bonnot, though no one for a moment attributed to him any extraordinary amount of sanctity.

The cases that link Garnier to the murder of children can be summarized as follows:

In August 1572, Garnier took a boy of twelve or thirteen near a forest, intending to eat him, but was interrupted by several men. Unfortunately the boy was already dead. The men stated that Grenier did not have the appearance of a wolf.

In September, "in the form of a wolf," Garnier attacked and killed a girl of ten or twelve in a vineyard, using teeth and claws. He moved her body to a wooded area, consumed most of it, and, because the poor victim was so enjoyable, he "brought some of the flesh home for his wife Apolline."

Peasants heard screams and howling coming from a wood on the eighth of November; they found a child, a girl, fighting off a "monstrous creature," which ran off into the dark forest. Some thought it a wolf, others the hermit.

On November 14, not far from Dole, France, Garnier, in the guise of a wolf, supposedly throttled a ten-year-old boy and ate him, even tearing away one of his legs.

***

What were the reasons for these attacks? Simply hunger—the need to satiate his own, and his wife's, appetites? A psychological condition perhaps associated with malnutrition, as some have suggested? Or were his actions driven by some kind of demonic possession? Finally, what was the "mechanism" by which Garnier, as a wolf, committed the crimes? Historical records provide a revealing account:

> Mr. Daniel d'Ange, then dean of the church of Sens, commented on the report of the trial of Garnier: Gilles Garnier, a lycanthrope (man-wolf), as I like to call him, lived a hermit's life until one day, having taken a wife and not having the means to feed a family, he took the habit, being bold and desperate, of exploring the woods and wild places. This is where one day he met a ghost in human form who told him that he could perform miracles. He claimed he could teach him the art of metamorphosing into wolf, lion, or leopard. Since the wolf is the most common animal in these regions, Garnier chose the wolf. He disguised himself in this animal, took shape through some ointment, committing all the terrible things he confessed before his death and recognizing the horror of his actions.

The shadow of the *loup-garou* loomed large in medieval France. The outrage caused by Garnier's case was such that a royal decree was issued stating that villagers from Dole and its surrounding areas could deliberately hunt and kill any "local werewolf" without written permission.

Garnier, found guilty of the crimes of lycanthropy and witchcraft, was burned at the stake on January 18, 1573.

End Thoughts: Criminals and Sadists in the Gévaudan?

The district of Gévaudan, located in what is currently the French *departement* of Lozère, was an isolated and inhospitable region in the time of the Beast. The economy was practically reduced to the subsistence labor of a small population in a poor rural environment. It was difficult to make a living and unemployment was high.

Suddenly, with the appearance of the Beast, the region became more dynamic. Functionaries, villagers, and the servants of local feudal lords were now involved in planning and carrying out organized hunts. The tempting rewards offered by the state and by local authorities for the hide of the murderous Beast created an influx of newcomers incentivized to try their luck. All kinds of individuals made the rounds of places like Mende, Le Malzieu, Saint-Chély-d'Apcher, Saugues, and Le Puy-en-Velay, thrilled for such a challenge, itching to bring down this formidable animal. They were of course not just thinking about the reward money, but the fame that would come with the elimination and "unmasking" of such a mysterious adversary.

Peasants and laborers were on the move as well, seeking employment as trackers or as simply serving as support for the troops stationed in the area. There were also outlaws, vagrants, mercenaries, and foreigners who were unemployed and desperate, in hopes of exploiting the situation. Local administrative and legal bodies, trying to deal with the chaos, were over-taxed by the wave of crime. Royal troops were sent to crack down on myriad offenders who settled in the region (lower Vivarais, east of Gévaudan, and also the northern portions, localities like Le Malzieu and Marvejols). Funding was provided to areas where criminality became so endemic that, more than a century later, in 1876,

Reconstruction of the terrifying creature of the 2001 film *Le Pacte des loups (Brotherhood of the Wolf)* in which a trained armored animal was responsible, at the hands of its master, for a series of attacks in eighteenth-century France.

the courts' expansion in Le Puy-en-Velay (resulting from the number of legal matters from neighboring Gévaudan) was the subject of study.

Further, groups of armed hunters were abundant everywhere. They were to be controlled and their firearms registered in Mende. No one could be in the region with arms without a certificate. "There would be reason to fear that, under pretext of these hunts, some ill-intentioned foreigners, or even some locals, would spread out in bands and commit crimes."

A Trained Animal?

Many authors and researchers have discussed possible connections between the murders of children and women in the Gévaudan with the actions of a sadistic madman. And because the Beast supposedly specialized in this particular type of victim (although the number of adult males attacked or threatened in some way was also high, more

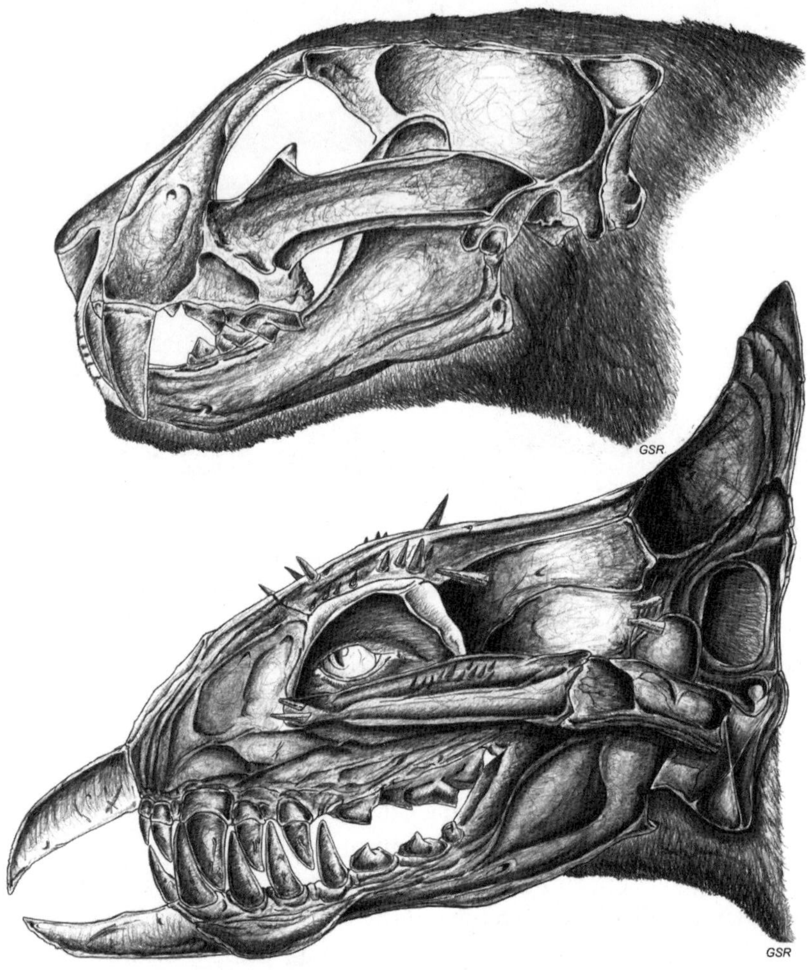

Close-up of the bone mask that enclosed the head of the Beast of the Gévaudan in the French film *Le pacte des loups (Brotherhood of the Wolf)* with a big cat (lion, tiger, etc.) skull for comparison.

than one hundred thirty-five, compared to one hundred twenty-four women), the parallelism is even greater.

In the early 1900s, medical doctor Paul Puech was the first to advance such a connection. Puech believed cases exhibiting characteristics of mutilation and sexual assault indicated human, not animal, intervention. He wrote that such macabre murders exonerated a "zoological" beast, and drew attention to the possibility that, owing to the ubiquity of the killings, several people may have been involved. For Puech, the Beast never existed. Instead, the killings were murders, the work of a sadistic madman, aided by henchmen disguised in animal skins. But what of the descriptions of many witnesses, who stated they saw large wolf-type beasts? We also have expert hunters identifying large canids in the countryside. And what of the vicious bites observed on the bodies of the victims?

Marguerite Aribaud-Farrère offers similar identification in her *La Bête du Gévaudan identifiée* (described in our Foreword), the cover of which shows a man wearing a wolfskin costume with a wolf's head. The individual wearing this attire is identified as an Parisian aristocrat, the Marquis de Sade.

After subjecting the pattern of killings to a complicated computer program that still leaves some loose ends, cryptozoologist Jean-Jacques Barloy, author of *The Beast of Gévaudan Unmasked*, holds that the murderers were two adult males acting in tandem, individuals who trained and handled strange beasts to carry out the attacks. This hypothesis was also adapted by film director Christophe Gans for his 2001 film *Le Pacte des loups (Brotherhood of the Wolf)*.

CHAPTER 21

Other Contenders: Prehistoric and Exotic Species

Some said La Bête was only wolves being more carnivorous than usual, while others, and this was the majority, said she was something very unusual and nobody knew how to destroy her.
—Abbé Pierre Pourcher

Members of prehistoric, introduced, and exotic species, owing to their unique characteristics, have been associated with the Beast. Some of these candidates could come from the pages of a thick volume on European vertebrate paleontology or the illustrations from a field guide on tropical carnivores.

Following is a review of various carnivore species that display similarities of one kind or another to the fabled animal or animals of the Gévaudan. Some were connected to the Beast and its frightful activities by eyewitnesses; other were represented graphically in historical documents of the time.

We will begin with a few candidates from prehistory and move on to other "suspects."

Prehistoric Bear-Dog (Amphicyon giganteus)

This huge and fearsome creature, more than eight feet in length, possessed the body of a bear and the head of a dog. Some in this group weighed up to 500 kilograms, more than half a ton. The bear-dog was distributed throughout Europe. Fossils have been found in France. However, this creature was extinct in the Miocene, about seven million years ago.

Giant Wolves? (Canis falconeri, Canis dirus)

Fans of the television series *Game of Thrones*, based on the series of novels by George R. R. Martin, wonder if the Beast could have been a dire wolf.

Fossils of Falconer's Dire Wolf, *Canis falconeri*, an Old World species that may be related to a dire wolf ancestor, has been found in Spain and in the Arno river valley of the Italian peninsula. With its large head and robust body, this prehistoric wolf species is a favorite contender for the Beast. Its dental (tooth) development suggests hyena-like habits, and its hyper-carnivore daily meal requirement (more than 70 percent flesh) could exceed forty kilograms, about eighty-eight pounds. Like the bear-dog, it had a European distribution. Fossils have been found in Spain and Italy, among other countries. But it became extinct approximately eight hundred thousand years ago.

Canus dirus was a beefier relative of *Canis lupus*, and probably lived alongside its cousin, but only in the New World, about ten to twelve thousand years ago. About 20 percent larger than its gray wolf counterpart, this powerful predator likely became extinct because of its bulkier build. The time period in which it lived was one of vanishing prey, whether from climate change, human overhunting, or both. Many dire wolf fossils have been found in the La Brea Tar Pits in California. The gray wolf, though smaller, was faster on its feet and, perhaps because of this advantage, survived and thrived.

Hyaenodon (Hyainailouros sulzeri)

The meat-loving hyaenodon, larger than a lion, was the biggest apex predator of its time (Miocene). Its lengthy skull was equipped with massive jaws. It may have developed the capacity to crush bones. Its fossils have been found in France. These specialized predators became extinct approximately 20 million years ago.

A New Species

One researcher believes the Beast was a member of a new species, a type of snow canid, a wolf-dog version of the snow leopard *(Panthera uncia)*. This creature would be able to negotiate steep valleys and snowy terrain. It would possess strong neck and shoulder muscles,

Prehistoric bear-dog, *Amphicyon giganteus* top, compared to ancient Hyaenodon, *Hyainailouros sulzeri*.

a reinforced waist and lumbar region, powerful limbs for traveling in deep snow, and wide paws that would have been used, snowshoe-like, to traverse challenging terrain.

Bear

Brown Bear *(Ursus arctos)*. The brown bear is a huge animal with a stocky body and short tail. Though the bear was suggested as a possible contender for the Beast, its morphology does not match descriptions of La Bête. Some researchers have suggested the possibility of a very strange hybrid, one resulting from a bear and a wolf/dog cross, something genetically impossible.

Monkey

Olive Baboon (*Papio anubis*). This is one of the most common species of baboon, widely distributed throughout Africa and found in many zoos, menageries, and private collections. Its elongated muzzle provides it with a profile close to that of a wolf-dog; because of this wolfish morphology, it was associated in Europe with the werewolf phenomena. In some historical accounts, the Beast is compared (morphologically) to this type of primate. For example, when La Bête is described as an animal capable of walking on its hind legs (bipedalism) when it wades through a river. However, this type of baboon is unable to survive in cold temperatures and snowy regions.

Armored Dog (Canis familiaris)

Some researchers have suggested that the Beast could have been an army-trained battle dog, protected from bullets by external armor.

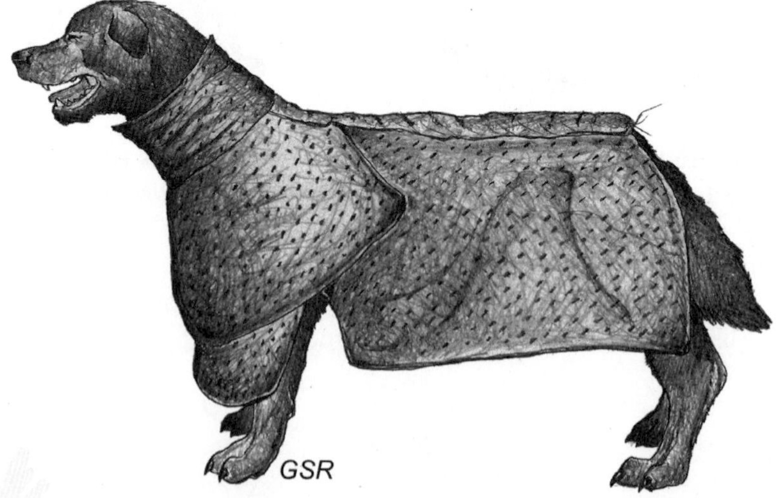

A seventeenth-century *Hundepanzer* (armored dog), protected to hunt large dangerous prey.

Napoleon himself used dogs in campaigning and for protection, although it is not clear whether or not they were armored. A German inventory of 1542 lists two "white" (steel) suits of armor for dogs. A seventeenth-century suit of armor for a *Hundepanzer* (armored dog) survives. It is made from four layers of linen, covered with buttonhole-stitched eyelets. This was probably worn by a boarhound—a large hunting dog, such as a mastiff or Great Dane or similar, bred and trained to attack large prey (boar, as well as elk, deer, etc.). It was protected this way from the deadly tusks of ferocious wild pigs.

Tiger Cat

The next section of our field guide to possible carnivores of the Gévaudan is devoted to some of the most charismatic flesh-eaters of all time, the big cats.

This inventory cannot be complete without mentioning an intriguing animal detailed in a March 25, 1765, letter from J. Bourgeois, a parson of Bouconville, France:

> Dear sirs, the fierce beast that ravaged the Gévaudan seems, according to the description that was made in the newspapers and gazettes, be a tiger cat; A strange animal and I think we cannot find anywhere but in the Yucatan Peninsula of Mexico, where there are many. M. Nicole in his geography, Volume 2 page 391, 1758 edition, says that these animals would be very frightening to people eating wild young calves that are abundant in the peninsula. Hence I conclude that this animal must naturally flee beef, cow, and even large dogs. But offering it its favorite food of calf could surprise by exposing him in the forest or in the countryside in different places. The bait, a calf six weeks or two months old would lie in the middle of several traps with poison spilled on the body (hide), or setting out a battery of several guns with attached ropes (they would fire if the animal would walk on them). This could be performed by your orders. That this animal is one or two of the unknown species in the Gévaudan, according to some relations, they would have been landed in France, probably by the Mediterranean, perhaps by the ocean. The desire to see the Languedoc soon free from this formidable animal is the only motive that led me to take the liberty to give you this letter, hoping that you will receive it as evidence of patriotic zeal. I have the honor, etc.

What could Father Bourgeois's "tiger cat" be? A real-life species, something new? Also—why is the Yucatan mentioned? The only living animal that could slightly resemble a "tiger cat from Yucatan" is the modern-day jaguar *(Panthera onca)*. This neotropical species has a wide distribution, ranging from southern North America (Arizona) through Mexico (including Yucatan and Belize, where they are numerous), south to Argentina.

This is the largest big cat in the Americas, and as many know, it has a beautiful pelage (coat) of open black spots over a yellowish background, similar to the color pattern of the African leopard. But a humorous and crucial consideration that also brings the "tiger cat" from Yucatan closer to the jaguar identity is the fact the jaguar is known in most of South America as a *tigre* ("tiger" in Spanish and French). By the way, the *tigre* usually prowls around villages and cultivated fields in search of prey. If it encounters a dog, even a big one, the cat will readily attack, kill, and devour. The same applies to cattle. South America is famous for its prime beef, cattle often maintained in fields that were once jungle. In such ranch-dominated habitats, cattle have become the jaguar's main food. The jaguar dispatches its prey with a deadly bite, the most powerful of all the big cats, often biting the back of the head, or employing a suffocating throat bite. It rarely attacks humans; usually this occurs when the big cat is provoked or harassed, for example during organized hunts, in which dogs and bloodhounds are used.

The connection between Father Bourgeois's Mexican "tiger cat" and the jaguar are clear. One can imagine an unfortunate animal, maybe one used to approaching Latin American villages to hunt some livestock from time to time, being captured and shipped to France to be displayed as an exotic living trophy.

Was La Bête an escaped jaguar roaming freely in the French countryside?

Tiger (Panthera tigris)

Classification:
Order Carnivora, Family Felidae

The tiger is the largest of all big cats, measuring up to 300 centimeters in length (head and body) and weighing as much as 325 kilograms. Subspecies of tiger are found in India, Russia, China, Indonesia, and North Korea. It is known, of course, for its magnificent coat, consisting of dark stripes against a red-orange or yellow ochre background. The tiger's habitat is varied, from tropical jungles to deciduous forests to the coniferous forests of Siberia. It's also at home in swamplands, grasslands, and savanna.

The tiger has a widely varied diet, ranging from types of deer, wild pigs, buffalo, antelope, and livestock, to rodents, invertebrates (beetles, locusts, etc.), birds, fish, and reptiles. A hungry animal may consume thirty to fifty kilograms (about 66 to 110 pounds) in one meal. In captivity they are fed approximately ten to twelve kilograms of meat per day.

Tiger attacks on people were reported in various regions of Russia in the nineteenth century; most were apparently somehow instigated by humans, but several were not. Tigers attacked and killed more than twenty people in eastern Russia and wounded others in the mid-1800s, but no such reports were made in the twentieth century. Accounts of tigers going after and killing dozens of people (such as workers in isolated conditions) occurred in China over the years until 1949. In India, where big cats compete for space with humans

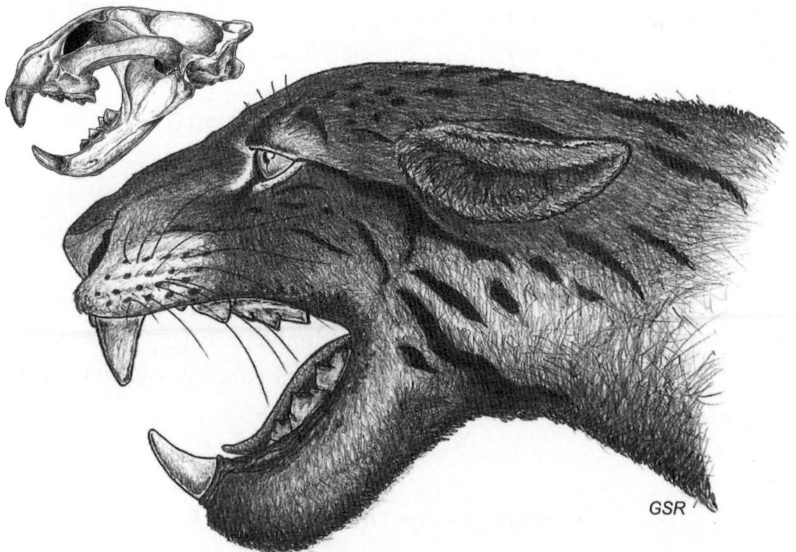

Tiger head and reconstructed skull. Some man-eating tigers in India claimed hundreds of victims.

and are unable to find natural prey, there have been many conflicts, with hundreds of people killed over the last two centuries. Because tigers attack their prey from the rear, humans who venture into tiger habitats are often advised to wear masks on the back of their heads.

Tiger/Beast of Gévaudan connection:

Some eyewitness descriptions that link the identity of the Beast with that of a tiger:

- A huge ferocious animal similar to some kind of big carnivorous predator, its head described as resembling that of a big cat *(Panthera spp.)*.
- In a letter dating from April 17, 1765, a curate of the diocese of Reims suggests that La Bête is a tiger cat, as discussed earlier.
- In November 1765, a dispatch listing animals most often mentioned in connection to the Beast includes tigers, leopards, lynxes, and hyenas.

Weakest characteristics for Beast identity:

- Conspicuous orange coloration
- Short muzzle
- Black stripes all over
- Long striped tail
- Retractable claws (non-visible when relaxed)

Strongest characteristics for Beast identity:

- Very large size
- A classic and much sought-after animal in all sorts of royal and aristocratic private collections and menageries
- A typical attraction in zoos and circuses
- May become a man-eater under environmental or health stress, although such individuals are rare
- The Siberian, or Amur tiger, is capable of surviving in cold temperatures/snowy regions

Leopard (Panthera pardus)

Classification:

Order Carnivora, Family Felidae

There are twenty-four recognized subspecies of the leopard found throughout the Middle East, Africa, Asia, and the Indian subcontinent. Leopards can measure up to 190 centimeters in length and weigh as much as seventy-one kilograms. Males are usually larger than females. Smaller than the tiger or lion, the leopard has a long body and is very nimble. It is noted for its spots, having black spots of two types, solid or annular (rosettes) against a background of yellow

Two typical members of the big cat family: leopard, top, next to a tiger, bottom.

or reddish-yellow color. Zoologist R. I. Pocock found the following trends in coloration for leopards in Africa:

- Savanna leopards are rufous to ochreous (rust-red to yellow ochre) in color.
- Desert leopards range from pale cream to yellow-brown in color. Those from cooler regions are grayer.
- Rainforest leopards are a dark or deep gold in color.
- High mountain leopards are even darker in color.

Leopards are found in forests, steppes, savannas, and mountain regions of extreme altitudes. Like tigers, leopards can feed on everything from insects and mice to large herbivores and antelopes. They favor medium-size herbivores weighing from twenty to eighty kilograms. Studies have found average intervals between leopard kills range from seven to twelve or thirteen days. Average daily consumption rates have been estimated at about three kilograms of meat, a little more for males, less for females. Other prey may include wild pigs, monkeys, wild sheep, hares, porcupines, birds, reptiles, crabs and other arthropods, and domestic animals.

There are human records of European Ice Age cave leopards, along with other carnivores, in paintings in Chauvet Cave in southern France (Upper Paleolithic), which are dated to about twenty-five thousand to thirty-seven thousand years before the present. The cave leopard became extinct in Europe about twenty-four thousand years ago. The modern leopard survived into the Holocene in Europe; remains have been found in France (a skull was recovered in 1924 in an Ariège cave in the Pyrenees), Spain, and Greece. There is some thought that leopards may have lived in areas such as Greece and the Ukraine into modern times. Remains from medieval Rome are believed to be those of leopards introduced from other countries.

Like the other carnivores discussed here, leopards will eat livestock if populations are stressed and natural prey is unavailable. A small number may become man-eaters, sometimes aggressively seeking prey by breaking into human homes. There are reports of this in Asia and Africa, and (rarely) in China. One Indian leopard is said to have killed more than two hundred people. Famed twentieth-century Indian-born British outdoorsman Jim Corbett—said to have killed more than thirty man-eating animals that had allegedly killed over one thousand people—noted that leopards are

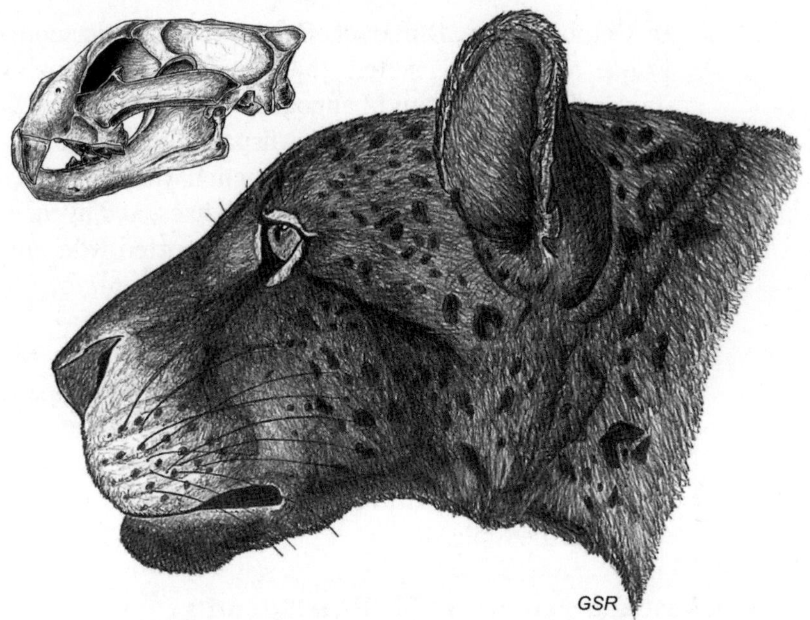

Leopard head and reconstructed skull. Their adaptability to live close to human settlements brings the felines in contact and conflict with people.

also known to consume human cadavers at cremation sites. Such cases are infrequent in Russia, though attacks were reported in the late 1800s in the Caucasus, and in Iran, an aged leopard with time-worn dentition unsuccessfully jumped a man in the early twentieth century. There are also accounts of leopards trailing people without attacking.

Leopard/Beast of Gévaudan connection:

Some Beast witness descriptions linked the creature with:

- A panther (black leopard) that escaped from a zoo, menagerie, or private collection.
- A huge ferocious animal similar to some kind of big carnivorous predator, its head described as resembling that of a big cat *(Panthera spp.).*
- In February 1764, subdelegate Montluc wrote a small report in which the Beast is described as having "a large head, pointed muzzle, and elongated body . . . believed to be a leopard."

- In October 1764, Duhamel, Captain of the Clermont-Prince volunteers, stated that "a leopard probably prowled the hills around Langogne."
- In November 1765, there was a dispatch listing the animals most often mentioned in connection with the Beast's atrocities, including leopards, tigers, lynxes, and hyenas.
- Monarchs and aristocrats routinely imported wild animals, among them the panther and the leopard, for use in hunting.
- That leopards were used for hunting is indicated by the existence of a Lombardic sketch of a hunting leopard from the fifteenth century.
- Big cats (especially leopards) were trophy animals, as reflected in some historical French medieval monographic works on the topic.

Weakest characteristics for Beast identity:

- Short muzzle
- Spotted all over
- Retractable claws (not visible when relaxed)

Strongest characteristics for Beast identity:

- The leopard is a classic and much sought-after animal in all sorts of royal and aristocratic private collections and menageries
- A typical attraction in zoos and circuses
- Also, as mentioned earlier, used as hunting animal
- Former European distribution
- May become a man-eater under environmental or health stress
- Capable of thriving close to human settlements
- Capable of surviving in cold temperatures and snowy regions

Lion (Panthera leo spelaea)

Classification:
Order Carnivora, Family Felidae

The lion's range today consists primarily of sub-Saharan Africa, though in the past it was distributed much further, even into Europe, where it apparently became extinct almost two thousand years ago.

The lion is the second largest big cat, with record measurements for length of a lion specimen at three and one-third meters (more than ten and one-half feet), including its tail. Record weight is 272 kilograms (about 600 pounds) for a male and 152 kilograms for a female.

The male lion is characterized by its mane, though some males are without. Both male and female have brown-yellow coats, though paler leucistic specimens are found. This is caused by a genetic loss of pigmentation (not albinism) and is also found in tigers.

The lion's natural habitat consists of savanna grasslands and scrub forest. Here, lions often scavenge for a meal, consuming injured or sick animals or, when possible, those killed by other predators. The lioness does most of the hunting. Like many predators, lions will eat what they can take, including rodents, but prefer animals such as zebras, impalas, wildebeests, and buffalo.

The mighty cave lion, *Panthera leo spealea*, was a Pleistocene species that probably survived into historical times (one to two thousand years ago) in the Balkans and Asia Minor. The most common prehistoric big cat, it was widespread in Europe, including France. It was 8 to 10 percent larger than the biggest African lions.

Problem animals (individuals that hunt humans) have been reported in southeast Tanzania and northern Mozambique. As we've stated, this occurs when natural prey is scarce or absent, when healthy individuals are crippled by natural causes or through injuries caused by humans (gunfire, traps, etc.), and sometimes when old exemplars are incapable of hunting wild game on their own (poor condition, issues with dentition, reduced mobility, etc.). See the sidebar on the man-eating lions of Tsavo, Kenya.

Lion/Beast of Gévaudan connection:

- There is one historical artwork (circa 1764) depicting a carnivorous predator resembling a big cat sporting a clear visible mane and a long tufted tail in the region of the Gévaudan. The creature depicted, which looks very

The Gévaudan "lion" attacking a girl. Note the mane, long tufted tail, and big-cat paws. Black-and-white engraving circa 1764. ***Private Collection/Bridgeman Images.***

much like a lion (with a relatively short muzzle), is attacking a young girl. We can also see the creature's back leg and one is tempted to see the typical big cat-furred paw with rounded toes without claws (which seem to be retracted).

- There are also some vague witness descriptions that stated the Beast was a "monster sired by a lion but with a mother of undetermined species."
- In Smith's book we learn that "Morangiès [the count] was among the first of the local inhabitants to hypothesize that the beast had African origins, and he signaled to Lafont his readiness to face a 'lion' if necessity required."

Weakest characteristics for Beast identity:

- Males have manes (they are shorter in very hot regions)
- Short muzzle

- Retractable claws (not visible when relaxed)
- Not capable of surviving long harsh winters
- Exotic/tropical hyper-carnivore

Strongest characteristics for Beast identity:

- Big size
- Some cold-temperature resistance
- Uniform color
- A classic, much sought-after animal for all sorts of private collections and menageries
- A typical attraction in zoos, menageries, etc.
- Former European distribution (becoming extinct here approximately two thousand years ago). A population of Asiatic lions survived until the tenth century in the Caucasus (southeastern Europe), their last Continental outpost
- May become a man-eater with environmental or health stress

The Man-Eaters of Tsavo: Parallels to La Bête

In 1898, the British Foreign Office appointed Lieutenant-Colonel J. H. Patterson to oversee the building of a portion of a railway from the coastal city of Mombasa, Kenya, into the country of Uganda. For nine months during construction, in the vicinity of the Tsavo River in Kenya, Patterson and his workers were the prey of two man-eating lions. Work completely stopped for one three-week period due to the cats' predations.

The lions were full size—over nine feet in length, and one measured just under four feet in height at the shoulder—and, like La Bête, they were extraordinarily bold. The animals would simply thrust their heads beneath the walls of workers' tents or in their tent doors, lock jaws onto the throat of the nearest man, drag him off, and consume him nearby. Patterson speaks of their "dreadful purring."

As the Gévaudanais found the Beast's behavior eerie, Patterson describes the lions' hunting tactics as "uncanny . . . the workmen finally believed they were not real animals at all, but devils in lions' shape." Patterson's workers told him it was useless to try to kill the lions. They believed the cats were two deceased chiefs from the area whose spirits had become lions to oppugn the building of a railroad through their land.

Like Duhamel, the d'Ennevals, and François Antoine, Patterson found his environment one that made hunting the man-slayers next to impossible. Tsavo's terrain was choked with undergrowth, such as the hook-thorned "wait-a-bit" bushes that grasped at clothing and impeded movement. An additional note on the environment: Research conducted by the University of Lausanne in 2009 concluded there were ecological and biological reasons for the lions' anthropophagic tastes. First, the area's grasslands and populations of natural prey (hoofed animals) had been diminished by elephant hunting. Second, the lions were of an advanced age, indicated by the fact that the pair had no manes. The cats also had bad teeth. Between the lack of normal food and the condition of their dentition, it makes sense that the lions would look to an alternative foodstuff: people.

Meanwhile, the lions grew more daring; they ignored fire, rocks, bullets, and poisoned bait in the form of deceased, tsetse fly-bitten service animals. Patterson says "the wily man-eaters . . . much preferred live men to dead donkeys." As in the Gévaudan, there was a generous helping of hoodoo: rifles misfired, the lions' trails were lost on rocky ground, the nocturnal-hunting cats were fired upon but vanished, seemingly unhurt, into Tsavo's total darkness. The hunters' misfortunes resulted in a number of workers from India becoming "more than ever confirmed in their belief that the lions were really evil spirits, proof against mortal weapons. Certainly, they did seem to lead charmed lives."

Finally, workers began to leave the site en masse, and construction stopped for three weeks except for the lion-proofing of the quarters of those willing to stay on. Some of the crew even dug pits in the earthern floors of their tents to sleep beneath them, after positioning logs above.

Nearly thirty workers were lost to the man-eaters before the cats were eliminated. And the men remained fatalistic until the lions' end. One worker, in relating how his late roommate was dragged from their tent in the middle of the night, commented, "Was he not fighting with a lion?"

Hyenas

Last but by no means least: For many researchers, the hyena is the favorite, and perfect, contender for the Beast.

***

Hyenas are carnivorous animals that also consume carrion, and externally they do physically resemble typical members of the canid group (wolves, coyotes, foxes, dogs, etc.). Because of these similarities—including a dog-like head, a wide snout, powerful jaws, large teeth, a stocky, furry body (approximately the same size as a big dog)—many people might misidentify one as a large wolf.

Upon a number of occasions, the Beast of the Gévaudan was described, and portrayed, as a hyena.

The Marquis de Lafayette, hero of the American Revolution, grew up in Auvergne, France, at the time. The young Lafayette and a friend reconnoitered nearby forests, eager to catch a sight of "the hyena of the Gévaudan." Later he wrote, "Even at the age of eight my heart beat in sympathy with the hyena."

Many illustrations, pictures, and historical images depict the Beast as such, explicitly expressing that the animal portrayed was a hyena. There are even historical documents in the collection of the *Muséum national d'histoire naturelle*, the National Museum of Natural History in Paris, connecting the hyena identification with the ferocious animal responsible for many human deaths in the Gévaudan region. Hyenas, with their typical predatory and scavenging habits, their capacity to inflict lethal bites, their wolf-like appearance, and insatiable appetites, can easily become a possible explanation for the enigma that we are investigating. Further, through a document that apparently shows the presence of hyenas in the Gévaudan, this species' man-eating monster candidacy seems more than justified.

We start with a prehistoric candidate from the hyena clan:

Giant Short-Faced Hyena (Pachycrocruta brevirostris)

Classification:
Order Carnivora, Family Hyaenidae

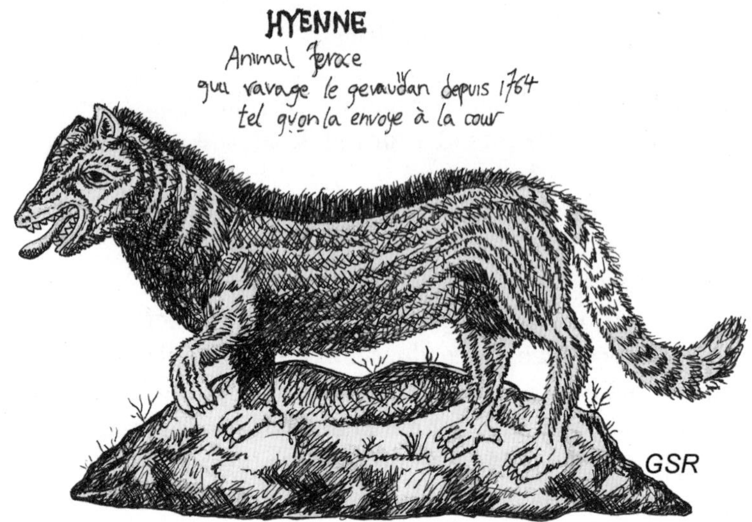

Reproduction of an illustration from 1764 that represented one of the ferocious animals loose in the Gévaudan. Original, *Bibliothèque nationale de France.*

This large hyena was distributed throughout Africa, Europe, and Asia. Said to be as big as a lion, it weighed approximately 160 kilograms (more than 350 pounds). Likely evolving from African prehistoric brown hyenas, it moved into Europe and Asia, making its home in cave settings in savannas and woodlands. An active hunter, as opposed to a carrion eater, it consumed large herbivores. Some researchers believe it also chased other predators away from their kills, and that it occasionally hunted in small packs.

Records from some parts of the world suggest that members of the hyena family *(Pachycrocuta)* commonly preyed on humans (Peking man, *Homo erectus pekinensis*, in China). There is also evidence of competition between archaic humans and giant hyenas for a mammoth carcass at a site in Spain (Fuente Nueva-3) dated to over one million years ago.

Giant short-faced hyena/Beast of Gévaudan connection: Mainly this animal's huge size, being as big as a lion. Some eyewitness descriptions describe a hyena-like animal of immense size, as large as a big cat.

Weakest characteristics for Beast identity:

- Extinct in the Pleistocene (approximately twelve thousand years ago)
- Cause of extinction: Competition with spotted hyena *(Crocuta crocuta)*

Strongest characteristics for Beast identity:

- Big size
- Relatively recent European distribution
- French fossils
- Flesh-eater, hyper-carnivore (not as much a scavenger)
- Probably similar morphology as brown hyena (big mane)

Spotted Hyena (Crocuta crocuta)

Classification:
Order Carnivora, Family Hyaenidae

This shy but robust dog-like hyena dwells in sub-Saharan Africa. Specimens may measure 160 centimeters in length, with heights of up to eighty-nine centimeters, and weights of as much as eighty-six kilograms (about 190 pounds).

Coats range from sandy to gray/brown with dark spots which may fade in time. Tails are thin but end in a dark bushy tip. As with other hyenas, the front legs are longer than those in the back, so the back slopes to the tail. The spotted hyena has massive jaws, a powerful neck, and a large head with rounded ears. Its wide feet each have four clawed toes.

The spotted hyena prefers savannas and mosaic forests (transitional areas between moist tropical zones and drier areas) and non-alpine altitudes. They avoid deserts except those along mountainous areas and waterways.

Spotted hyenas are often thought of as scavengers and carrion eaters, but they are also skilled hunters, killing as much as 95 percent of their food. Spotted hyenas sometimes attack and kill livestock in rural parts of Africa, creating conflicts with humans.

The awesome late-Pleistocene predator, the cave hyena *(Crocuta crocuta spelaea)*, ranged from Africa to Europe. The modern African species was also distributed in Europe during the Pleistocene,

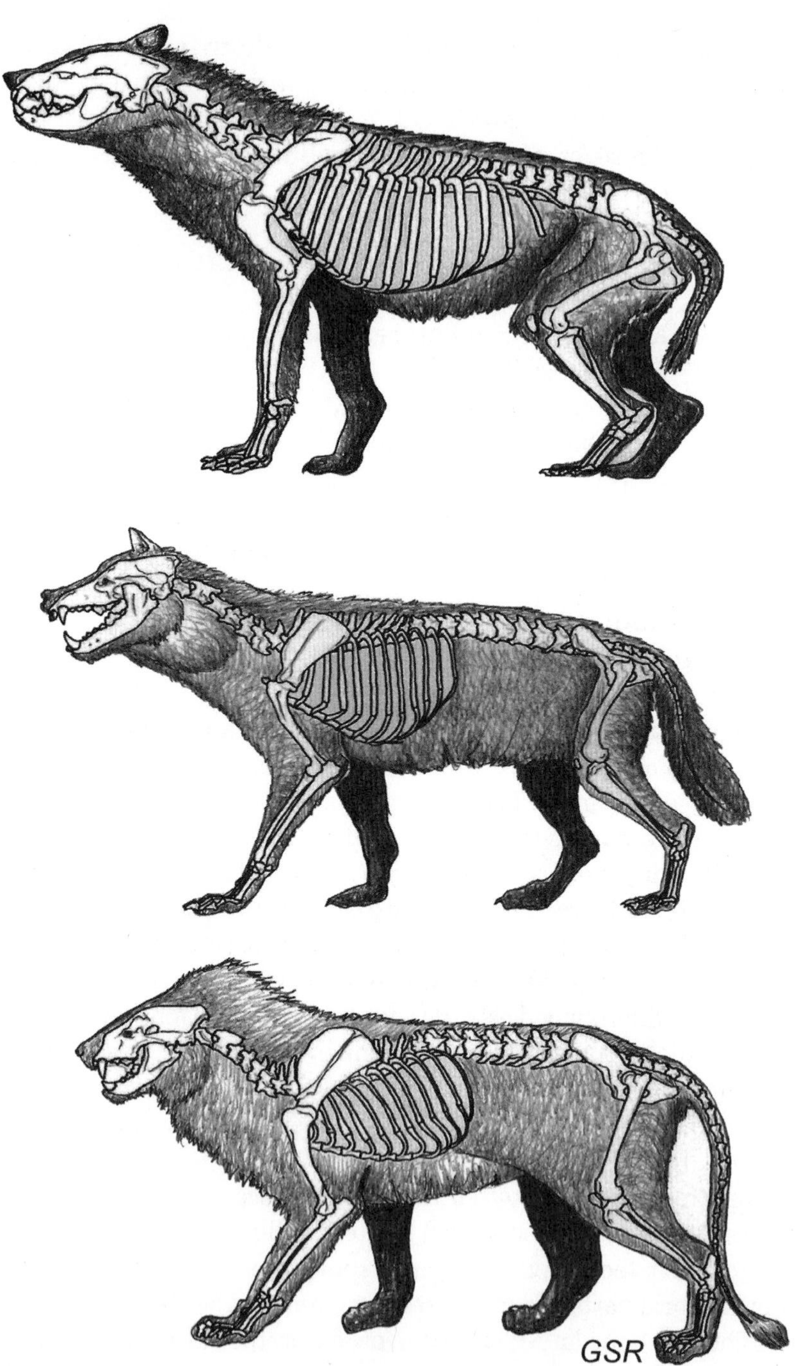

Skeletal reconstructions and body outline of different carnivores. Top, spotted hyena; middle, wolf; bottom, lion.

but it was smaller than its relative, not much larger than the spotted hyena of today.

Though rare, spotted hyenas are reported to injure or kill rural Africans each year. These events occur usually when victims are sleeping outside unprotected or are in country areas near dawn or dusk. This hyena may also enter tents when they are open, or when there is meat inside the tent.

Spotted hyena/Beast of Gévaudan connection:
Basically, the many historical artworks depicting carnivorous predators identified as hyenas in the region of the Gévaudan.

Weakest characteristics for Beast identity:

- Conspicuous dark spots all over body
- Incapable of surviving long harsh winters
- Poor and clumsy jumper

Strongest characteristics for Beast identity:

- Former range (Pleistocene) includes most of Europe, including France
- This is a powerful predator capable of taking large prey, including adult humans, easily
- Highly mobile; strong runner, capable of reaching 55 km/h
- Extinction in Europe is recent, historical

Striped Hyena (Hyaena hyaena)

Classification:
Order Carnivora, Family Hyaenidae

The striped hyena is a large and powerful animal that can be confused in the distance with a German shepherd dog or similar. It is found northern Africa, the Middle East, and Asia from Turkey to India. Length-wise, the striped hyena measures a little over 100 centimeters, and is about sixty to seventy-four centimeters high at the shoulder. Males weigh up to forty-one kilograms, females thirty-four kilograms.

This hyena has shaggy gray/tan fur, with black vertical stripes covering its sides and legs, a dark muzzle, and a black throat patch. The back, from its neck to its rump, is covered with a thick, erectile mane (which can be raised, making the hyena appear quite large; it is used in combative displays against other hyenas). Body and neck are thick and heavyset. All hyena species present a sloping profile as their front legs are longer than their rear legs, making the animals poor jumpers but good runners. Tails are fluffy and long.

Habitat-wise, the hyena prefers a dry environment: steppes scrubland, woodland savannas, semi-desert, and mountainous surrounds. It cannot survive at temperatures of minus fifteen to minus twenty degrees Celsius.

These are carrion eaters, consuming the flesh and bones of large vertebrates killed by other predators. They are also opportunistic, feeding in gardens and trash dumps and consuming smaller animals as they can: birds, mice, reptiles, turtles, and invertebrates.

The prehistoric form, sometimes regarded as a different species *(Hyena prisca)*, was widespread in Europe, especially in France, until approximately ten thousand years ago (Pleistocene). It was a somewhat larger animal.

Striped hyenas rarely attack livestock or people and are unaggressive, even allowing dogs to attack them without attempting to defend themselves. If cornered by dogs, they may choose flight rather than a fight. And if unable to get away, they may foil dogs by playing dead. Then, with their attackers off guard, they are likely to jump to their feet and bound away to safety. There are, however, reports of hyenas attacking humans. In the 1880s, Russian news outlets reported a number of attacks south of the Caucasus mountains. These were mostly nocturnal attacks on sleeping children (in one year, twenty-five children were hurt) and on people overnighting outdoors on their properties. Random attacks on other adults were also reported, and bounties offered. Attacks were reported in 1908, and in the 1930s and 1940s, hyenas were again said to be seizing youngsters resting outside at night. Other reports of more than twenty children being carried off by hyenas came from India in the 1960s and 1970s, though one asserted that, when incidents involving other dangerous animals were taken into account, such attacks were low.

Striped hyena/Beast of Gévaudan connection:

The hyena hypothesis is supported by certain sources. Let's start with the comments of the foremost authority on zoology in the eighteenth century, French naturalist Georges Louis Leclerc, comte de (Count) Buffon. The killings in the Gévaudan region could have been linked to the African striped hyena. This connection can be seen in Buffon's famous *Natural History,* specifically *Volume IX, Quadrupeds VI,* 1761. Buffon tells us that the hyena:

- "Though in size equals the wolf . . . has, nevertheless, a contracted appearance."
- "The hair of his body and mane is of a dark grey . . . yellow and black . . . disposed all along in waves."
- "He lives like the wolf, by depredation, and is more strong and daring."
- "He resides . . . in dens, which he forms for himself under the earth."
- "It is a solitary animal."
- "When at a loss for prey he scrapes up the earth . . . [and] the carcasses of animals and men."

***

In the 1990s, Franz Jullien of the Collection Conservation Services of the National Museum of Natural History in Paris, France, located a museum-published pamphlet dating to 1819. In it, there is a reference to the Gévaudan in connection with both a live hyena on display and a specimen hyena. This document states the following:

> Description of what there is remarkable in the Menagerie and the Cabinet of Natural History. About the life and habits of wild animals that are enclosed both the Menagerie in the Valley of the Swiss; monitoring Places that lie [in] the Cabinet of Natural History. At the end of the garden, on the edge of the Seine, the ferocious animals are living, the care of MM. Richard Rousseau and whose familiarity with them is frightening. The king of beasts, the lion, seems to forget

his voracious instinct. Note: To use this form, it is necessary, by entering through the gate, turn right. The first animals found are namely:

- No. 1 and 2: A gray wolf, given the Menagerie by Mr. Sachai, and is tamed like a dog when his master comes, is done out in the yard and he lavishes his caresses. With him, the wolf-dog.
- 3. and 4. Both male and female Cape of Good Hope porcupines, sent by Mr. SM Jansens, Governor of the Cape.
- 5. Striped Hyena from the East. She was taken to Tippoo (Tipu) Sarb (Sahib) by the English, and bought in London by the French governor, brought to Paris by Bernard Lazardi, former keeper of the Menagerie. This fierce and indomitable animal is ranked in the class of lynx: he lives in Egypt; he traveled the tombs to pull the corpses, during the day attacks men, women, and children, and devours them. Sports a mane on his back, crossed like the royal tiger, it is the same species as we see in the Cabinet of Natural History, and devoured in the Gévaudan a large amount of people.
- 6. Speckled Hyena from Africa sent to France by Captain Baudin, during his expedition to Botany Bay.
- 7. Jaguar or Adive, private American animal, arrived at the Menagerie on November 14, 1817.
- 8. Belle Constantine, widow of the king of beasts [obviously a lioness], she lost her husband four years ago, was ten years old.
- 9. The lioness with dog Braque, who was raised with it.
- 10. The African Lion.

For obvious reasons the most interesting number from the list is number five, in which the eastern striped hyena (clearly differentiated from the speckled/spotted hyena, number six) is identified with a man-eating animal associated with the Gévaudan region. The connection seems important: This animal, donated by an Indian sultan, Fateh Ali Tipu (also known as Tipu Saib, 1750–1799), to the British, and later purchased by the French, is undoubtedly compared to one specimen of the museum collection that then roamed the Gévaudan–responsible, it seems, for devouring a large amount of people. This would mean that in 1819, there was a striped hyena registered in the museum's collections as an animal coming from the Gévaudan (and responsible for attacking many people there). Is this the right interpretation? Or could this document actually be stating that a similar type of hyena, not necessarily "that one animal," attacked and devoured people in the Gévaudan? (In other words, perhaps predators were misidentified and erroneously labeled as hyenas.)

To French researcher Franz Jullien, taxidermist and collection manager of the Grand Evolution Gallery of the National Museum of Natural History in Paris, here at last is part of the solution to the enigma. For him, "one" of the Beasts of the Gévaudan was obviously "this particular striped hyena." Here are the key factors in Jullien's hypothesis:

- Antoine Chastel, son of Jean Chastel, owned this animal (theoretically brought it to the Gévaudan region from Africa) as part of a menagerie and trained it to attack.
- What is certain is that when the Chastels were imprisoned in Saugues in 1765, the crimes ceased, but resumed soon after their release.
- Deaths apparently permanently ceased after Antoine's father Jean finally killed the Beast in 1767 (according to witnesses, the animal also behaved in a strange manner in those final moments, as if it recognized the elder Chastel).
- Allegedly, Chastel brought his Beast to Versailles to show the king, but, owing to the poor condition of the animal's remains, Louis ordered it to be buried immediately.
- According to Jullien, the animal killed by Chastel could not be buried in the gardens of Versailles. Parisian scientists, including naturalists Buffon and Louis-Jean-Marie Daubenton, at this, the time of the Enlightenment, were on the lookout for unique discoveries. Further, the remains were kept in the king's office (the building site of the future zoo and *Jardin des Plantes*, the botanical garden) after being studied by Buffon. Later it would have been mounted and included in the collections.
- Therefore, Chastel's animal would have been the striped hyena responsible for the attacks in the Gévaudan, and later compared to the Indian specimen in the museum as discussed above.
- Guy Crouzet, the author of *La grande peur du Gévaudan (Gévaudan's Greatest Terror)*, 2001, agrees with Jullien's thesis.

However Jullien's hypothesis has been questioned in different ways:

- Folklorist and French researcher Michel Meurger suggests that this idea was at the time in tune with the historical context, but nothing justifies it beyond that time.

- If this was indeed a singular specimen, the remains of a fabulous Beast responsible for so many deaths, why wasn't its skin or skull preserved or prepared for further conservation, especially if it was a specimen possibly acquired and mounted by the eminent Buffon? Wouldn't the king himself be eager to exhibit this trophy in order to evidence the state's success in dealing with this man-eating monster?
- As the second Beast autopsy indicates (see page 268), the composite morphology/anatomy of the animal shot by Chastel was a wolf-dog hybrid. If this animal was a striped hyena, its unique and distinctive morphology would have been recorded in the available autopsies.
- In Jay Smith's book we read: "According to local lore . . . Chastel . . . arrived at Versailles and managed against all odds to secure a royal audience, whereupon the king promptly insulted Chastel and ordered the swift burial of his rotting and odoriferous creature." It is not clear if Chastel actually got the chance to meet Louis XV, although Smith writes that this story seems to be one based on the memory of M. Estaniol, mayor of Saugues, and embellished as the years went on. It is also in part included in Pourcher's book and Franz Jullien's *La deuxième mort de la Bête du Gévaudan*: "Estaniol, who died in 1858, would recall hearing elderly locals of ancient memory agitatedly stating that only complots at court had deprived Jean Chastel of the honor of victory and the prize money promised to the man who defeated La Bête."
- Too, why had nobody even talked, showed, pictured, illustrated, or exhibited this formidable killing hyena of the Gévaudan, a perfect contender for the Beast, until 1819, more than half a century after the events began to occur?
- According to Smith's research, Chastel's hyena/Beast apparently never entered the museum's collection and Buffon never mentioned it (which seems odd if the specimen was so unique and notorious).

In a personal interview with Jullien at the National Museum of Natural History, he informed us that neither the alleged Gévaudan hyena (nor the Indian hyena) were part of the museum's current collection. Both would have been very early examples of taxidermy and were probably damaged over time or destroyed by insects. The museum has specimens of striped hyena specimens on display and in storage, but these animals come from known and more recent sources.

***

From the fifteenth century into the nineteenth century, each summer a huge fair and international trade show was held in Beaucaire, France, attracting hundreds of thousands from Europe, Turkey, Greece, and the Middle East. The fair plays a role in *The Count of Monte Cristo* by Alexandre Dumas, and Napoleon wrote of a soldier's conversation with merchants here in *Supper in Beaucaire*. Those who believed La Bête was a hyena speculate that it may have escaped from a menagerie at this fair.

***

Barnson cites a 1929 write-up in the *Brioude Almanac,* in which author C. Chacornac tells how a friend took advantage of a trip to Paris in order to view the Beast's remains in the National Museum of Natural History. He was told the skin had lost its hair, and the remains had recently been discarded and burned, in keeping with state collections policy. Thompson also mentions that François Antoine's Chazes wolf was the subject of an official painting, but this artwork seems also to have disappeared.

Between 1739 and 1752, acclaimed artist Jean-Baptiste Oudry painted eleven stunning life-size portraits of animals from the (live) royal menagerie at Versailles, including a famous rhinoceros named Clara, a lion, other cats, exotic birds, and a hyena. The suite of paintings was exhibited in 2007 at the J. Paul Getty Museum in Los Angeles. Regarding the painting entitled *Hyena Attacked by Two Dogs*, exhibition catalogue editor Mary Morton states, "the precision with which [the hyena] was painted indicates the painting

Striped hyenas with erect mane (top) and normal (relaxed) position.

must have been inspired by a live specimen." In a 1750 letter written by Oudry, the artist says he painted his subjects from life. The portrait (more than four feet wide by six feet long) is of a striped hyena, though it was identified as a *"Loup curvier de la Louisiane,"* or a Louisiana lynx, in one 1739 exhibition, and as a "Lynx of the Menagerie . . . painted for the King" in a 1746 showing. It is believed Oudry placed the hyena in confrontation with two dogs in order to give prominence to the dark dorsal "crest" raised when the animal displays its "electrically charged defiance." The Getty catalogue notes, too, that the hyena painting is the only animal-in-combat portrait in the suite and at least one expert has stated it was actually not part of the original commission Oudry received from Louis XV's surgeon, François Gigot de La Peyronie. The paintings belong to the collection of the Staatliches Museum Schwerin in Germany.

***

After reviewing the presented facts we are inclined to think that the hyena at the museum mentioned in the 1819 publication was simply a misidentification of some sort. There is a chance that it could represent a real hyena (sighted, or perhaps attacking people while temporarily free), perhaps an escaped animal from some menagerie, zoo, private collection, circus, etc., as has also been suggested. Another option is that it could have represented an animal smuggled into France aboard a merchant ship via the Mediterranean, maybe even already mounted, making its way to the museum collections after being purchased because of its exotic origin and nature. The connection could have been created simply because of the many rumors circulating at the time of the Beast and the historical artworks that represented the Beast of the Gévaudan as a hyena (because of its odd morphology). Therefore, in the early 1800s, a dubious stuffed museum specimen was linked with the Gévaudan in a remote and anecdotal way.

Weakest characteristics for Beast identity:

- Chastel's La Ténazeyre Canid's morphology differs too much from that of a striped hyena (color, stripes, etc.)
- Distinctive black throat patch
- Vertical stripes (5 to 9) on sides
- Clear black transverse and horizontal stripes on four legs
- Hunting abilities rather poor (simple chases and grabs at prey)

- Mostly nocturnal (active at night)

Strongest characteristics for Beast identity:

- Certain historical documents and artworks
- Capable of surviving in cold temperatures
- Former range (during the Pleistocene) includes most of Europe and France
- Attacks solitary humans at night, especially sleeping or unattended children and babies, or adults lying or sleeping uncovered in the open
- Known to excavate human graves, carrying away bones and/or remains (thus developing a taste for human flesh)
- Became extinct in Europe in recent historical times

Tables 1 and 2. Prehistoric and modern species discussed in this chapter, each with morphological, behavioral, and paleontological aspects, and percentage matches with the Beast of Gévaudan's descriptive key features.

Prehistoric species

Name	Long tail	Long Muzzle	Visible claws	French Fossils	Relatively recent	% Match
Prehistoric striped hyena	YES	YES	YES	YES	YES	100
Cave hyena	**NO**	**YES**	**YES**	**YES**	**YES**	**80**
Bear-dog	YES	YES	YES	YES	NO	80
Falconer´s dire wolf	**YES**	**YES**	**YES**	**YES**	**NO**	**80**
Hyaenodon	YES	YES	YES	YES	NO	80
Short-faced hyena	**NO**	**YES**	**YES**	**YES**	**NO**	**60**
Cave lion	YES	NO	NO	YES	YES	60
Cave leopard	**YES**	**NO**	**NO**	**YES**	**YES**	**60**

Wolf head, top, compared to a hyena. The latter species has a more conical appearance and distinctive rounded ears.

Modern species

Name	Long tail	Long muzzle	Large size	Visible claws	Individually aggressive	% match
Wolf-dog	YES	YES	YES	YES	YES	100
Dog	**YES**	**YES**	**YES**	**YES**	**YES**	**100**
Striped hyena	YES	YES	YES	YES	NO	80
Spotted hyena	**NO**	**YES**	**YES**	**YES**	**YES**	**80**
Wolf	YES	YES	YES	YES	NO	80
Bear	**NO**	**YES**	**YES**	**YES**	**YES**	**80**
Wolverine	YES	YES	NO	YES	YES	80
Lion	**YES**	**NO**	**YES**	**NO**	**YES**	**60**
Tiger	YES	NO	YES	NO	YES	60
Leopard (Panther)	**YES**	**NO**	**YES**	**NO**	**YES**	**60**
Smaller cats	YES	NO	NO	NO	NO	20
Baboon	**NO**	**YES**	**NO**	**NO**	**NO**	**20**
Lynx	NO	NO	NO	NO	NO	0

CHAPTER 22

What of Wolves and Hybrids?

"The Beast . . . was . . . in all likelihood a large, powerfully built, highly intelligent, and undoubtedly somewhat warped representative of the species Canis lupus.*"*

—Richard H. Thompson

From all accounts, the Gévaudan overwhelmed hunters Duhamel, the d'Ennevals, and even François Antoine. Only Jean Chastel, a native, seems to have been at ease in his surroundings. When you consider wolf ecology, the region was the ideal habitat for *Canis lupus*. Wolves are built to thrive in and prefer cold weather; their coats provide insulation to forty degrees below zero, Fahrenheit and Celsius. They are extremely sure-footed; their paws have the capacity to spread and adjust to different types of terrain on the run, a boon in the variable Margeride mountains. The area provides plenty of rocky, secluded nooks in which to locate dens. Its high pinnacles and immense vistas would allow wolves to easily perceive animal and human activity.

La Bête traveled seemingly vast distances between attacks, but this seems to agree with what wildlife ecologists have learned of *Canis lupus*. An Alaskan pack of ten wolves was observed ranging an average of twenty-four miles between kills, from six to forty-five miles each time. Wolves in Isle Royale National Park, Michigan, would average twenty-three miles, and feed approximately every forty-eight hours. Wolf specialist L. David Mech states that "It appears at present under most conditions wolves hunt merely by traveling widely until they meet up with prey." A November 2014 Associated Press news story reported that a female gray wolf from the Northern Rockies traveled hundreds of miles to the North Rim of the Grand Canyon in Arizona, the first time *Canis lupus* had been seen in this area since the 1940s. The animal was killed months later by a hunter who mistook it for a coyote.

Optimal prey for wolves is an animal they can kill without risk, by stalking, by chance encounter, or by scent, says Mech. When they get close to their target, they abruptly surge in, seeking a direct hit. The prey animal may run; this prompts the wolf to give chase. If the animal is swifter than the reported speed of a wolf (twenty-five to forty miles per hour) they may escape, and the wolf ceases its pursuit. Wolves favor young, old, and injured prey. States Mech, "No doubt a lone wolf or even small packs would have to rely on only the very oldest and weakest moose." Simply the sight of a potential target on the ground, resting or rolling on its back, etc., may initiate an attack.

Wolves use canines and incisors to kill, their mighty jaws applying up to 1,500 pounds of pressure per square inch. Their carnassials, or "shearing teeth," then cut away "bite-size pieces." The injuries inflicted on the people in the Gévaudan were as grisly as those inflicted by predators upon prey animals. Victims' throats were slashed, limbs torn away. There were sixteen decapitations.

It has been said that perhaps this animal or animals acquired the taste from the flesh of fallen soldiers. There are accounts of instances in which wolves have consumed human cadavers. It is recorded that the corpses of the English vanquished by William the Conqueror were to be eaten by "worms, wolves, birds, and dogs—*vermibus, atque lupis, avibus, canibusque voranda.*" Scandinavian poets were said to have sung that Norman soldiers slaughtered by Danes in 1069 provisioned "a choice banquet for the Wolves of Northumberland." Centuries later, in the New World, wolves ate bodies of Native American victims of smallpox. Famine-crazed wolves have also been known to disinter corpses from graves. In Scotland, in such cases, bodies were laid to rest on wolf-free islands off the coast, such as that of Handa, Green Island, and St. Mungo, or in lochs, such as Ross-shire.

In North America, Bruce Hampton, in researching the historical interactions of indigenous peoples with wolves, states that accounts of canid predations on humans generally took place in locations where buffalo were scarce or nonexistent, "suggesting that wolves may have been less of a threat to humans where natural prey was abundant." French writer Jacques Delperrie de Bayac and others tell us that in the Gévaudan region, there was a loss of domestic prey through disease that decimated sheep herds in the 1700s.

Wolf expert Barry Lopez speaks of a "conversation of death," the moment in which a wolf and its natural prey, such as a moose, make direct eye contact. The split-second interchange seems to determine whether the prey will stand firm or turn tail. In the story of the Beast, few victims were able to stand up to the Beast's aggressions. There were cases when cattle and pigs resisted attacks and protected caregivers.

The Beast preferred certain organs and parts of its victims' bodies. According to the Abbé Pourcher, "La Bête Féroce, it was said, did not eat the whole of the corpse only the liver, the heart, the intestines, and part of the head." Perhaps this is akin to wolves that often stop eating after consuming select portions of cattle or sheep? Wild prey, on the other hand, is generally eaten in its entirety. According to a US government study conducted in Yellowstone National Park, a wolf pack cooperates in disemboweling a kill and first devours the most nutritious organs. Muscle tissue is the second course, hide and bone the third.

Super Wolves

Those interested in the lives of wolves have likely come across the work of wildlife writer Stanley P. Young. His stories of super wolves of North America, and of the US Bureau of Biological Survey hunters charged with exterminating them, have been for some readers compelling, for some melodramatic, and for many people for many years, convincing.

The 1970 book *The Last of the Loners* by Young, who was employed by the US Fish and Wildlife Service for forty-four years, profiles a number of "lobo wolves" with "almost unbelievable intelligence" that hunted livestock in Colorado and other locations in the early twentieth century, evading skilled Biological Survey hunters for months and years. With nicknames such as Old Lefty of Burns Hole and the Phantom Wolf of Big Salt Wash, these marauders were said to be both hated and admired by their human hunters, known as "wolfers." The canids were not man-eaters, like the Beast, but were said to have destroyed tens of thousands of dollars worth of livestock in their careers. Like La Bête, they sidestepped traps, eschewed poison, and evaded bullets. Time and again, their hunters commented that they could not believe how savvy these canids were.

Because of their smarts, many of these lupine desperados supposedly grew older than typical wolves, old enough to become "gummers," like three-footed Old Lefty of Burns Hole, Colorado (one of its feet was destroyed escaping from a trap), along with the Greenhorn wolf of Colorado, with "cruncher teeth worn down close to red sockets, . . . wolf fangs blunted and broken." At that age, according to Young, all a famished wolf can do is go for its prey's windpipe and hang on, and subsist on the easier-to-chew portions. A letter from a grateful stockman thanking Young for the destruction of outlaw wolves comments: "I presume that the fact of the she-wolf having a hind foot gone, and the he-one's teeth being badly worn, accounts for their taste for calves more particularly than the older stuff."

Like La Bête, the Custer Wolf of Custer, South Dakota (and parts of Wyoming) was said to be "not a wolf—not merely a wolf." This individual had an entourage; a pair of coyotes (*Canis latrans*) that followed from a distance as the wolf went on supposed killing sprees and lone rambles (his mate had been extirpated by hunters). He was said to have ranged a circuit forty miles wide and sixty-five miles long. The Survey sent one of its best hunters after the Custer Wolf in March 1920; the wolfer did not succeed until October 11 of that year. After the hunter did so, locals gathered to see the remains of the renegade wolf (bringing to mind the displays of La Bête in Versailles and Courtaud in Paris). It turned out to be a white, ninety-eight pound specimen, "smaller than the average male wolf."

According to contemporary biologists, however, Young's yarns (some referenced in American congressional hearings related to control of predators) were likely embellished to develop support for control programs and should be cited with caution. The same is true for naturalist and writer Ernest Thompson Seton, perhaps most well known for the tragic story of "Lobo, the King of Currumpaw," first published in *Scribner's Magazine* in 1895. However, some historians believe these tales are valuable in offering understanding, if not of wolves, of the culture of the United States in the early 1900s and the "coming together of science and folklore in a modern state bureaucracy."

In any case, it turns out that, unlike the remains of the enigmatic La Bête, said to have been burned long ago, some of the remains of the now-called "Famous North American Wolves" exist. In 1998, in two studies, one published in *Wildlife Society Bulletin* and one in the

The outlaw Custer Wolf of South Dakota was alleged to have caused $25,000 worth of damage, but estimates may have been overstated. The wolf turned out to be smaller than expected, just 98 pounds. ***The Denver Public Library, Western History Collection, Z-1553.***

Canadian Field-Naturalist, scientists studied famous wolves from the late 1800s and early 1900s. Findings may relate to the Beast.

We learn that pre-WWI, North American ranchers raised longhorns. This is a bolder breed of cattle, known to vigorously protect offspring. But individuals take up to a decade to mature. By the late 1920s, the preference was for breeds such as the Angus and Hereford. These types of cattle are ready for market much sooner, in as little as two years, but milder temperaments make them more susceptible to predation.

Famous wolves were often made so by mutilation. In their desperation to escape hunters' traps, they lost toes and feet and broke their teeth. Upon the killing of Lobo Giant Killer Wolf of Minnesota, it was discovered the animal actually had had a "partially severed trachea" for some time. Foot injuries helped locals and hunter identify individuals by their tracks.

Study researchers also believe the popular accounts of wolves by Young, Seton, and others may have intimidated the wildlife researchers who followed these respected writers. It was only in the 1940s and 1950s, after wolves had vanished from locales frequented by famous lupines, that more unbiased studies were published, and so it is impossible to confirm the writings of Young and others. The researchers even describe possible fraud: The body of a suspiciously large three-toed wolf may have been a "stand in" for Three Toes of Harding County, South Dakota, supposedly destroyed by a Survey hunter in just fifteen days, after being hunted for thirteen years by 150 men.

A photographic mystery involves an image of Old Whitey of Bear Springs Mesa, Colorado, the photo of which is included in Young's *The Last of the Loners*. This wolf reportedly exhibited bizarre behavior, such as "bobtailing" (biting off calves' tails). The same image is identified in a photo caption provided by the US National Conservation Training Center Archives/Museum as "Old Three-toes, a Northern Rocky Mountain Wolf, endangered, Wyoming. C. J. Bayer, Photographer. July 26, 1920." The US Fish and Wildlife Service library cites the wolf as "Old Three Toes, notorious Split Rock Wolf, trapped in 1920."

Wolf identified as "Old Three-toes, a Northern Rocky Mountain Wolf, endangered, Wyoming. C. J. Bayer, Photographer. July 26, 1920." ***National Conservation Training Center Archives/Museum.***

Researchers Gipson and Ballard reported that the photo and last caption mentioned appeared in a 1928 report on Wyoming wildlife damage control.

The studies' authors state, however, that it is likely that some of the famous wolf stories were free from error or embellishment but these must stand up to continuing research.

Moving on, "surplus kills"—when a famous wolf was reported as causing extraordinary damages (Three Toes of Harding County, fifty-thousand dollars; Custer Wolf, twenty-five thousand dollars) with regard to loss of livestock, the researchers showed that in twenty-nine of the reports, not one but two or more wolves, or packs, could be accountable. Various factors could lead to surplus kills; an example is given of seventeen still-bleeding, newly dehorned, defenseless yearling calves in New Mexico, thought to be killed by one wolf, El Lobo Diablo, after they were turned out in a distant grazing area.

Hybrid Damage

Perhaps most related to the Beast is data based on reports of behavior and bodily characteristics, indicating that seven of the famous US wolves may have been wolf-dog hybrids: Gray Terror, Phantom, Rags the Digger, and Unaweep from Colorado; the South Dakota Custer Wolf; and Old Angora and Red Flash from Wyoming. As far as wolf coloring goes, thirty-nine of the canids were gray, sixteen white or almost white, and two black. The last two were odd-colored, again indicating hybridism: Phantom was collie-dog tawny, and Red Flash had a "glossy, red-tipped" coat. Gipson, Ballard, and Nowak state that wild dogs (*Canis familiarus*), wolf-dog hybrids, or coyote-dog hybrids—animals frequently confused with wolves—may have caused most of the damage. These types of animals "are sometimes aggressive and unpredictable . . . at times chasing and mutilating many individuals. Wolves usually kill more efficiently."

In 1924, in New Mexico, dogs, coyotes, and wolf-dog hybrids were actually responsible for 75 percent or more of the losses said to have been caused by wolves. The authors state, "If, historically, dogs and hybrids were often mistaken for wolves, then the high killing rates reported may have resulted, not from exaggerations, but attributions of kills to the wrong predator species."

A taxidermy specimen identified as a timber wolf-collie cross from 1919. *NGS Image Collection/The Art Archive at Art Resource, N.Y.*

In 1971, Canadian zoologist C. H. D. Clarke brought forward the concept of "hybrid vigor" in relation to the Beast to Western audiences in *Natural History* magazine. He explained how the first generation of a wolf-dog mating may be bigger in size than its parents and wolfish looking, despite the breed of dog involved. The coats of these individuals may also present more varied hues than wolves, blackish or rufescent (reddish) with possible random white coloring, a canine trait. He states that coyote-dog individuals observed in Canada were "more cunning than dogs or coyotes, not the least bit tame, and far more destructive than the wild parent, with less fear of man." Hampton speculates that Native Americans perhaps crossed wolves with dogs to obtain bigger, stronger service animals, but echoes Clarke in saying that first-generation animals "can be high-strung and difficult to train, often unpredictable, and perhaps even dangerous."

Ernest Thompson Seton mentions a hybrid incident occurring in 1919 in Westchester County, New York. A farm family thought they were losing chickens to a fox, but when the trap-evading creature began taking poultry from the henhouse's highest perches, they determined it must be something bigger. A pair of creatures was then observed; they did resemble foxes, albeit very large examples. Finally, the farmer shot one of the pair after the creatures attempted another raid (in which the invaders fought and injured the farm's dogs). The farmer took the animal's remains to a New York City taxidermist who stated he did not know what it was. Seton says its coat was of a fine texture and fox-red and its ears were short. Prominent naturalists Dr. Roy Chapman Andrews (famed for discovering fossil dinosaur eggs in the Gobi Desert, among myriad other accomplishments) and Dr. Harold E. Anthony of New York City's American Museum of Natural History, after deliberation, identified it as a second or third dog-coyote cross, the offspring of a dog-coyote hybrid "with a collie, common shepherd, or possibly a police dog." The skull was broad, and the brain cavity too large for a coyote, yet too small for a dog.

Regarding the Beast of Gévaudan, Richard Thompson contends that the individual "was . . . in all likelihood a large, powerfully built, highly intelligent, and undoubtedly somewhat warped representative of the species *Canis lupus*." He also believes that it was two or more wolves.

He may be right.

Wolf Attacks

Lupine predations upon people were not exceptional, neither in France nor in Europe. In England, where wolf populations were so overwhelming that wolf taxes were required in some parts, dedicated hunters were to render services "daily." Hospitals (originally the word meant "an inn or resting place for travelers") were constructed to protect wayfarers from wolves during the reign of Athelstan (927–939) in order that "they should not be devoured by them." Wolves were so rampageous in Scotland's highlands that in 1577, Scots set up "spittals" to serve the same purpose. Wolves were hunted to extinction in both countries, but they disappeared much earlier in England, during the reign of Henry VII (1485–1509). In Scotland, where conditions were much like the Gévaudan, with "vast tracts of forest and moor, rugged and well-nigh impenetrable in parts . . .[an] absence of roads, and the consequent difficulty of communication between scattered and thinly populated hamlets," the wolf survived until 1743. And in Ireland—nicknamed "Wolf-land" at the time of William and Mary—wolves hung on until about 1760. The redoubtable Irish wolfhound, or *Wolfe Dogge* (forbidden by Cromwell to be exported), was in great part responsible for their final extermination.

In France, in the region of Vosges, near the German border, there was a saying, "If the he-wolf doesn't get you, the she-wolf will." Devlin cites Allier river valley sharecropper Tiennon Bertin recalling childhood apprehensions about wolves while watching over sheep with his sister in the nineteenth century. Moriceau has studied the accounts of wolf attacks, both rabid and otherwise, from early medieval times to the nineteenth century. He believes non-rabid attacks are indicative of clashes between predator populations competing for space and the "dysfunction of rural society," with, for example, children perhaps as young as four years old caring for farm animals.

Still, Richard Thompson and C. H. D. Clarke hold that the average gritty teen or adult Gabalitan could probably fend off the typical wolf with pikes, by throwing stones, by clapping their wooden clogs together, etc., or with the assistance of their cattle, known to boldly defend their own young and their caregivers. It is curious that many of the rural people, who would have been familiar with wolves, who lived "in a culture featuring twilight herding by unarmed children," would find the Beast, if it was a wolf, exceptional.

CHAPTER 23

Two Dead Beasts

Toward the end, the bishop of Mende attributed the attacks to Bêtes Féroces, his Vicar settled the costs for the destruction of Bêtes Féroces (i.e., more than one).

—Abbé Pierre Pourcher

In the end, two Beasts were destroyed. The first, known as the Chazes Wolf, was hunted by royal gunbearer François Antoine and his hunting party in September 1765 near Saint-Julien des Chazes, France. This was a big animal: It measured approximately 190 centimeters (6.23 feet) in length (body plus tail), and weighed 56 kilograms (123.46 pounds). (It was heavier according to other sources, as we shall see.)

Jean Chastel was responsible for shooting the second Beast, known as La Ténazeyre Canid, in June 1767 along the slopes of Mont Mouchet. Chastel destroyed a canid that possessed 42 teeth and measured 151.54 centimeters (4.97 feet) long (body and tail). It weighed 47.4 kilograms (104.50 pounds). This hefty animal had a strange morphology, presenting rather short and stocky front legs, unlike wolves. But since this animal had 42 teeth, as most canids do (including wolves, with 20 upper-jaw teeth and 22 lower), perhaps it could have been some sort of "strange dog."

A problem: The descriptions of various witnesses did not in all cases match the anatomy of the specimens killed. However, we may actually examine the Beasts' anatomical details, thanks to the historical autopsies of these animals which have been preserved.

The Reports

The following summarizes the data known about the two Beasts killed.

An artistic recreation of the Beast, including the typical witness-described features, such as a massive head, huge jaws, thick snout, a long spiky mane, a powerful, stout body, and formidable claws. This rendering is depicted next to an adult human for scale.

<u>Beast Number 1 (The Chazes Wolf)</u>

Date: September 20, 1765
Place: Saint-Julien des Chazes (Pommier woods)
Hunter: François Antoine, assisted by a group of royal gamekeepers, as well as his son, Robert-François Antoine de Beauterne
Animal sex: Male
Animal length/weight: 190.7 centimeters, body and tail; 56.5 kilograms. According to François Antoine, the measurements were 1.85 meters and 63.6 kilograms, respectively. Per author Sánchez's personal communication with researcher Alain Bonet, according to the autopsy, measurements were 190 centimeters, body plus tail, and 73.4 kilograms.
Autopsy by: Charles Jaladon
Corpse/taxidermy: Exhibited for King Louis XV and court at Versailles in October 1765. Later destroyed as a result of inadequate preservation.

<u>Beast Number 2 (La Ténazeyre Canid)</u>

Date: June 19, 1767

Place: d'Auvers swamps, or the Sogne d'Auvers, near Auvers, La Besseyre-Saint-Mary (La Ténazeyre woods).
Hunter: Jean Chastel, in conjunction with other locals and the Marquis d'Apcher
Animal sex: Male
Animal length/weight: 151.54 centimeters (body 97.44 centimeters, tail 54.1 centimeters); 47.4 kilograms
Autopsy by: Boulanger, father and son. Notary: Roch-Étienne Marin.
Corpse/taxidermy: Rotting body buried upon the king's orders. Some researchers argue that this animal could have been mounted and preserved (but later destroyed by parasites) by then-prominent naturalist Buffon and stored for some time at the National Museum of Natural History in Paris.

What Were They?

After reading these accounts we can summarize the more unusual characteristics of both animals in the following manner:

Beast Number 1 (Chazes Wolf, hunter François Antoine)

Length: 190.7 centimeters body plus tail, 56.5 kilograms. According to François Antoine, 1.85 meters, 63.6 kilograms. According to autopsy, 190 centimeters body plus tail, 73.4 kilograms [per author's personal communication with Alain Bonet].

Initial anomalous characteristics:

- Reddish flank colors, whitish throat, black portion running down to end of tail
- Huge eyes
- 40 teeth, 18 upper jaw, 20 lower, later 41 (1 coming up). Wolf: 42 teeth (20 upper jaw, 22 lower); Hyenas, 34 teeth (17/17)
- Very thick and robust neck/shoulder region
- Powerful hind legs
- Massive lower jaw muscles
- Speculative similarities with a hyena, although later, and after comparison to sets of measurements for this species made by the French naturalist Buffon, there were differences mainly in:

- Snout length (1.27 centimeters longer than Buffon's measurements)
- Ear length (2.54 centimeters shorter than Buffon's)
- Size of longest claw: 2.6 centimeters (Buffon's hyena specimen measurement was shorter)

Eventually, and after being dissected and mounted for King Louis XV for exhibition at his court, most of those who actually saw the prepared animal (a wooden model covered by the animal's skin) stated it was a wolf of quite unusual size.

Following is a summary of the reactions of those who looked into the eyes of François Antoine's Beast of Gévaudan (sometimes, later, in exchange for a small admission fee):

- *A big wolf*, François Antoine.
- *A monster wolf*, Mr. Ballainvilliers, the king's representative in Auvers (in a letter to François Antoine).
- *A carnivorous wolf*, medical personnel at Clermont.
- *A robust wolf no bigger than a large mastiff dog*, William Cole, English traveler. Cole also bought two prints which allegedly portrayed the Beast and said, "*neither were like the creature in shape or color.*"
- *It is an exceedingly large wolf, of enormous size, and, in some respects, irregular conformation . . . and the expression of agony and fierceness remains strongly imprinted on its dead jaws*, Horace Walpole, British writer and politician.

The *Gazette de France* newspaper published a short article about the Chazes Wolf, stating that "the most experienced hunters have concluded that the beast was a true wolf that boasted nothing extraordinary, neither in its size nor in its composition." The king reacted to this, stating, "There has been nothing extraordinary about the source of the nation's anxiety."

<u>Beast Number 2 (La Ténazeyre Canid, shot by Jean Chastel)</u>

Length: 151.54 centimeters body plus tail. Weight: 47.4 kilograms. Initial anomalous characteristics:

- Big claws and wide paws

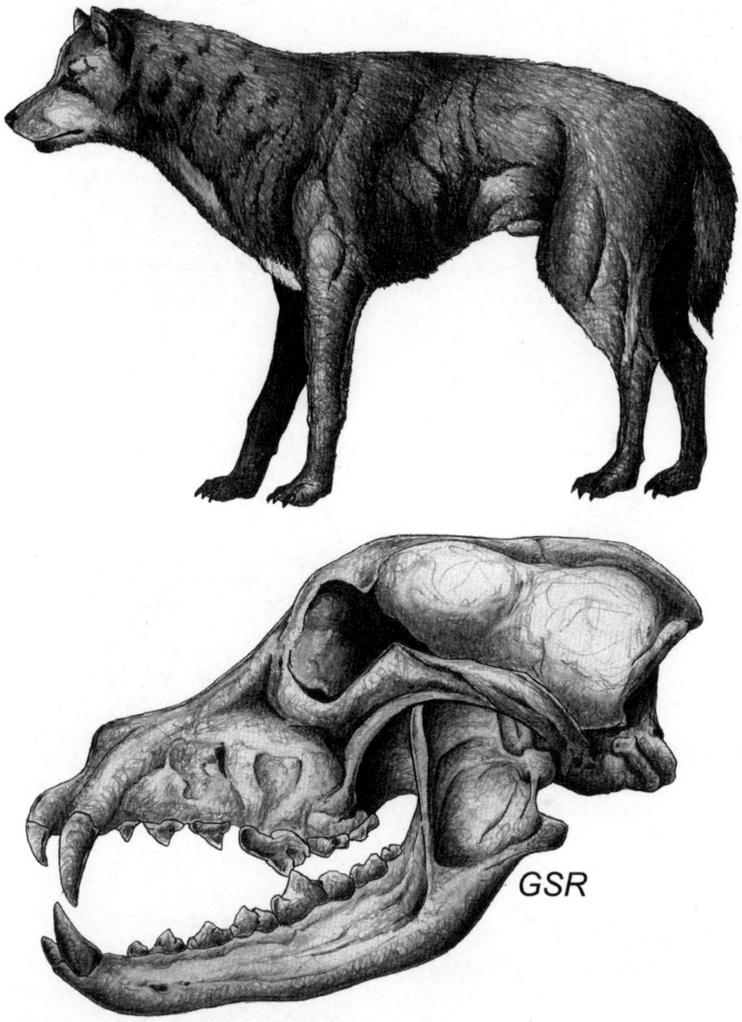

La Ténazeyre Canid full body and skull reconstruction, based on Marin's autopsy measurements and adapted from the French documentary *La bête du gévaudan: autopsie d'un mythe*, by David Teyssandier, Paris: *La compagnie des Taxi-Brousse.*

- Hindquarters similar to a wolf but more powerful
- Short front legs, but very robust, more so than in a wolf
- Big head, with a robust skull presenting a bony ridge at top. In the end, some said it was no bigger that a man's closed fist.

Top left, wolf skull reconstruction, long snout (top view). Top right, La Ténazeyre Canid skull reconstruction, wide and short, more dog-like (top view). Below, La Ténazeyre Canid reconstructed head, based on Marin's autopsy measurements and adapted from the French documentary *La bête du gévaudan: autopsie d'un mythe,* by David Teyssandier, Paris: *La compagnie des Taxi-Brousse.*

Based on the weights recorded for both Beasts killed, and according to François de Beaufort, these specimens represented robust canids, weighing slightly more the average recorded for French wild wolves (36 kilograms males, 28 kilograms females). Beaufort also records that the heaviest French wolf shot was a male that weighted 82 kilograms, exceptional for Europe, and a hefty female of 48 kilograms, also a heavyweight for European populations.

In order to clarify this question further, presenting the reader with more data in this sense, we include now, in table format, average measurements and weights for the gray wolf (*Canis lupus*) from the scientific literature.

Table 1. Average measurements and weights for wolves worldwide in meters, centimeters, and kilograms. In the *Handbook of the Mammals of the World*, we find maximum "average" sizes: body and tail of 2 m (or 6 ft, 6.75 in), shoulder height of 1 m (3 ft, 3.25 in) and weight up to 62 kg (136.69 lbs). According to Geneviève Carbone, in 1942 an exceptionally large wolf was shot in the Carpathian Mountains. Its length—body plus tail—measured 213 cm (nearly 7 ft), and its weight was recorded at 96 kg (more than 211 lbs)—a true monster wolf!

Sex	**Male**	**Female**
Head to back (cm)	100-130 (115 average)	87-117 (102)
Tail length (cm)	40-52 (46)	35-50 (42.5)
Weight (kg)	20-79.4 (50)	18-55 (36.5)
Shoulder height (both sexes cm)	66-81 (73.5)	

To some international researchers, including Phil Barnson, and taking into account the measurements reported, morphological aspects (color, spots, chest mark, leg appearance, etc.), and the dental formula corresponding with that of a canid (42 teeth, as in wolves, dogs, coyotes, etc.), the Beast shot by Jean Chastel was probably a wild dog.

If we assume that this theory is right, we could ask ourselves: A dog, but what kind? And what about its unusual appearance, which confused hunters and others familiar with wolves and wild carnivores? The answer could lie in the middle, and Chastel's Ténazeyre Canid could represent some kind of mixture, a creature with both wolf and dog characteristics, a hybrid, hence its odd morphology. Such specimens may result from habitat fragmentation (more common in Europe), low population densities, or when feral dogs encounter solitary wolves (living apart from a pack).

Female and male wolves (and also coyotes) usually become sexually active once a year, in the springtime. Female dogs, on the other hand, are sexually active two times a year, approximately each six to eight months for around twenty days. Thus a female dog in heat can mate with a wolf or coyote only during the male's limited breeding period, but a male dog encountering a female wolf or coyote in estrus (heat) is prepared to mate anytime.

Therefore it is much more probable that if the La Ténazeyre Canid, was a wolf-dog hybrid, its father was a dog mated with a female wolf (a bigger chance for the pairing, and therefore mating, to happen—the male dog is ready to mate all year round). That being said, and in order to establish a wolf-dog identity in a more confident way, we must now look to some of the key characteristics presented by this alleged Beast.

Table 2. Key characteristics of La Ténazeyre Canid, shot by Jean Chastel on June 19, 1767. Data obtained from the Roch-Étienne Marin autopsy report.

La Ténazeyre Canid key characteristics	Present in wolves	In wolf-dog hybrids
Chest marking (white, heart shaped)	NO (never)	YES
Stripes (thin, dark, scarce)	NO (never)	YES
Spots (some)	NO (never)	YES
Mixed color: brownish red	NO (uniform)	YES
Squared skull	NO (wedge-shaped)	YES
Short snout	NO (long)	YES
Stop (the degree of angle change between skull and nasal bone near the eyes)	NO (smooth, angle greater than 90°)	YES (high % dog blood) NO (high % wolf blood)
Face mask	NO (blended)	YES (high % dog blood) NO (high % wolf blood)
Short, robust front legs	NO (four long legs in relation to the body)	Depends on % of wolf-dog blood

The animal shows clear characteristics associated with wolf-dog hybrids, canids very similar to a wolf in general appearance and size, but which retain certain dog features not present in "pure-bred"

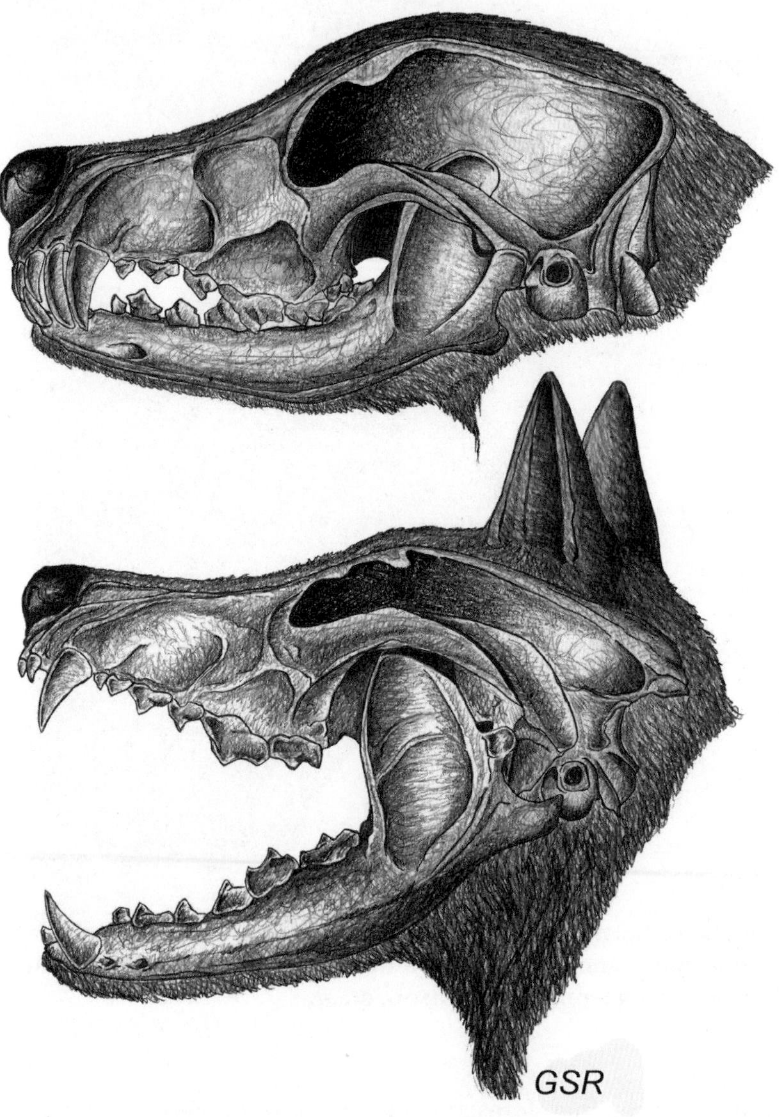

Top, dog skull and reconstructed head profile. Bottom, wolf skull and reconstructed head profile.

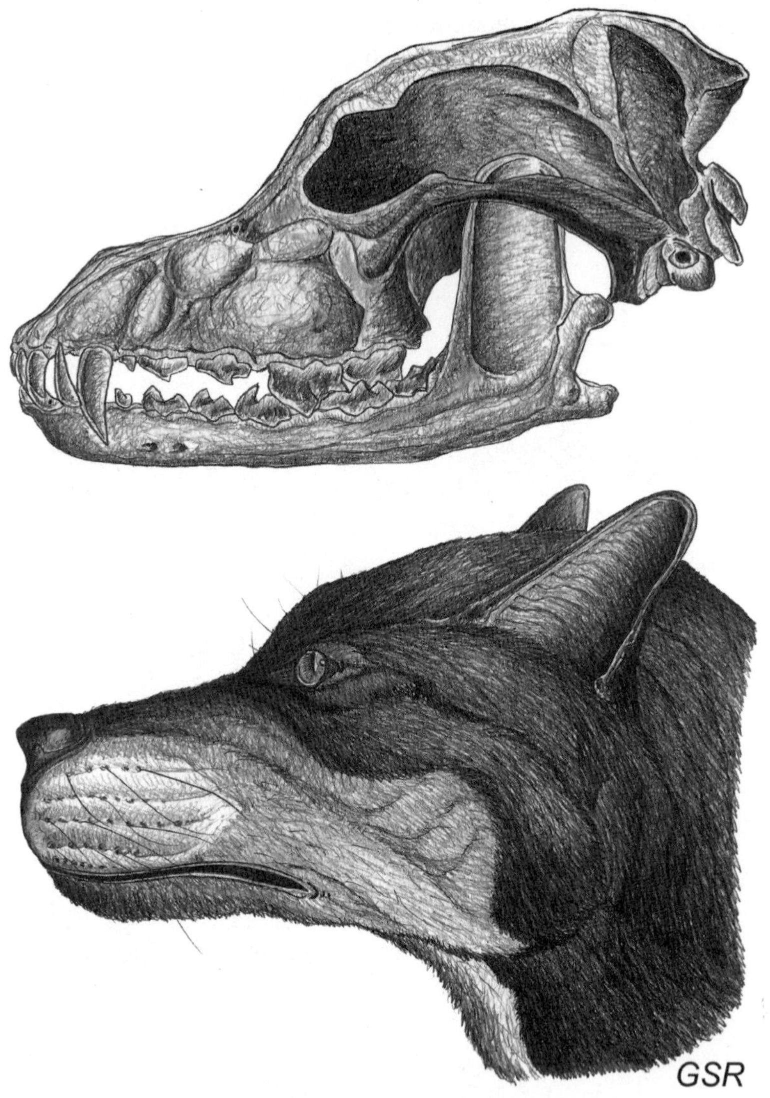

Top, La Ténazeyre Canid skull reconstruction. Bottom, possible external appearance of the same animal, showing a rather long snout. Based on data from Phil Barnson, et. al.

wolves. We can therefore conclude that some of these characteristics confused hunters and experts alike, thus the attribution to the Beast of an unknown identity or unclassifiable morphology.

Illustration showing reconstructed head and skull of Jean Chastel's Beast, La Ténazeyre Canid.

Up to now we have discussed wolf-dog hybrid physical characteristics, important in trying to get a better picture of some of the odd-looking canids prowling in the Gévaudan at the time of the Beast . . . but what about their behavior and aggressiveness? In this sense, how do they differ from a typical wolf way of behaving, and what differences exist, if any, when compared to a typical dog, which has interacted with humans since prehistoric times? Most experts, mainly archaeologists and geneticists, agree that modern dogs may have originated from *Canis lupus* (though there is new evidence that wolves and dogs may have both descended from a common extinct ancestor) twelve to fifteen thousand years ago. Smaller, less aggressive wolves may have followed nomadic tribes; wolves may have been adopted as puppies; or wolves frequenting human villages and dump sites in search of an easy meal became tamer, and over time, became primitive dogs, companion animals progressively bred for various tasks, for guarding, herding, etc. (Anthropology professor Pat Shipman contends that early modern humans and their wolf-dogs caused the extinction of Neanderthals.) In the process, these proto-dogs retained natural instincts and behaviors, which were adjusted, with some patterns being modified or reduced. As we saw earlier, wolf-dog hybrids retain a mosaic of physical characteristics from both races, resulting in a composite animal approximately half dog, half wolf.

According to Dr. Robert Willems, in terms of behaviors, a composite also occurs: Hybrids may inherit a range of behavioral traits, some of which may be conflicting. For example, wolves normally seem to fear humans, avoiding all contact except when raised in captivity, when they become less fearful animals. Dogs, on the other hand, socialize readily with humans, even preferring human company to that of other dogs. Wolves are tremendously successful hunters. Many dogs would starve if left to fend for themselves in the wild. Additionally, wolves rarely bark, something obviously not true for most dogs. The mixture of potentially conflicting genetic traits results in less predictive behavior patterns in the wolf hybrid, compared to either wolf or dog. This is not to say that the behavior of a specific hybrid is unpredictable or erratic. It would, however, be unlikely that someone unfamiliar with a particular hybrid, even someone with considerable experience, would be able to predict that animal's behavior with reasonable certainty. The adult behavior of hybrid pups also cannot be predicted with anything near the certainty of dog pups, though the behavior of an individual wolf hybrid may be predictable.

Another aspect that has been subject to controversy is related to aggression. How aggressive would these hybrids be, and how is aggression connected with their genetic background? Would it make them unstable? Could they become highly aggressive individuals, more so than the specialized flesh-eating wolf? The absence of an objective behavioral study of this type of animal has contributed to the wolf hybrid controversy, and most opinions of their behavior can be readily divided between two opposing camps. One side describes them as being destructive, unpredictable, and untrustworthy around humans, especially children. The other sees them as gentle, playful, intelligent, and loving animals, similar to the dog in their relations with people. In fact, many hybrid owners claim their animals are less dangerous than some breeds of dogs. Adding to the confusion, national statistics regarding canine attacks on humans compiled by the US Centers for Disease Control and Prevention (CDCP) have been used by both sides to support their differing positions. The aggressive tendencies of these animals and documented attacks on humans have caused many to have concerns about wolf hybrids. But others question whether they are as dangerous as many claim. When CDCP statistics on canine attacks are used to compare hybrid attacks to those committed by various breeds of dogs, hybrids appear to be no more dangerous than some of the more aggressive dog breeds. But these statistics may be misleading, since they only list the number of attacks by breed without taking into account breed population figures or circumstances surrounding the attacks. The following tables summarize some information on wolves, dogs, and wolf-dog hybrid behaviors, aggressiveness, and the evolution of such responses.

Table 3. Wolf, Dog, Wolf-Dog Hybrid Behavior (adapted from Dr. Robert Willems).

A1. Wolf *(Canis lupus)*			
Social behavior	**Predatory behavior**	**Aggressive tendencies**	**Aggressive restraint**
Pack animals Complex structure Social hierarchy established through dominance behavior	Present, hunting animal Carnivorous (flesh-eating)	Reduced, detrimental to pack survival	Present, due to complex social structure
A2. Dog *(Canis lupus familiaris)*			
Associated with humans, all humans, in general, being dominant to the dog	Absent by becoming domestic	Sometimes potentiated in certain races	Absent because of different social structure
A3. Wolf-dog hybrid (*Canis lupus familiaris*)			
Usually associated with humans Sometimes in wild packs	Both present (wolf) and absent (dog)	Both reduced or potentiated	Both present or absent

B1. Wolf *(Canis lupus)*			
Degree of aggressiveness	**Increased aggres-siveness**	**Evolution of aggressive behavior**	**When aggression usually occurs?**
Relatively low.	Never potentiated	Reduced, detrimental to pack survival	• Territory defense • Protection • Social dominance
B2. Dog *(Canis lupus familiaris)*			
More than wolves	A number of dog breeds were developed specifically for their fighting ability and aggressive tendencies	Not subject to the same selec-tive pressures as wolves; individual's survival de-pends on other factors	• Organized fights • Contests • Protection • Defense • Social dominance
B3. Wolf-dog hybrid *(Canis lupus familiaris)*			
Variable, depend-ing on the percent-age of wolf/dog blood present	If crossed with potentially dangerous or aggressive races (pit-bull, Rottweiler etc.)	Reduced in wild packs; domesticated individual's survival de-pends on other factors	• Organized fights • Contests • Protection • Defense • Social dominance

That is why, according to Willems, we must take into consideration the following:

- Most attacks by wolf-dog hybrids have been on small children. Many occurred when the animal's predatory instincts were triggered by some unwitting behavior by the child, causing the hybrid to regard the child as prey.

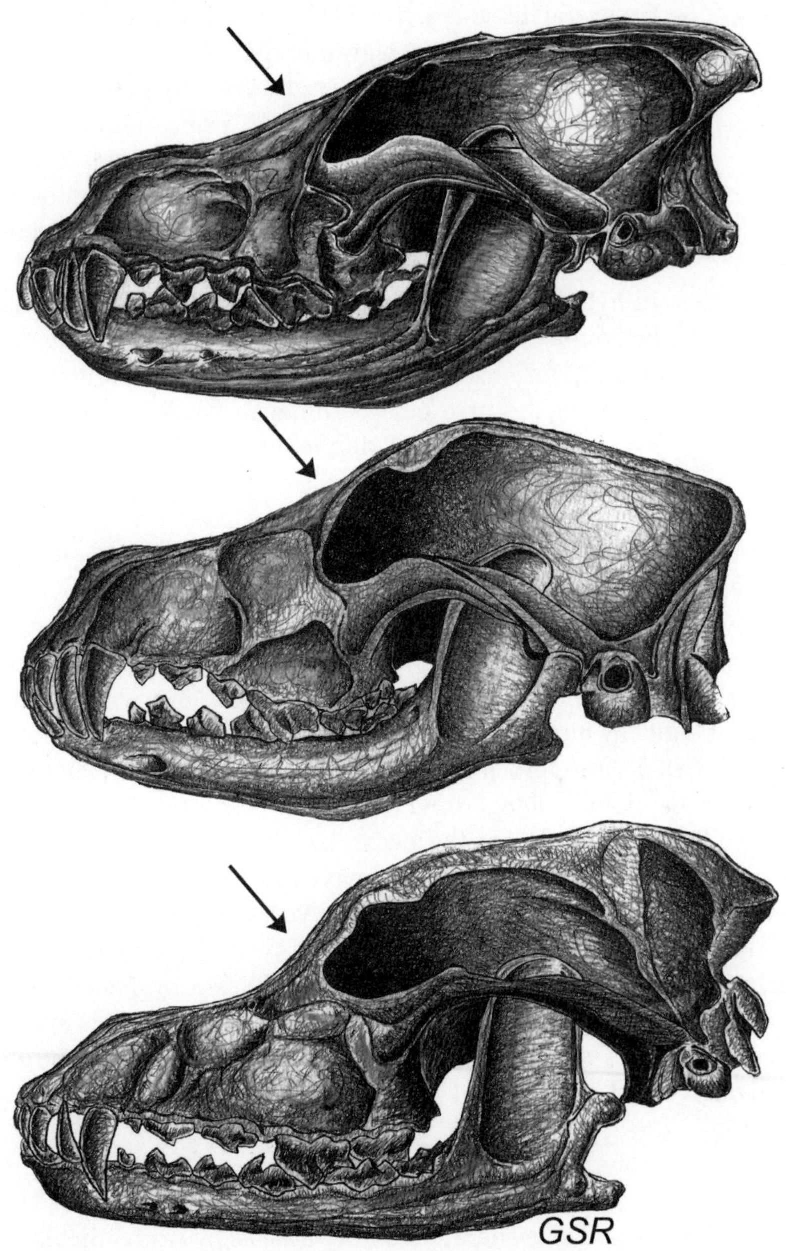

From top to bottom; wolf, dog, Jean Chastel-associated Beast skulls. Note (arrows) different stop angles on all drawings.

In several instances, hybrids have even attacked children with whom they have played in the past.
- In some hybrids, the timidity of the wolf may be replaced by the aggressiveness of the dog, while the predatory contribution from the wolf ancestry may remain relatively intact. Thus, hybrid attacks on humans can be related to both the aggressive tendencies of the dog and the predatory nature of the wolf.
- In hybrids, where the aggressive nature of the dog may be coupled with an absence of the wolf's aggressive restraint, serious injury or even death to a human can result in the case of a dominance challenge. Hybrids, having strong natural dominance tendencies, may be particularly dangerous.

According to scientist Stephen Spotte, wolves and wolf-dogs make inappropriate pets, and their use for this purpose should be outlawed. Wolves in nature are timid with regard to the presence of humans unless habitually fed, which increases the danger of being bitten. There is almost no chance of being attacked by a wild wolf not domesticated by humans. Captive wolves are different, and crossing a wolf with a large ferocious breed of dog produces offspring that can be exceptionally dangerous.

Following the story of the Beast, based upon physical characteristics and aggressive/predatory behavior (eleven attacks and ten deaths, victims all children under fifteen years old, in a three-month period from April to June 1767, Auvers, France, vicinity), we can be pretty confident that the La Ténazeyre Canid shot by Jean Chastel was a wolf-dog hybrid. We cannot be 100 percent sure this animal was responsible for all deaths recorded then, or that this was the one and only "Beast."

***

In France and elsewhere, predatory attacks by wild animals occurred fairly often, both in time and space. Could some of the *other* Beasts from other years and far-away regions have been some kind of wolf-dog hybrid? Unusual descriptions, in which the typical wolf profile seems to be diluted with strange canid characteristics, cou-

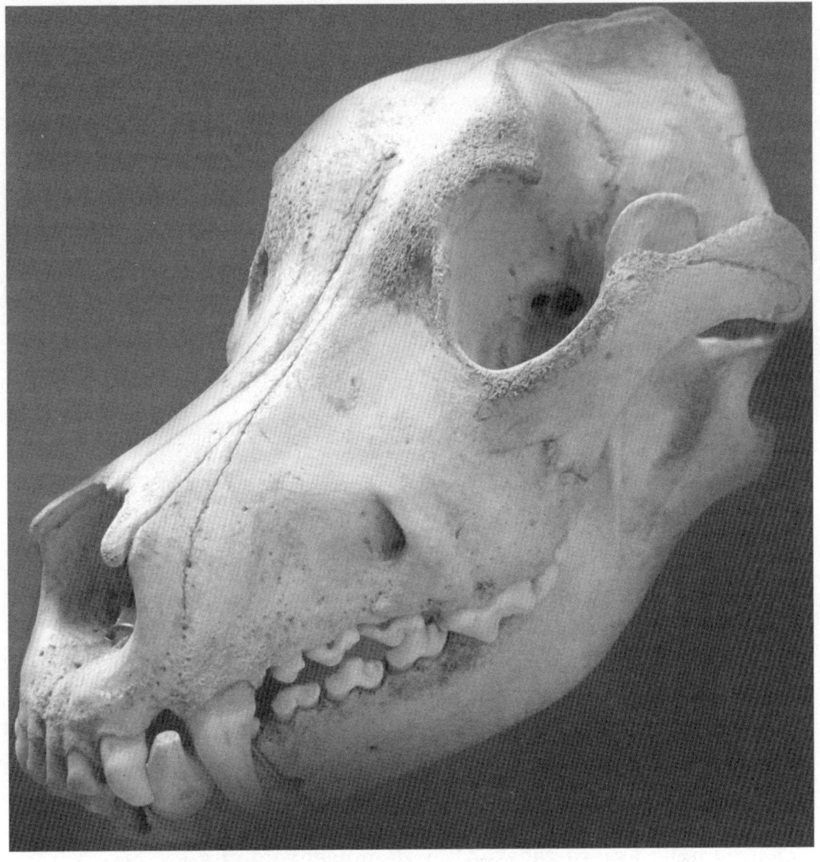

A typical dog skull showing the steep stop angle.

pled with cunning, extremely aggressive behavior, and sometimes a huge size, seem to correspond exactly with what we would expect from an animal born from a wolf-dog cross. This possible explanation for the Beast's identity could be entitled the "Big Wolf-Dog Hybrid Theory." We include the word "big" here for obvious reasons:

- First of all, we have many eyewitness accounts in which the Beast is compared to a donkey, calf, or an animal bigger than a wolf.
- This large animal probably carried the genes from a big, heavy wolf, probably a specimen well over normal weight and size.

- The pairing probably took place with a large male dog, belonging to some heavy race (a Dogue de Bordeaux, a Great Dane, or mastiff).
- The oversized offspring, later an adult "Beast," probably showed what is known as "hybrid vigor," or heterosis, outbreeding enhancement. This is the opposite of inbreeding (in humans known as endogamy). The result is that the offspring is usually larger than its parents' individual average sizes. Sometimes its measurements may surpass its biggest progenitor in size, resulting in true-to-life monstrous animals—what we might expect in an animal deemed La Bête Féroce, "the ferocious Beast".

We want to finish this chapter in which additional contenders for the Beast have been proposed—that is, a large wolf (the Chazes individual), and a probably confirmed wolf-dog hybrid (La Ténazeyre Canid)—by bringing into play, with regard to the hybrid (maybe a one-of-a-kind animal because of its huge size and unique behavior), some morphological data on French dog breeds from the eighteenth century. Here are some possible candidates for a "Father of the Beast."

Table 4. French dog breeds from the eighteenth century (We include the Irish wolfhound and Alaskan malamute because these, too, are ancient giant races. All male measurements.):

Race	**Great Dane**	**Neapolitan Mastiff**	**Bordeaux Dogue**	**Irish Wolfhound**	**Alaskan Malamute**
Shoulder height (cm)	76-86	65-75	58-75	71-90	61-66
Weight (kg)	54-90	60-70 90 record	55-65	40-70	36-43
Origin/ Race age in years	Wolfhound mixed with old English mastiff and greyhound. Approx. 3,000 years.	Roman Molossus. Approx. 2,500 years.	Bulldog, Tibetan mastiff, or Roman Molossus.	Approx. 3,000 years.	Arctic wolf 2,000 to 3,000 years.

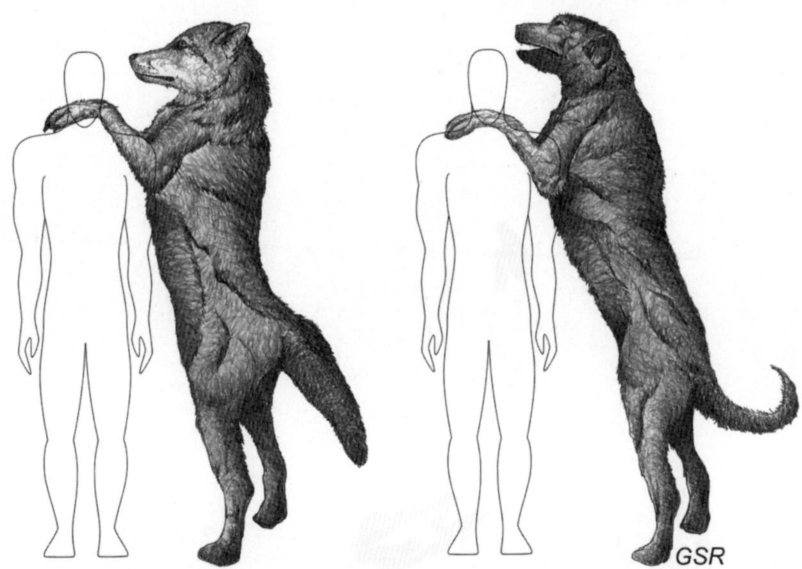

Left, Alaskan malamute, and right, Irish wolfhound, compared to a 1.67 m (5 feet, 6 inches) tall adult French man from the eighteenth century (average height at the time).

CHAPTER 24

Cold Winters, Killer Wolves

Now, toward the midwinter of that year, 1764, the frosts were excessive and the wolves became ferocious.
—Guy de Maupassant, "The Wolf"

Canis lupus is a top predator that normally attacks large prey. In Europe, these would include deer, roe deer, ibex, chamois, and, to a lesser extent, wild boar and elk. However, the wolf is a carnivore of great adaptability and is able to subsist on small prey as well: rabbits, hares, squirrels, and other micro mammals. In order to survive, the wolf can also exploit a particular group in a particular season, as in Russia and Canada, where beavers are favored in periods without snow cover. And in extreme situations, wolves do not hesitate to attack domestic livestock such as goats, sheep, and pigs.

Still, wolves will always prefer wild prey to domestic animals. But what about the humans who attend to livestock? Could the wolf discover that this other food "option" is a viable one, easy to take down and consume? There is no doubt wolves normally avoid humans; the animals seek refuge in remote areas, dense forests, and alpine regions.

But during extreme winters, wolf clans move from mountain regions into valleys and plains where there are greater concentrations of prey and better conditions; as a result, they come into direct conflict with human inhabitants. And this is where problems begin—for both sides.

Environmental Disequilibrium: Hunting Livestock and Young

To begin to understand the motivation of the Beast of the Gévaudan in attacking humans in such a systematic way, we first must pay attention to the environmental and social circumstances in the Gévaudan region of France during the eighteenth century. The country was immersed in a bleak post-war period following the Seven Years' War, which pitted France against the British Empire, among other powers, over colonial expansion and control of trade routes. The rural areas of France were plagued with disease, hunger, and unemployment, and the environment was altered by human activity. Decades of uncontrolled hunting drastically reduced populations of wild herbivores, wolves' natural prey. Forests were logged and cleared, and grazing areas expanded, resulting in a relative abundance of livestock. Wolf populations were pressured to find sustenance among these domestic animals. *Canis lupus* was observed more and more frequently near human communities, stalking grazing goats, sheep, and cows. And the only thing separating the jaws of the wolf from the throats of its animal victims were shepherds, who were, in eighteenth-century France, mostly children.

And so, the Beast's attacks follow a pattern. The victims (more than one hundred deaths out of more than two hundred attacks) are mostly children (less than sixteen years old) of both sexes (up to 47 percent, sixty-eight deaths out of one hundred forty-five attacks) and adult women (55 percent, sixty-seven out of one hundred twenty-four attacks). In contrast, the number of men killed is approximately half (25 percent, thirty-three out of one hundred thirty-five attacks). Some say this is because the men carried on their farm work together in groups with tools, while children and women tended to be more isolated.

Further, most of the children attacked are between eight and twelve years old. Why might this be? Because children under eight are still at home and children twelve years old and over are more capable of defending themselves. Coincidence or premeditation?

Recent studies indicate that during the Middle Ages, wolves in Lombardy and eastern Piedmont, Italy, developed a preference for human infants. For many wolf experts this is indeed plausible. The animal confuses the child with potential prey, according to Patricia A. Goodmann of Wolf Park, Indiana, and Jean-Marc Landry of France, both specialists with regards to wolves and ecology.

Says Landry, "The movements of a little boy are reminiscent of prey in distress, [and this] can be accentuated by . . . heavy winter

The peasants and farmers from the Gévaudan defended themselves with sticks and spears, and sometimes with help from their guard dogs. ***The Fantastic Museum of the Beast of the Gévaudan, Saugues, France. Photo G. Sánchez Romero.***

clothing that prevents movement. A child who moves clumsily or quickly [and whose actions are] accompanied by loud shrieks, can trigger a predatory behavior in any canine, including the dog."

Goodmann gives the example of her pet schnauzer, which often confuses children with other dogs, especially youngsters seen at a distance in the company of adults.

According to sources, the typical Gévaudan attack was quick, occurring in the open during the day or near human settlements at night. The victim was usually bitten in the region of the neck or collarbone, beheaded by the animal's teeth and/or claws, and consumed, to a greater or lesser degree. Internal parts, such as the liver, heart, intestines, and brain, were favored. If an attack was interrupted, the Beast tore off an arm or leg and escaped with this small reward. The animal also consumed large amounts of victims' blood, returning for more later, even the next day if not sated.

The first Beast, the Chazes wolf, is dead. ***The Fantastic Museum of the Beast of the Gévaudan. Photo G. Sánchez Romero.***

When experienced hunters tried to poison the body of one of the victims, the Beast declined the offering, seemingly detecting the contamination. When the hunters planted bait in hopes of ambushing La Bête, it refused to appear. The Beast even abstained from carefully placed "dummies" made of fur- and leather-covered animal parts.

Wolf Populations, Winter Mortality, and Food Intake

Wolves have been hunted and their populations decimated the world over since ancient times. At first, as humans began to settle into an agrarian lifestyle, with domesticated dogs, they found the wolf a threat to the livestock that provided them with so many benefits and indeed, survival itself. Thus, wolves were hunted to protect domesticated animals. They were also hunted for their skins, as trophies, and for sport. In France, the *Luparii*, an elite force created by Charlemagne, controlled wolf populations during the Middle Ages. The economy depended on livestock, mainly goats and sheep; the *Luparii* were considered heroes by pastoral communities. Even until relatively recent times, rewards were given for each wolf killed.

The practice of organized hunting waned after the Middle Ages, especially during periods of war. And once again, forests, mountain ranges, valleys, and other habitats in France began to harbor wolf populations. Still, according to wolf expert Jean-Marc Landry, about twelve thousand wolves were killed in France between 1797 and 1798. Sixty-five percent of these animals were wolf cubs: Younger animals confined to burrows were easier to destroy and hunting them did not require scarce and costly firearms. However, after the French Revolution, the wolf population increased significantly compared with the previous two decades. The government was not always able to pay the rewards offered, and hunts were disorganized. At the end of the nineteenth century, researcher Françoise de Beaufort estimates that France harbored some three thousand to seven thousand specimens. By about 1923, the population had dwindled to only one percent of original numbers.

Today, after wolves began returning to France via the Italian Alps in the 1990s, it is believed that there are a few hundred wild specimens. Based on the historical data, then, we could assert that during the eighteenth century—when the Gévaudan attacks occurred—wolves numbered in the thousands.

What other factors, besides human pressure, influence wolf populations? Ecologically speaking, population size can be linked directly with the density of prey available. If there is more prey, or if the available prey is easier to catch, populations will be larger. The same circumstances regulate the survival of wolf cubs and adults. In autumn and winter, the biomass of available prey within a territory is crucial. The higher this biomass, the more cubs we find (although approximately half of cubs die before reaching one year of age). In parts of North America and Canada, the survival rate for both adults and puppies is 61 to 82 percent. Winter temperatures and conditions are the litmus test the species must overcome to survive.

But how much food is needed on a daily basis? This is a critical consideration when investigating the Beast of the Gévaudan. The numbers of killings perpetuated by the animal were significantly higher in winter. Was this increase pure coincidence? To put it another way, is it possible a large carnivorous predator could survive harsh winters in south-central France on the flesh of the human children it killed?

The amount of food a wolf should eat each day depends upon its weight. Heavier variants, such as those from Canada and Russia, must eat about 3.5 to 4.5 kilograms, or 7.7 to 10 pounds of meat per day. Lighter, gracile breeds from countries with more benign climates, such as India, where adult wolves weigh from 18 to 22 kilograms, or 39 to 48 pounds, need less to sustain them: 1 to 1.5 kilograms, or 2.2 to 3.3 pounds per day. What weight might we estimate for La Bête? As we know, winters in the Gévaudan were severe, lasting six to nine months, and only a little less cold than in parts of Canada or Russia. Male wolves in Europe weigh about 36 kilograms, or 79 pounds, and females approximately 28 kilograms, or 62 pounds However, according to Beaufort, the record weight for a very large male is 82 kilograms, or over 180 pounds; for a huge female, 48 kilograms, or 106 pounds. And there is an exceptional yet verified 1942 record from the Carpathian Mountains of a massive wolf weighing 96 kilograms, or over 211 pounds, and measuring 213 centimeters, nearly eighty-four inches long—seven feet!—from its snout to the tip of its tail.

We know the Beast of the Gévaudan was very large. Contemporary estimates give us the following figures: The wolf killed by François Antoine near Les Chazes woods on September 20, 1765, weighed 56 kilograms, or about 123 pounds. According to François

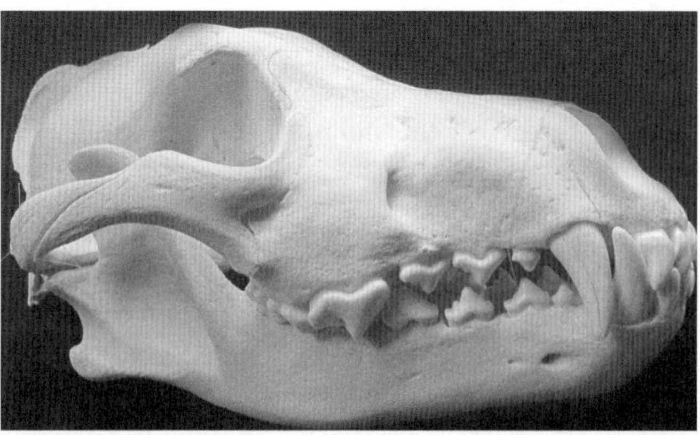

A wolf (*Canis lupus*) skull, showing its thick jaws and very strong teeth. *G. Sánchez Romero*.

A female victim lies on frozen ground: The deadly Beast has struck again. *The Fantastic Museum of the Beast of the Gévaudan. Photo G. Sánchez Romero.*

Antoine, it measured 185 centimeters, about six feet, from snout to tail tip and weighed 63.6 kilograms, or about 140 pounds; according to its autopsy, it measured 190 centimeters (body plus tail), 6.23 feet, and weighed 73.4 kilograms, nearly 162 pounds.

Veteran hunter Jean Chastel killed the second Beast on June 19, 1767, a canid with 42 teeth measuring 151.54 centimeters (body 97.44 plus tail 54.1), 4.97 feet, weighing 53.4 kilograms, over 117 pounds. (Other sources provide a weight of 47.4 kilograms, or 104.5 pounds.)

So these were rather stout wolves within the known range for French populations, although slightly skewed toward the upper end of the scale.

If we speculate a bit, giving the Beast a record weight close to the 211 pounds of the great Carpathian wolf, we would then know it would need to eat approximately eleven to eighteen pounds of meat per day. Knowing that a ten- to twelve-year-old boy may weigh on average fifty-five to sixty-six pounds, is it feasible La Bête was able to obtain from its young victims the amount of sustenance required to survive? From our sources, we estimate that removed muscle/tissue mass—a limb carried away, or a generous portion of flesh, or internal organs—from the bodies, not entirely eaten, was equivalent to several pounds. Further, the Beast aimed its attention at protein-rich organs, such as livers, hearts, or brains. Such nutrients could sustain an animal like the Beast until the arrival of spring.

Why Did La Bête Attack So Viciously?

This question has puzzled researchers, historians, and naturalists since the time of the Beast. What could lead this creature to kill so many people in such dreadful ways? To answer this question, we must try to establish parallels between the Gévaudan and similar cases, better known and studied, such as the man-eating lions of Tsavo, Kenya, or the Indian tigers and leopards that hunted men.

The infamous African lions terrorized workers in the late 1800s during the construction of a railroad that apparently crossed their territory. This fact, coupled with a severe drought and resulting dramatic shortage of natural prey, prompted two large, old—an important fact—males to kill humans. The advanced age of the specimens is crucial; we now know their teeth were very imperfect and incomplete, unfit to eat tough meat and crush large bones. Therefore, after developing a taste for human flesh, and learning that some individuals are easily overcome and weak, the lions became hardened murderers, daring even to enter tents at night in search of prey.

The second case—that of the man-eating cats of Asia—is similar: Here, big cats (tigers and leopards) learned to stalk and hunt people, and quickly "got hooked" on human flesh, which they began to seek at alarming rates from village to village. Research has also now shown why Asian big cats turn into man-eaters. The reasons may be multiple:

- A taste for human flesh. During famines, epidemics, and war, unburied corpses were available. After these events, the animals would continue killing people to maintain their new diet.
- Aged animals are not always capable of running down normal prey, such as antelopes or wild pigs. Loss of teeth is another factor.

A second beast is shot by Jean Chastel, a somehow anomalous canid having both dog and wolf characteristics. *The Fantastic Museum of the Beast of the Gévaudan. Photo G. Sánchez Romero.*

- Animals become injured; for example, there is a well-known case involving a severely injured tiger with broken porcupine quills embedded in its paws and snout.
- Individuals are wounded and handicapped by human gunfire. These animals become highly dangerous, often specializing in hunting people after being shot and left in the wild, with for example, a broken paw or limb. Such creatures also become so wary of human activity interrupting their meals, they flee immediately at the slightest disturbance, never eating enough; hence, killing much more than needed.
- Learned behavior. Cubs learn from their mothers to prey on humans in areas where man's presence is abundant.
- Lack of prey. Forest habitats depleted of natural prey may force weaker individuals, with territories sometimes located at the periphery of natural reserves (and in contact to human settlements) to kill livestock and then farmers, herdsmen, and those gathering food in the forest.

- Mistaken identity. People outside who are physically keeping a low profile (resting), or who are bending over as they work in a field or garden, may confuse the predatory animal. After a human stands in an upright position, tigers seem to lose the interest in this target.

Such man-eaters may also, in the minds of their human prey, become supernatural beings, were-tigers and were-leopards, creatures of legend. Why? A man-eating predator, through a combination of luck and increasing natural wariness, manages to evade attempts to kill it, continuing to prey on people for months or even years on end with what seems like extraordinary cunning. Asian man-eaters, too, will travel long distances, up to twenty miles between kills, while patrolling extensive territories. To local villagers, such behavior (the man-eater's ability to stay one step ahead of its pursuers) is clear evidence of supernatural intelligence.

***

The Gévaudan case fits with almost all the patterns described above. A large and powerful veteran predator, likely a wolf, likely advanced in years, develops a taste for human flesh, perhaps enhanced by having consumed remains from cemeteries, battlefields, or communal graves of epidemic victims. It then learns to subdue living individuals, mostly children, the weakest and easiest prey to take. (It should be noted, too, that wolves possess extreme jaw and neck strength; they can easily subdue and transport prey two or three times their own body weight.) From its kill, the Beast discerns edible material offering maximum nutrition—nourishment vital to its survival in its severe environment.

The Beast's vast territory provides abundant "two-legged food," and the predator makes it the basis of its diet. All it must do is spy on the movements of the bipedal creatures it craves and wait for the right time. All of its other instincts remain the same: Be wary of lures. Never lose track of hunters and their dogs. Discern poison hidden in traps. Dodge bullets: Like a dog that recognizes our movements if we scare him with a stick or throw a stone, the Beast knows when man lifts his "fire stick," it must duck and run to avoid the deadly "fire."

A large wolf in threatening display at the National Museum of Natural History, Paris. *Photo G. Sánchez Romero.*

Because of its years of experience, the Beast is a cunning creature indeed. It exploits a vast territory, which it knows by heart. It is extremely mobile, capable of covering long distances (more than twenty kilometers, more than twelve miles per day). It traverses dense forests and steep, rugged terrain to avoid human contact. Hence, La Bête is especially difficult to track, even by large groups of experienced hunters assisted by dogs.

Rabies?

Could the Beast have been a rabid wolf or wolves? Rabies, also known as hydrophobia, is a deadly virus that invades the nervous system and slowly makes its way to the brain. Here it takes over, initiating the frenzied outbursts for which the disease is best known. The affected creature, near death, can no longer control itself; it is simply a convulsed agent of its infector, biting whatever it can reach to pass the lethal pathogen along. C. H. D. Clarke states that there were many rabid canids in France at the time of the Beast and feels that locals, because of the consequential nature of the disease (it "kills nearly one hundred percent of its hosts in most species, including humans") would have been conditioned to recognize such an animal.

The attack pattern shown by a wolf or a dog infected with rabies is very different from the Gévaudan-reported attacks of genuine predatory episodes where an animal hunts a human victim, an individual specialization. During rabies rage episodes, which may last one or two days, rabid animals bite anyone or anything crossing their paths. Further, rabies attacks are uncontrolled; the affected animal lunges wildly and bites its victims anywhere on their bodies. And it does not devour them, although rabies-infected creatures are capable of killing their victims. Finally, a fact that is vital when considering the attacks of the Beast—rabies paralyzes the muscles of the throat and the affected animal has trouble swallowing (causing it to produce "foam at the mouth") and is thus unable to consume its victims. In addition, after about a three-week incubation period, the individual usually dies at about the fourth week.

The Beasts of the Gévaudan: Experienced and Dangerous Carnivores

After analyzing the data presented, as regards the Beast's behavior, attack mode, and morphological characteristics, and after reviewing the literature published on the subject, we venture to make the following assumptions about the possible identity of the ferocious animal of the Gévaudan: First, the attacks were carried out by a small pack or clan of large and bloodthirsty wolves, perhaps a pair, at most a trio. Hence the mobility of the group and the disparity in their morphological features as reported. Some of the observed behaviors, such as the indiscriminate slaughter of lambs while consuming only a few and a total aversion to watchdogs, tell us much about the animals' nature. If we consider that, in a large percentage of cases, witnesses stated they spotted a large, strange wolf, the puzzle is more easily solved. We must also remember that at the time of the killings, the region harbored numerous wolves that were considered a genuine threat to farmers and their livestock. The members of this small but seasoned clan of predators could recognize poisons, traps, and firearms. They had the skills and instincts necessary to hunt humans, especially children and babies as well as women. They developed a taste for human flesh (it is said to be addictive) and determined which individuals were most vulnerable to their attacks and most vital to their nourishment; hence, their predatory efficiency.

It is also possible that members of this clan suffered from mange and its resulting skin lesions and loss of hair; therefore, they craved protein-rich organs, such as livers and hearts, to counteract the constant loss of body heat during the long winters (more human deaths were recorded this time of year than any other) and unseasonable weather during the other seasons. The animals' hairless backs and sides would reveal the contours of their spines and ribs, providing grist for the eyewitness descriptions of the Beast's odd appearance and color.

The backbone of the wolf has robust vertebrae crowned with bony protuberances, known as *apophyses,* where the wolves' powerful dorsal and neck muscles are attached; these muscles are used for taking down and subduing heavy prey. These bony projections could lend the Beast a distorted silhouette, as if it were embellished with dorsal ridges.

It is probable that as a result of advanced adulthood, these creatures had incomplete sets of teeth and related oral infections, resulting in inflammation and swelling of the nose and mouth. This is another reason the animals targeted young and tender human prey: Soft flesh and fragile bones were easier to chew and digest. Witnesses also noted pungent odors about the Beast, a characteristic associated with oral infections and abscesses.

***

At this point readers may ask: What happened to these animals? Why were they never found? There are several possible explanations. The most likely is that these wily individuals finally succumbed to old age, starvation, or disease, and, feeling the inexorable call of death, sought refuge in caves or isolated underground caches to die. After their demise, scavengers such as foxes, crows, and rats, along with carrion eaters and creatures such as worms and beetles, along with climate—humidity, heat, snow, and ice—would reduce the carcasses to bones. Over time, of course, these are transformed into invisible organic matter, perpetuating the mystery of the identity and whereabouts of the extraordinary Beasts of the Gévaudan.

For wolf biologist Jean-Marc Landry, author of several books and studies on the great predators, the idea of an experienced pair or trio of wolves suffering from skin lesions and tooth loss fits well with the possible identity of the Beast of the Gévaudan. Landry states that people in Switzerland, where he has been working, are often surprised when they spot a wolf with a thin rather than a thick coat. It's an image they are unfamiliar with and the odd-looking animal is immediately perceived as an "unknown" creature. Moreover, Landry believes the *apophyses* of a large and scabby animal could definitely give it a grotesque profile or silhouette, topped as if "crowned by thorny projections." As stated earlier, this feature was noted in several eyewitness descriptions of La Bête.

Landry also tells us about current fears among French shepherds about the reappearance of wolves on their land. The animals are migrating from neighboring Italy via the Alps. Landry, who, among other activities, heads a European project to mitigate wolf attacks on sheep and goats through the use of protective collars, states that shepherds are concerned about the presence of wolves, especially at night and in conditions of low visibility, such as snow, rain, and fog. As such, more shepherds are carrying rifles. Landry tells us wolves may be kept at bay with the odd shot, but could the episodes from the time of the Beast be repeated? Today's shepherds will open fire on them, depending on circumstances and as a last resort. A major part of the solution to this problem lies in the wolves' finding adequate food in the wild. Perhaps we humans can assist in this regard by providing food, whether manufactured or surplus, in specific places. Another measure discussed by Landry is the zoning of areas where wolf and livestock populations overlap in order to avoid contact between the two groups. This will only work, however, if the wolves are capable of finding natural prey.

While it is difficult to close the case of the eighteenth-century French attacks in the Gévaudan, we have taken a small step to provide a possible scientific explanation to the enigma of the animal or animals responsible for such aggressions.

Possible Beast candidates (from the top down): Large mange-infected wolf (see projecting vertebra on its hairless back) with dental infections and swollen snout; baboon; and spotted hyena.

CHAPTER 25

Beasts Past and Present

Concerning the cruel Bête, it is possible to recall that history mentions a fairly similar one, which existed about two hundred years before and which devoured more than one hundred fifty people in the forest of Fontainebleau before they could destroy it. This makes more understandable the long duration of the killings ours is committing.

—Abbé Pierre Pourcher, quoting a March 16, 1765, letter from Paris

France is a large country with an area of approximately 550,000 square kilometers (212,356 square miles). It is the third largest Eurasian country after Russia and the Ukraine. It is also bigger than California, but not as large as Texas. In its central and southern portions, one finds large tracts of forest once home to countless wolves. In this vast wilderness, there was more than enough space for all kinds of beasts. In the previous chapters, we have discussed the best-known Beast, notorious mainly because of the extraordinary number of deaths and injuries for which it was apparently responsible. But it was not alone.

Historical documents, parish records, antique works of art, and contemporary descriptions depict a fair number of other creatures, other Bêtes, as bloodthirsty as that of the Gévaudan, some so infamous that merely mentioning their names invoked the dark arts, secret pacts with the devil, and absolute terror. Most of these animals are now just vague memories, represented in pages of archives or realistically portrayed in modern publications synthesizing data on such zoological phenomena. But apparently, some "die hard" and are revived by contemporary sightings.

These accounts sometimes correspond with sightings of wolves, which have recently been returning to France. Others are far more mysterious because the physical descriptions of the animals seen or even photographed do not conform with the general anatomy of *Canis lupus*. These animals are labeled as Alien Big Cats (ABCs) or believed to be exotic species either accidentally or deliberately released into the wild. But they are flesh and bone creatures, roaming free within the vast French interior. Their silhouettes in many cases recall the typical profiles of large carnivorous predators. In others, they are reminiscent of unknown and powerful prowlers, deadly marauders of a not-so-distant past. Are these new Bêtes féroces, modern incarnations of the legend of the Gévaudan?

Courtaud and the Wolves of Paris
Paris, France, Winter 1439

Bitter temperatures grip Paris and its surroundings; the falling snow is as suffocating as a coating of wet plaster.

Outside of the royal city, desperate peasants struggle to survive in raw conditions, but are often simply unable to move about in the accumulations. Firewood is scarce and wet, crops have been ruined, everything is frozen. Those lucky enough to have a horse, donkey, or mule, and something resembling a cart, flee the country in caravans, hoping to find relief, help, and a bit of nourishment within the walls of Paris. It is a blind bet. No one knows for sure what they will find within the labyrinthine city, a chaotic urban complex overwhelmed by people, poor public services, and an alarming lack of food and supplies.

Whiteouts, severe temperatures, and hunger are not the only dangers the travelers must face: There are whispers of shadows, *loups-garous*, necromancers, cannibals, and murderers haunting the roads. At night, unnerving howls and shrieks cut through the frigid air like blades separating flesh from bone. These haunting utterances result from nocturnal bloodbaths, in which people begin dying. (In the end, there were approximately forty deaths although eighteen were officially registered.) As nights pass and victims accumulate, news of the slayings spread. Superstitions are amplified.

Through fog, snow, and sleet, wolves are sighted by those atop the city walls. The animals begin to acquire an almost mythic status, forming a pack, dwelling in the woods north of Paris on the highest

The mighty Courtaud ("Bobtail"), reconstructed here based on large modern wolf-dog specimens.

point in the area: Montmartre, the Roman Mount of Mars. (Today Montmartre, in the eighteenth *arrondissement*, is part of Paris.)

Rumors circulate. It is said that this spectral pack of animals is led by a creature from hell, with a thick coat of fur and fiery red eyes that emit a ghostly glow at night. The animal is capable of walking on two legs and can even speak: When about to dispatch one of its victims, it names him or her in perfect French.

***

What can modern readers make out of these stories? Clearly here are classic elements of medieval superstition regarding sorcery and werewolves, in which a frightening animal such as a wolf, under certain circumstances, can acquire such notoriety. But, if Courtaud and his pack were nothing more than ordinary wolves, as others of the time stated, what would we really know about them in reality, without the veneer of the fantastic, without a werewolf's magical ointment?

To find out, we must delve into one of the best books on the topic, and almost the only one written in recent times: Daniel P. Mannix's *The Wolves of Paris*, published in 1978. Though a novel, it includes a great deal of information on the animals that terrorized the French capital that dark winter long ago.

Mannix's work was also influenced by Ernest Thompson Seton's *Great Historic Animals* and by Roger H. Guerrand's *Le Journal d'un bourgeois de Paris sous Charles VI et Charles VII (The Diary of a Paris Bourgeois Under Charles VI and Charles VII).* (An English translation of the last title entitled *A Parisian Journal, 1405–1448*, translated by Janet Shirley, was published by Oxford in 1968.)

Mannix's novel covers wolf biology, behavior, and ecology. In trying to acquire an understanding of these wolves of Paris, we wish to study their actions, motivations, and their achieving almost supernatural status in the minds and hearts of the Parisians of the time.

In order to present a fair amount of data in an orderly and condensed way, we will ask a series of questions connected to certain aspects of Courtaud and its pack and their shadowy existence. The first thing we must ask is rather obvious if we want to learn more about these wolves:

What kind of animal was Courtaud and why did it receive that nickname?

Courtaud, in Mannix's novel, is a hybrid wolf-dog cross, even though nothing is known about its true nature before it appeared at the gates of Paris in 1439. The name *Courtaud*, in French, means "bobtail," "cut-tail," and was also the name for a docked horse, and according to witnesses the pack leader did have a short tail or none at all. This condition could be the result of a conflict with another animal, with a human, or perhaps some infection or disease.

We have extensively discussed the predatory nature and natural aggressiveness of wolf-dog animals. In general, *Canis lupus*, the wolf, is normally fearful of humans and avoids all contact. Wolf attacks on people seldom occur, and when this happens, the animal is probably infected with the rabies virus.

On the other hand, wolf-dogs are far more aggressive as they may retain the predatory instincts of the wolf and the innate aggressiveness of the dog, an independent animal that does not require pack structure (where aggression is controlled for the benefit of all members) to survive. Dogs may live a comfortable life in our homes where everything is provided, they may work for us in various ways as guard dogs, herd dogs, hunting dogs, and so on. From time to time they may challenge us, perhaps as feral dogs, reviving ancient hierarchies and forgotten social structures. Feral dogs are known to attack humans, especially children (at times confusing them with smaller game or prey).

How was Courtaud physically described?

Courtaud was an extremely large individual, much bigger than the average wolf, and as Mannix states in his book, "such a brute would have been unusual enough in the far north" (referring to the much bigger size and weight typical for northern wolves in Canada or Russia). Courtaud was also a very long animal, measuring more than 2.2 meters, an incredible 7.21 feet (imagine how awesome it would be if, as the peasants said, it stood on its hind legs). Its paws were also huge, leaving a track wider than a man's open hand (and well over the thirteen centimeters maximum width for big wolves). Courtaud was much heavier than an adult male; let's say almost 100 kilograms, or over 220 pounds. Its fur color was unusual: Witnesses stated that it was completely reddish, except for a clearly defined white mark on its chest. This is consistent with hybrid identification, since generally speaking, wolves range in color from black to white, being normally grayish (without any kind of rosettes, spots, stripes, or other color pattern). Courtaud's head was wide, robust, and somehow rounded, with a very short snout. It was wider than that of a normal wolf, which has a pointed skull and long snout. Again, the Paris wolf's head is consistent with the hybrid profile; wolf-dogs usually have stocky, massive skulls, with prominent stops (the indentation between forehead and snout) and short muzzles, revealing the genes of *Canis lupus familiaris*, the domestic dog.

Why did the wolves of Paris attack humans?

Courtaud and its pack became man-eaters for multiple reasons, summarized as follows:

War and Battlefields

Animals existing in the proximity of war zones will alter their behavior. Throughout history, there are accounts of wolves and other predators devouring the fallen in the field of combat. The presence of dead or wounded human cadavers (or those of horses, etc.) on a battlefield furnishes an easy meal, and predators are known to take advantage of such situations, overcoming their natural fear of man. Emboldened by the experience, and now familiar with the taste of human flash, the predator expands its targets to include families of the soldiers, peasants, farmers, etc., in the vicinity, women, children, and the elderly, now living in poor conditions with little cover (their villages having been sacked, homes destroyed, farms burned, etc.). At the time of Courtaud and the wolves of Paris, the Hundred Years' War between England and France (1337–1453), which, divided into sub-war periods, actually lasted one hundred sixteen years, took an enormous toll in lives: France lost up to half of its total population (according to different historians, between 6.3 and 10 million persons, out of approximately 17 to 20 million) and England up to 30 percent (although the Black Plague also contributed).

Reduced Fear of Humans

With their instinct to avoid people reduced, these wolves began, more and more, to feed on human flesh. Slowly, the wolves of Paris, led by an animal unafraid of humans—Courtaud was half dog, so its reaction and behavior toward people would be different from its wolf companions—had learned to tolerate the scent of man and now associated it with a new and readily available prey. Too, rival animals might vie not just for cadavers, but for those humans badly wounded and helpless, a "gateway" experience perhaps leading to even bolder behavior and attacks on the living. However, most persons who could defend themselves or those carrying firearms were left alone; the predators recognized the threat posed by such individuals. Some packs may have become parasitic, tailing troops and armies into combat zones to feed on anticipated dead and wounded. In this way, they became dependent on flesh, "hooked" on it. (Similarly, the man-eating lions of Tsavo, Africa, would ignore wild game or livestock set out as bait, preferring human victims.)

Ecological Imbalance

Wild populations of European animals, especially large herbivores, were greatly reduced during medieval times. Massive organized hunts, usually led by royalty and those of the upper classes who were fond of wild meat as well as the sport itself (a connection here to a former primitive lifestyle in which organized parties of hunters and trackers would provide meat to prehistoric clans), had a decidedly detrimental impact. This systematic way of hunting, with more efficient firearms, specially trained dogs, swift horses, and large numbers of assistants (peasants who lived within the feudal district), who were forced to literally "beat" the bushes and frighten game out into the open, extirpated untold numbers of animals. Some animal populations moved to distant, less populated territories, perhaps to the east, far beyond Germany and Austria. Wolves not killed in the hunts and deprived of natural prey started hunting agricultural livestock, which obviously brought them into human contact. Hamlets expanded into villages, towns grew bigger, cities developed. More cultivated land was necessary to feed ever-increasing human populations. The conflict for territory and resources had begun. Only stronger wolf packs, living deep within the woods, where natural prey was still available, could survive. Those pushed closer to human settlements came into contact with this new kind of "animal." And some were easier to kill than deer or wild goats.

Why were the wolves of Paris so difficult to track?

Wolves' intelligence and unique attributes allow them to be elusive. Accumulated life experience is also very important, since an aged animal has faced situations where, in order to survive, intelligence has played a key role. Wolves learn fast and are highly inquisitive. Let's list some behaviors that make them remarkable:

- Wolves usually range a territory well-known to them, and they use multiples routes or tracks in their travels, so they can avoid passing through the same way twice.
- They have a superb sense of smell, and circle their "headquarters" in order to detect any threatening or unknown scents in the air. They usually travel upwind, air-scenting continuously and remaining undetected.
- Their eyesight is also excellent. (Dogs, on the other hand, rely more on their noses.) Wolves are capable of differentiating the slow, calm, solid gait of cattle, the mad rushing of fallow deer, the athletic bounds of red deer, and the movement of wild pigs (a slow walk, stopping from time to time to raise their heads). They assess the

strength, sex, and health of an animal based on its motions and postures.

- In that sense, wolves can obviously differentiate humans from wild animals, and the distinct, heavy, more rigid footsteps of men versus the usually lighter gait of women. Children running would almost always trigger a predatory response.
- Their hearing is also exceptional, enabling them to recognize and identify human voices, animal sounds and calls, bird shrieks, the calls of crows and ravens, barking dogs, and, of course, hunting horns.
- They are highly mobile, capable of covering great distances in a short time, usually traveling single file, especially on heavy snow, stepping in the paw prints of their leaders.
- Wolves have a complex way of communicating their moods and desires through a variety of body postures and movements of the tail (which is used as a signal flag). The pack moves in a coordinated way, acting as one (for example, in the case of danger, the pack in unison will crouch, wait, smell, and observe). Body contact is also important to establish dominance. Howling secures territories and avoids wars.

How do wolves avoid manmade traps, poisons, and bullets?

Courtaud's pack, and almost any wolf in the wild, will automatically mistrust any artifact or object found in the forest that has a human scent. This is a basic way wolves recognize traps and snares. Trial—and sometimes fatal error—is another way wolves learn about hidden dangers. For example, when an inexperienced young wolf eats a baited piece of meat filled with poison or other injurious contents, and dies shortly thereafter, the pack would recognize that there is danger in the bait, associating its scent with the result of consuming it: death. As Mannix reveals, balls of meat were stuffed with sharp wooden splinters bent in a circle and tied together with horsehair. The horsehair would dissolve within the animal's stomach, causing the splinters to snap violently, resulting in internal bleeding and horrible death. In this case, even the wolves could not understand the tricky mechanism that caused a clan member's death, and so there is now an automatic association made between "foreign" meat, especially human-scented, and death. Courtaud's wolves generally followed basic rules:

- Don't meddle with anything that may have a human origin.
- Be extremely careful with items that seem out of place, like pieces of meat and strange man-made objects that simply don't belong in the forest.
- Keep senses sharp to detect the smallest clues that may lead to anomalies or possible trap sites, such as displaced leaves or freshly cut wood.
- With regard to poison, it is again trial and error. If a clan member died after eating a certain piece of meat, the survivors would gather "data" from the dead wolf's mouth, saliva, and blood, and in future, would be able to recognize and avoid the poison.
- After a time, as Mannix writes, "the pack never ate anything they had not killed themselves. Courtaud went a step beyond. He seldom ate anything but humans, whom he was convinced were safe food." Therefore the pack leader hermetically reinforced its man-eating conventions and in that way, "became" (to Parisians) a *loup-garou*, a satanic creature craving only human flesh and blood.
- Human movements are quite conspicuous when we hold a gun or a rifle. Our arms usually are separated from our bodies, kept horizontally, and at the end is a "stick" or blunt object that opens fire. This is more or less the rough picture a wolf may create in its brain, immediately associating this posture as a threat, with its successive loud blast, smell of powder, and perhaps pain.

How was Courtaud destroyed?

Courtaud and its pack began to rely more and more on human victims for sustenance, something that almost irremediably made them dependent. This highly irregular and completely unnatural condition was, in the end, turned against their survival. The pack left its wooded Montmartre stronghold, moving near Paris proper, following the human exodus from rural France, as earlier described. The wolves established a new den in proximity to the city walls, where food had become plentiful, as, inside the walls, Paris functionaries were coping not only with a weather disaster, but also with the difficulties of dealing with the remains of those who'd succumbed to one of the worst calamities humanity has faced: the plague.

There was no sewer system, garbage dumps made everything unsanitary, medicines and vaccines were unknown. Rats were everywhere. The Parisians' solution: They simply threw the corpses of plague victims over the walls every day, to dispose of the bodies and in hopes that the ravenous wolves below would become infected. They didn't. The humans' situation was horrendous; the wolves' nirvana. The animals became even more confident, starting to enter the city through sections of crumbling ramparts. By now they were also attacking people, especially the weak and injured, easy prey for healthy apex predators craving the over-abundant human flesh. The king and his officials were panicking. Something had to be done. And a plan was created.

Initially deceased and beaten beggars, alcoholics, and prostitutes would be used as bait to lure the wolves further inside the city, setting up a human trap from which the animals could not escape. The wolves fell for it, little by little. In the beginning, they ventured cautiously down a couple of streets. As time passed, they gained confidence, roving the narrow byways of Paris, memorizing the ins and outs of alleys and passageways, a labyrinth of alien scents and unknown dangers. The wild animals were no longer "home," in a natural habitat, where the world was understood. Goaded by the ready supply of meat, they began to forget Courtaud's "rules."

In the end, according to Mannix, the pack was reduced, hunted down in the streets, and cornered.

According to *A Parisian Journal*, Courtaut (a different spelling) was killed, placed "into a wheelbarrow with the jaws wide open and taken about all over Paris. Everybody left whatever they were doing . . . to go and look at Courtaut. They got more than ten francs in takings."

Other Infamous and Ferocious Bêtes

Wolves have inhabited France, and Europe, since prehistoric times. Archaic predecessors of modern wolves appeared approximately two million years ago in Italy during the Pleistocene. The valley of the Arno river harbored the prehistoric species *Canis etruscus*, a true wolf, though a bit smaller in size than the modern species, but

A historical engraving depicting the *Bête du Gâtinais* (1653), a short-snouted, long-legged dog-like animal.

almost identical in general appearance, anatomy, and morphology (and possibly in ecology and behavior). *Canis lupus* (more precisely *C. l. mosbachensis*) appears at the middle of the Pleistocene (around 500,000 years ago). The Lunel-Viel wolf, even closer to the modern specimens, lived around Montpellier, southern France, about half a million years ago. During all this time, interaction with humans was nearly impossible to avoid. In prehistoric times, such contact was probably scarce, although as *Homo sapiens* developed and expanded its territories and populations, the two species tracked closer to one other. French historian Jean-Marc Moriceau has been documenting such episodes with available written records. As anyone can imagine there have been all sorts of wolves which have allegedly attacked humans: cursed wolves, ferocious beasts, *loups-garous*, man-eating clans, rabid individuals, sick and injured wolves, wounded animals in poor health, desperate females with litters to protect, and so on. The following list is somewhat exhaustive but shows the sheer variety of animals that, through time, have accompanied the well-known Bête from the Gévaudan:

Bête de l'Orléanais
Bête de l'Yveline
Bête de Touraine
Bête du Chartrain (1660–1662)
Bête du Gâtinais
La Bête (1690–1695)
La Bête d'Evreux (1633–1634)
La Bête de Bailleau (1687–1695)
La Bête de l'Auxerrois (1731–1734)
La Bête from the Eure valley (1711–1714)
La bête de Xaintrie (1742–1744)
La Bête du Gévaudan (1764–1767)
La bête from the región of Othe (1713–1714)
La bête du Toulousain (1600–1605)
La malbête ("bad beast") du Limousin (1698–1700)
La maudite bête (the cursed beast) (1482–1483)
The wolf Courtaud (1439)
The wolf from La Croix-en-Touraine (1711)
The wolf from Primarette (1746–1752)
Les bêtes de Touraine and Vendômois (1742–1755)
The ten wolves of Varzy (1801)
The wolves from Bourgogne
The wolves from Dauphiné
The wolves from the interior of Cannes (1714–1715)
The wolves from Ville-aux-Clercs (1595–1600)
The wolves from Saint-Aignan (1715)
The wolves from Cévennes (1809–1817)
The wolves from Bourbonnais (1596–1600)
The wolves from Genevois (1748–1752)
The wolves from Livradois-Forez
The wolves from Lozère (1625–1636)
The wolves from Morvan
The wolves from Valromey
The wolves from the Jura Mountains
The wolves from Varassieux (1697)
The wolves from the lower Dauphiné (1752–1756)
The wolves from Lyonnais (1755–1756)

Since a detailed analysis of each of these cases is beyond the scope of this book, we will offer the reader a condensed table

LA BÊTE D'ORLÉANS

Gravure moderne faite pour la publication de cet article dans l'*Astrologue de la Beauce et du Perche*, année 1859.

FIGURE DE LA BÊTE FÉROCE, qui ravage les alentours d'Orléans.

Æ. C-M. Lith. Hebert, Chartres.

(*Réduction fac-simile.*)

Two historical documents representing the infamous Beast d'Orleanais, showing its scale-covered body. ***L.-F. Coudray-Maunier, La Bête d'Orléans, légende beauceronne, Chartres: Petrot-Garnier libraire, 1859.***

including concise and most relevant data connected to the better known "beastly" episodes.

Map Number	Year	Province/ Towns	Victims	Animal(s) Description(s)
1	1636	Santerre	Many (exact numbers unknown)	Province devastated by plague. Wolves raiding many villages.
2	1653	Le Gatinais	Mainly infants, children, and some women, wounded and killed	Killer wolf shot April 11, 1653, and taken to the court of King Louis XIV.
3	1670	Dauphiné	Many (exact numbers unknown)	A wolf. No further details about its description.
4	1691	Dauphiné	Many (exact numbers unknown)	Man-eating wolf. Could be a descendant of the previous wolf. 21 years after.
5	1693–1694	Indre et Loire (township of Bourgueil)	Many infants and children tending livestock. At least 200 victims	*Benais Bête*. Like a big wolf with very wide mouth. Probably a small clan due to high number of victims over a wide territory.
6	1691–1700	Northern Orleanais (towns like Cercottes, Orleáns, Chevilly, etc.)	More than 200 attacks, over 40 fatalities	Animal described as a *Bête* or predatory wolf, covered in scales (immune to bullets). A man-eating clan operating in a huge wooded area.
7	1719, 1730, 1732 and 1734	Dauphiné	Many (exact numbers unknown)	Possibly man-eating clan based in this region. Descendants from the previous man-eaters of the same region?
8	1731–1734	Auxerrois	28 persons total	Wolf.
9	1747, 1748	Dauphiné	Mainly children	*Bête Féroce*. The animal preys almost exclusively on children tending livestock (ignoring the sheep). Possible descendants from previous Dauphiné man-eating clan.

10	1754–1756	Lyonnais. Mountain regions of Thelzé, de Moire, de Fronnac, de Saint-Bel and de l'Arbresle	17 children and infants	Size of a wolf, with short legs, very hirsute/shaggy hair, spotted or striped, multi-colored pelage. Possibly a wolf-dog hybrid.
11	1764	Vivarais	8 killed	Province east of Gévaudan. Animal described as *Bête*.
12	1766	Perigord	Around 20 persons	Sarlat Bête, a rabid wolf.
13	1798	Nievre	Around 10 persons	Wolf.
14	1801	Nievre (Varzy department).	17 victims, wounded and dead	Two wolves. Probably a man-eating clan, together with the previous one.
15	1809–1816	Cévennes	Around 20 persons	South of Gévaudan. Known as Cévennes *Bête*.
16	1814	Orleanais	2 dead, 8 wounded (women and children)	*Chaingy Bête*. Beast is shot dead near Cercottes.
17	1817	Nievre	Around 6 persons	Around the town of Clemency, multiple attacks in the whole area.
18	1823	Somme	Unknown	Wolf packs.
19	1830	Orleanais (Orléans Forest)	2 women, 8 men, and 2 children attacked	Wolf packs. A female wolf and 2 males shot dead, non-rabid.
20	1854, 1868	Orleanais (Chaingy)	2 attacks, children	A wolf is preserved at the Natural History Museum in Orléans.
21	1878 and 1880	Dauphiné	Unknown number of victims	The attacks reach the cities of Lyon, Bron, and Saint-Priest. A huge animal, some said similar to a tiger.
22	1880	Orleanais (Orléans Forest)	Around 10 persons are attacked and wounded	A wolf pack, attacking in Chanteau, Cercottes, and St. Lyé. Wolf preserved at Natural History Museum, Orléans

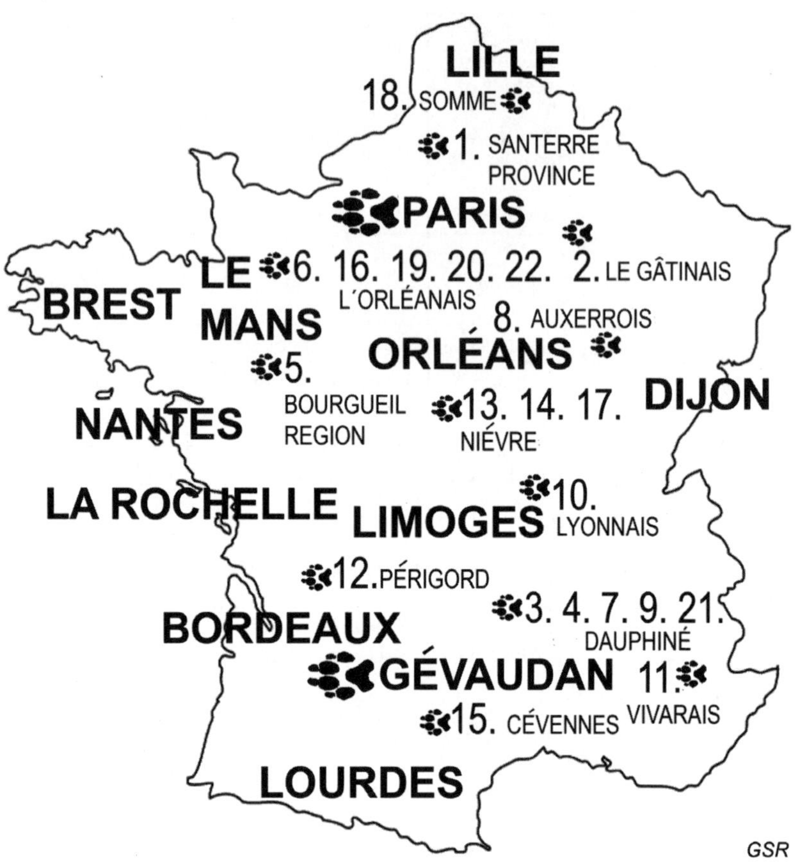

Modern mystery marauders. The French countryside is idyllic and inviting. River birds swoop along the water's edge. Sheep bleat far off in the distance hills. Cow bells clang softly in the meadows. But . . . something disrupts our bucolic scenario: A feline silhouette, sleek, silent, and disturbing. Rare cats supposedly roam free through cultivated fields and dairy farms. What is their true nature?

French researcher Michel Meurger has written extensively about this topic, and his analysis establishes two crucial periods in which there have been numerous sightings of mystery carnivores allegedly identified with big cats:

Wild wolves shot in Indre (Argenton-sur-Creuse, central France). Top row, right, head of a wolf-dog hybrid, all of them shot in 1884. *Revue d'Histoire Naturelle.*

- 1946–1956, called by Meurger "the Bête from Cézallier cycle."
- Post-1960 period, in which a number of "beast" sightings occurred, including that of the famous Vosges Bête. During this period, 1977–1988, the Eurasian Lynx (*Lynx lynx*) was controversially reintroduced in France, sometimes illegally, complicating matters.

The following table and map synthesize much information about these well-known and well-documented cases. We include at the end other less-known "beastly" animals, some modern examples, and a few reports from neighboring Spain and Switzerland, which received media coverage at the time.

Map Number/ Name	Year/ Location	Animal Description	Other Details/ "Beast" Candidates
1-Cézallier Beast	1946–1951 Auvergne (Central Massif)	Described as a lion/ lioness. Deep longitudinal claw marks on attacked cows. Wild dogs and wolves also sighted in the area. Described also as a lynx, hyena, and as an elusive plantigrade (bear, raccoon, wolverine).	Heavy livestock raiding (mainly sheep) induced by a post-war situation. In 1951 the Grandrieu wolf is shot (Haute-Loire province). An old shepherd recounts seeing big cats on nights with full moons and recorded a jumping attack on cows (a typical feline hunting maneuver, not seen with dogs or wolves). Cattle highly disturbed by creature (they would have confronted dogs or wolves, normal enemies since historical times).
2-Valais Monster (Eischoll wolf)	1946, Valais Province, Switzerland	Short, rounded head, feline, pointy ears. Reports of spotted big cats also on file. Also a puma or a panther clan (leopards) escaped from an Italian zoo (European lynx usually shows dark body spots).	Tracks found identified as lynx (probably from Savoy region, French Alps) by Lausanne University zoologists. A wildcat *(Felis silvestris silvestris)* later shot and identified. In 1947, Bern Natural History Museum experts state that another set of tracks corresponds with those of a lion. That same year, a large wolf is shot and exhibited at Sion Natural History Museum. Genetic analysis reveals eastern European or Russian origin. More livestock-raiding specimens shot in later years.
3-Vosges Beast	Vosges Mountain Massif, Lorraine region, France, 1975–1988 1994 (a wolf-like animal is filmed)	Bigger than a German shepherd, reddish or fawn-colored, pointed ears, 60 kg. Hair sample analysis results: Canid, no further data.	250+ animals attacked (cattle, sheep, goats, foals, etc.). 26 organized hunts, more than 250 persons involved in more than 150 km² (army and policemen). Unknown carnivore tracks. Killing method similar to a wolf (not wild dog). Hypothesis: An escaped, out-of-control large hunting dog trained to kill big game.
4-Noth Beast	1982 Creuse Department, Noth Forest	Animal the size and appearance of a lion, as big as a calf.	Cattle (mainly sheep and some cows) attacked and killed by the mystery marauder. A family of puma-like animals sighted.

5-Pornic Panther	1982 Loire-Atlantique Department	A jet black animal resembling a panther.	A big black wildcat *(Felis silvestris silvestris)* shot.
6-Esterel (or Valescure) Beast	1983 Var and Alpes-Maritimes, French Blue Coast (massif formation)	Described as a very big cat, or a puma-type of animal.	Probably a big feral dog or a big hybrid canid. Organized searches failed to locate the animal.
7-Arize "Mountain Lions"	1980–1986 Aragon Pyrenees (Huesca, Spain) and Arize massif (French Pyrenees)	Two big animals very similar in general appearance to a puma (mountain lion) with long tails.	Sightings reported by local people who spied the animals in the distance. Some say they might be big feral dogs.
8-Malataverne Beast	1988 Drôme Department	Tiger, puma, or lynx.	Some puma-type tracks are obtained. Probably a lynx.
9-Modern French Cases	1993–2014 1993: Ariege Department. 1994: Paris area (Chantilly forest). 1995: Chizé forest (Poitou-Charen). 1997: Herault. 1999: Vienne Department. 1999: Haute Province Alps and Upper Var 2000: Picquingny (Somme dept.).	Big cat species, lynx.	1993: Panther, puma or lion? 1994: Puma? (fawn color sheep dog) 1995: Puma? 1997: Lion? (big feral dog) 1999: Puma? Previous animal? 1999: Lynxes? Hundreds of sheep lost, woman scratched by a lynx-like animal. Sighting of a sleeping lynx 2000: 2 puma/tigers? (2 domestic cats)
10-Gorliz Panther	2005 Basque country (northern Spain, contiguous to French territory)	Panther.	A jet black panther-like animal. Various sightings. A policeman opens fire on the running animal; it takes cover in dense woodlands.
11-Huesca Puma	2005 Granada mountain chain, Banastás, Huesca Province (Pyrenees, Spain)	Big cat species.	Many sightings of an animal described as a big cat with short brownish/fawn fur, very elusive and shy. Tracks obtained. Organized police searches failed to locate the animal.
12-Extremadura illegal hunts	2005 Monterrubio de la Serena, Badajoz (Central Spain)	Big cat species.	Local police discovers a network of illegal organized hunts on private lands. Targets: Illicitly imported lions and tigers.

(continued)

Map Number/ Name	Year/ Location	Animal Description	Other Details/ "Beast" Candidates
13-Mijas (Malaga) Panther	1995–2007 Comares, La Cala, Campillos, Atajate, Benadalid, Jimera de Libar, Genal, Andalucía, southern Spain	Big cat species, panther.	Puma (not afraid of humans) tracks (4 cm) are obtained. Big brown cat, 50 kg. Long tail. A young horse, 15 sheep, and other farm animals missing. A big black panther is sighted perched in a tree. 15 pigs reported dead, but not eaten. Wild dogs? New tracks found, animal must weigh over 80 kg. A short video of a panther-like animal is obtained. Much larger than a domestic cat with a very long tail.
14-Rhone Panther	2009 Rhone, Chenières, Cutry, Fresnois-la-Montagne, Lorraine region (France)	Jaguar, panther.	Witness description: a large jet-black non-aggressive carnivore (panther-like) walking in the countryside. Later, fresh tracks identified as "jaguar" are obtained. Baited traps are set without success.
15-Berja (Almería) Panther	2013 Andalucía, southern Spain	Big cat species, panther.	Many sightings (even the city mayor spots the animal). A black panther-like feline. Organized parties (employing helicopters, baited traps, and infrared cameras) capture a fox and a domestic cat. Tracks are obtained: similar to jaguar or puma.

Quite clearly, the previous maps and tables indicate the activity and an anomalous presence of large carnivores in Europe, including the vast expanse of France. These elusive animals seek refuge in mountainous areas, massifs (peaks), and woodlands, as any wild animal would do. The maps also clearly indicate the movements of some of these creatures from country to country via natural boundaries, for example, mountain ranges such as the Pyrenees and the Alps. It is typical to find sightings and evidence on both sides of each boundary, such as the Huesca and Arize massif cougars (Spanish and French Pyrenees, respectively).

Called Alien Big Cats (ABC) in English, this phenomenon is also extensively found in the United Kingdom. Within continental Europe, such carnivores may be trying to establish small populations.

The southern region of Spain should be carefully studied as its mild climate could be ideal for some highly adaptable tropical species, such as leopards or jaguars. These creatures, possibly escaped from private collections or illegally introduced, may pose a serious threat to local wildlife. Are these cats the modern equivalents of ancient wild beasts of France? Some of the descriptions given and certain historical evidence seem to corroborate it.

CHAPTER 26

The Beast and Wolves Today in France

[The Beast] . . . was returned to Monsieur de Beauterne [gun-bearer François Antoine], who kept him till the Revolution came, and amongst other institutions swept away the terror of the Cévennes.

—*Charles Dickens*

On the Trail of the Beast Today

Two and a half centuries after the time of the Beast, its home turf—the Massif Central, Lozère, the Cévennes—is no less impressive. A car trip here from the direction of the south of France allows one a jaw-dropping portal to the Beast's world through the sky across the Millau Bridge. A modern wonder of the world, the cable-stay bridge, completed in 2004, is more than one and a half miles long, with a central pillar taller than the Eiffel Tower. Or one could follow in the footsteps of Robert Louis Stevenson and walk his "frontiers of hope," the GR70, as well as other "Beast walks" and trails across undulating mist-covered mountains, volcanic peaks, and seeming lunar landscapes. Guidebooks and tour services are readily available through Internet searches. Throughout the region, one finds echoes of the former Gévaudan and its Beast in signs, sculptures, and emblems of multiple municipalities. Polite requests may yield information from locals about key sites, such as the area where young Portefaix fought back, or the neck of the woods where Jean Chastel did his deed. Driving at night along the area's narrow, twisting byways above fathomless river gorges might transport one back to 1764, as is the case with author Sánchez, when he and his wife came across an immense black dog on a murky, mist-fogged road.

Depictions of the Beast and Its Adversaries

Impressive statuary of our subject includes a giant wood-carved Beast licking its chops upon a hill overlooking Saugues. One cannot miss the statue of Marie-Jeanne Valet confronting La Bête in the hills of Auvers. There are two sculpture groupings in different settings in Le Malzieu; one depicts children fighting the animal, the other represents the theory of the sadistic wolf master. A bronze Constructionist-style statue and an abstract sculpture are found in Saint-Privat d'Allier and Marvejols, respectively. Weathered road signs mark the trail of La Bête between communities. And there is the *stèle*, or monument, to Jean Chastel, depicting our hero in profile, scowling, blunderbuss in hand, along the roadway at La Besseyre-Saint-Mary.

Bas-relief silver wolf head medallions dot the streets of Saugues, and painted wolf tracks lead to its Fantastic Museum of the Beast of the Gévaudan (www.musee-bete-gevaudan.com), where three-dimensional models and sound effects provide a glimpse of life in the Gévaudan in the 1760s. Note: The museum's hours vary, and off-season it is only open by prearrangement; check before planning a trip. Les Loups du Gévaudan Wolf Park (www.loupsdugevaudan.com), Hameau de Sainte-Lucie, founded in 1985, is a forty-acre preserve and home to about one hundred wolves from various countries and regions, such as Poland, Canada, Siberia, the Arctic, and Mongolia. Its mission is to create awareness and understanding of wolves. It also possesses some documents related to the Beast.

Twilight of the Wolf in France

Thirty years after the reign of La Bête, following the French Revolution, the wolf seemed to be making a temporary comeback. A footnote to a story about a trip to Paris published in the *Gentleman's Magazine* in June 1797 reported, "Since the Revolution and the abolition of the *corvées* [roads constructed by means of forced labor], the roads have

Approaching our exit. *Photo Schwalb.*

been so generally neglected as to be in many places almost impassable. This is not the only sad consequence of the horrors of war and revolution. In proportion as depopulation and neglect have thinned the country, wolves and other wild beasts have renewed the depredations frequent in uncultivated countries; and the race of the celebrated beast of Gévaudan have lately produced an extensive destruction."

Devlin tells us that, at this time, wolves were indeed menacing areas such as Eure-et-Loir, in central northern France. However, extermination was actively underway. As the years went by, there were fewer and fewer wolves to kill. By 1918, it was believed that there were about two hundred indivduals in France. The last one is reported to have been killed in 1937, though some say this took place in the 1950s. A wolf was killed in Lozère in January 1951, per Jacques Delperrie de Bayac.

Reconquering France?

There are wolves in France today, apart from those kept in wolf parks, in zoos, as pets, and so on. In the early 1990s, wolves were observed moving across the mountainous border between Italy and France into the Mercantour National Park in the French Alps. "Nowadays," reports the website Wolf in France (http://www.rdbrmc-travaux.com/loup/index.php?lang=en, page no longer accessible at time of publication), "the wolf population . . . spreads on all the Alps (up to Switzerland in the north) and starts to reappear in the Eastern part of the Pyrenees, in the Massif Central, and in the Jura mountains." Wolf populations today are monitored by over twelve hundred trained field professionals who report their findings the National Office for Hunting and Wildlife (ONCFS).

The species *Canis lupus* is protected under the Bern Convention, a binding legal initiative that aims to conserve wildlife and habitats in Europe, as well as a European Union Habitats Directive, aimed at protecting animals, plants, and habitats. In France, an action plan launched in 2013 by ministers of agriculture and ecology, in consultation with the French National Council for the Protection of Nature, aims to promote biodiversity and protect wolf populations yet restrict livestock damages.

But the presence of wolves here, as is the case in the United States, Germany (where the species has been recently taking over immense Soviet training grounds largely unused since the Cold War), and other countries, is highly controversial.

There are many reasons for this, according to Véronique Campion-Vincent, one being that wolves, unlike other predators such as bears and lynxes, "have traditionally carried the strongest and most negative image in European societies, not only in folktales and legends but also in naturalists' descriptions since classical antiquity. In such stories, wolves regularly attacked livestock, especially sheep, occasionally humans, and especially children acting as shepherds." Still, a large portion of the French public is in favor of the wolf. Campion-Vincent cites this striking modern turnaround, which has "launched a major rehabilitation campaign of the animal" (even recasting the Beast's story, making man the culprit), and thus overhauling the nation's "symbolic bestiary."

She traces the complex peregrinations involved in the re-establishment "of species formerly considered as pests or vermin . . . [which] . . . rests upon new conceptions of Nature." The wolves' unexpected reappearance two decades ago excited the public imagination, but understandably consternated mountain sheep farmers in the Alps region. The farmers try to maximize meager incomes, supplemented by subsidies, by grazing as many sheep as possible with few or no caretakers. They also view themselves as preservationists of the traditional French rural landscape. And so clashes with environmentalists have ensued, amid the formation of various organizations taking sides. The State provides compensation for predator-killed sheep via certification by ONCFS agents. Campion-Vincent points out that the wolves' comeback was not truly "natural," and was more like "the outcome of measures of protection of the species adopted in Italy in the middle of the 1970s." Still, many believe stray dogs cause much of the damage. There have also been "conspiracy theories" about the wolves being deliberately reintroduced by over-zealous nature-lovers.

As of 2013, according to the website of the International Wolf Center, www.wolf.org, there are an estimated 250 to 300 wolves in France, with about two dozen packs (about one hundred more individuals than a century ago). The media reports that the species' "reconquest" of the country is progressing with surprising speed; wolves, we are told, may once more prowl Louis XV's forest of Fontainebleau, south of Paris, in a few years' time. French farmers have reported newsmaking wolf sightings in the Auvergne in 2012, and sheep and other livestock predations, even in unforested farm and vineyard areas, such as "Little Champagne," a two-hour drive from Paris, in the fall of 2013. In February 2013, it was determined that government hunters may kill twenty-four wolves per year, in favor of farmers, and trained shepherds may defend their livestock in the case of an actual attack. But, as mentioned above, and as suspected by US researchers in cases made famous in America one hundred years ago, wild dogs may be to blame for attacks on livestock. Wolves are carrion eaters, and may be seen consuming the remains of prey killed by dogs, and are thus mistakenly considered culprits. Sheep farmers are urged to employ herders, sheepdogs, and pens to protect defenseless livestock from all predators.

Ecologists remain hopeful about our potential to co-exist with the wolf in the twenty-first-century and beyond. Campion-Vincent says, "The stakes of the manipulations of wild fauna . . . would be clearer if there was less invocation of sacred principles, less conjuring up of the loaded term of 'Nature.' . . . Nature, yes, but nature shaped and organized by humans, whether to cultivate it or to re-establish animal species that had previously been removed."

Historian Jean-Marc Moriceau says the eighteenth-century tale of the Gévaudan is "an indicator of relations" between man and wolf, and man and nature. He believes the "profoundly original" story of the Beast may be used as a cultural tool with regard to new discussions on wolves, forestry, urban growth, the management of space, and so on. "All these subjects put the field of history in a new light."

Appendix

Details of the Autopsies

We begin by examining the animal shot by François Antoine, the Chazes Wolf, in September 1765. Here is the full account, with author notes and contemporary measurements in brackets [ ].*

Jaladon Report on Les Chazes Dire Wolf

On September 27, 1765.

I the undersigned Charles Jaladon, master and demonstrator of surgery, lieutenant of Mr. the first surgeon of the King, army surgeon of the regiment of Riom, member of the Academy of Sciences and Arts in this town of Clermont-Ferrand, certify that under the terms of the ordinance of my Lord of Ballainvilliers, steward of the province of Auvergne, I visited his mansion with the intent there to see and visit the wild animal that caused so much devastation in Gévaudan and the mountains of Auvergne. On which I noticed the scars and wounds of which mention is made hereafter, and having it transported to my home I made the most exact searchings on all the parts of its body in the presence of Master Benoît du Vernin, doctor in medicine and dean of his college, and MM. François Fargeon, Master in surgery, provost of his company, J.-B. Raymond, also master and demonstrator in surgery, who kindly helped me with the examination and dissection of the aforesaid animal, after which searchings the following remarks result:

- *That the animal had started to putrefy, which appeared by the smell, the fall of the hair and the skin.*
- *A scar to the inner face of the beginning of the right shoulder which penetrates to the muscle.*

- *Several scars to both wrists or the lower front part of the forelegs.*
- *Two holes located on the hind part of both thighs which appear to have been made by a bullet.*
- *A shot which pierced the right eyeball, penetrated the head, and fractured the bones at the base of the skull and resulted in the death of the animal, said blow apparently caused by a bullet.*
- *A scar behind the left ear.*
- *Another scar penetrating the flesh obliquely on the front-facing, middle part of the right shoulder.*
- *The skin pierced in various places by shot or buckshot especially on the left side.*
- *Several shots of various sizes were found in the various lower parts of this animal.*
- *The lumbar muscles of the neck and of the lower jaw are masses of flesh of a strength much superior to ordinary wolves; all the other proportions are also more considerable than in such animal species.*
- *After removing the teguments* [outer covering: skin and hair], *grease and the already gangrenous muscle parts I desiccated the fleshy parts with the liquor indicated by Mr. de Buffon. Then, with the spirit of turpentine I placed in the interstices* [closely-set crevices] *of the muscles the powders and the balms that are used in embalming, the cavities are filled with odorous powders and balsamic gum and penetrating salt, all the external parts covered with the same powder over the ordinary lignement, the whole covered with its skin . . .*
- *The skin of this animal had been so damaged that all its long hair had fallen, the part which covers the abdomen, especially between the thighs, has been stripped of skin, as well as some other parts of the skin, as a consequence of decomposition.*
- *All the other proportions decreased in volume through desiccation* [dehydration and loss of mass], *as one can notice from the following table:*

<u>Proportion</u> *(at the time I made the measurements [?]):*

- *Length from the tip of the nose to the end of the tail: 5 feet, 10 inches, 6 lines (after dessication: 5 feet, 9 inches, 4 lines)* [190.7 cm].
- *Length from the tip of the nose to the root of the tail: 4 feet, 5 inches, 1 line (after dessication: 4 feet, 4 inches)* [138.62 cm].
- *Length from the nose until the occiput* [or occipital, back portion of the skull]*: 1 foot, 1 inch (after dessication 11 inches, 10 lines)* [35.18 cm].

(. . .)

- *Length of the hind paw: 2 inches, 9 lines (after dessication: 2 inches, 6 lines)* [7.2 cm].
- *Length of the fore paw: 2 inches, 11 lines (after dessication: 2 inches, 9 lines)* [7.6 cm].
- *Length of the largest nail: 1 inch, 1 line (idem after dessication)* [2.9 cm].
- *Length of the fangs or defenses: 1 inch, 3 lines (idem after dessication)* [3.3 cm]. *In wolves up to 5 cm 2 inches.*

<u>Number of teeth:</u>

- *On the upper jaw eighteen, to wit six incisors, two defensives and ten molars, six on the right side and four on the left side, and one ready to emerge on the same side.*
- *On the lower jaw twenty-two, to wit six incisors, two canines or defensives, and four* [read: fourteen, as the following sentence shows] *molars. There are seven on each side.*

This official report is sincere and true, in witness whereof I signed with the aforementioned, in Clermont-Ferrand on September 27, 1765. J.D. F.R.
(Archives departementales du Puy-de-Dôme c. 1736).

We now move on to examine the report of the Beast shot by Jean Chastel, La Ténazeyre Canid, an unusual animal that fortunately was better examined, resulting in a much more detailed autopsy.

Here is the full account, again with author notes and contemporary measurements in brackets [ ].*

Autopsy from notary Roch-Étienne Marin

The Marquis d'Apcher, who lived in the Castle of Besques near Charraix, had for some time been trying to hunt the Beast, with the people of his lands. In the course of this, on 19 June 1767, Jean Chastel killed the Beast (a male specimen). A statement preserved in the French National Archives and drafted on June 20, 1767, by master Marin, royal notary of Langeac, reports as follows:

The Marquis d'Apcher, having had the animal moved to his castle at Besques, parish of Charraix, we deemed fitting to go there to verify this, and being at the Castle of Besque the Marquis d'Apcher had this animal shown to us, which seemed to us a wolf, but extraordinary and very different in shape and proportions from the wolves one can see in this area. This was certified to us by more than three hundred people from the whole neighborhood who had come to see it.

Many hunters and knowledgeable people indeed pointed to us that this animal only resembles a wolf through its tail and hind-quarters. The head, as we shall see from the proportions below, is monstrous: its eyes have a strange membrane which starts at the lower part of the eye-socket, rising when the animal wishes to cover the eyeball [a nictitating membrane, or third eyelid, a translucent membrane which provides eye protection and lubrication]. *Its neck is covered by a very thick, reddish gray hair crossed by a few black stripes. It has, on its chest, a great heart-shaped white mark. The feet have four toes armed with large nails that extend much longer than those of ordinary wolves. They are, as well as the legs, which are very big, especially the front ones, the color of a roe deer's. This seemed to us a remarkable observation because, in the opinion of those same ~~hunters~~* [word purposefully crossed in the original] *knowledgeable people and all the hunters, never have such colors been seen in wolves. It also seemed fitting to observe that its ribs do not look like a wolf's, which gave this animal the ability to turn around easily, whereas the ribs of wolves, being set in the oblique, do not allow this faculty.*

The proportions we had taken from this animal are:

- **A. G.** *Length from the root of the tail to the tip of the head: 3 feet* [97.44 cm]

- **P.** *From top of the head to between the two great angles of the eyes: 6 inches* [16.2 cm]
- **Q.** *From the great angle of the eyes to the tip of the snout: 5 inches* [13.5 cm]
- **U.** *Width from one ear to the other: 7 inches* [18.9 cm]
- **S.** *Mouth aperture: 7 inches* [18.9 cm]
- **B.** *Horizontal length of the neck: 8 inches 6 lines* [22.8 cm]
- **C. O.** *Width of shoulders: 11 inches* [29.7 cm]
- **E.** *Width at the root of the tail: 8 inches 6 lines* [22.8 cm]
- **D. H.** *Length of the tail: 8 inches* [21.6 cm] [Correction from another document incites to read: 1 foot 8 inches, 54.1 cm].
- **F.** *Diameter of the tail: 3 inches 6 lines* [9.3 cm].
- **V.** *Ear Length: 4 inches 6 lines* [12 cm]
- *Width of the forehead under the ears, 6 inches* [16.2 cm]
- **W.** *Distance between the two great angles of the eyes: 2 inches 6 lines* [6.6 cm]
- **I. L.** *Length of the humerus/femur (upper leg bone): 8 inches 4 lines* [22.4 cm]
- **J. M.** *Length of the forearm: 8 inches* [21.6 cm]
- **K.** *Length from the last joint to the nails: 7 inches 6 lines* [20.1 cm]
- **R.** *Length of the jaw: 6 inches* [16.2 cm]
- **X.** *Width of the snout: 1 inch 6 lines* [3.9 cm]
- **3.** *Width of lower molars: 1 inch 3 lines* [3.3 cm]
- **1.** *Length of the incisors, 1 inch 3 lines* [3.3 cm]
- **4.** *Length of lower molars: 6 lines [1.2 cm]*
- **2.** *Length of upper molars: 1 inch 1 line* [2.72 cm]
- *Length of the tongue: 14 inches from its root* [37.8 cm]
- **Y.** *Width of the eyes: 1 inch 3 lines* [3.3 cm]
- **T.** *Head thickness: 7 inches* [18.9 cm]
- **N.** *Hind legs from the first to the second joint: 7 inches 2 lines* [19.3 cm]
- **Z1. Z2.** *From the second to the third joint to the nails: 10 inches* [27 cm]
- **Z3.** *Leg width: 4 inches 6 lines* [12 cm]
- *From the "chataîgne"* [literal French: chestnut] *to the extremity of the leg: 6 inches* [16.2 cm]

- *Length of the penis: 7 inches* [18.9 cm]

The upper jaw is garnished with six incisors, the sixth being longer than the others. Two large strips or hooks far from the incisors and 1 inch 4 lines high [3.6 cm] *with a diameter of 6 lines* [1.4 cm], *three molar teeth, of which one is fairly small and two are large, a fourth molar larger than the others and to which is nearly joined the fifth and penultimate one, which is divided into two parts, one of which extends perpendicularly and the other stretches horizontally in the interior of the palate, and finally a sixth molar.*

The lower jaw is garnished with 22 teeth, to wit 6 incisors, and on each side a row similar to the upper ones, 7 molars, the first very small and far from the strip, the next three are larger and similar to the second and third upper molars, the fifth larger and longer is divided into three parts, the anterior of which is shorter, the sixth, quite large, has with two anterior and lateral protuberances, the seventh is very small and almost equal. (...)

They also pointed to us that this animal, from the front legs to the spine, is 2 foot and 4 inches high [75.76 cm] *and that its eyes are the color of red cinnabar.*

We offer this second testimony from the Archives departementales du Puy-de-Dôme:

*Letter written from Auvergne to the Count of **** [name purposefully blanked in the original document], *relative to the destruction of the real dire beast, its female and its five young, that used to ravage Gévaudan.*

*Mr. de la M**** [we know from other documents this was Mr. de la Mothe] *made his examination. He observed that the head was monstrous, square in shape, much wider and longer than that of an ordinary wolf, the muzzle a bit obtuse, the ears straight and wide at their base, the eyes black and fitted with a very singular protruding membrane; it was a prolongation of the lower eye muscles. These membranes served it to cover both eye sockets at will, by rising and gliding under the eyelids. The mouth opening was very large; the incisors, resembling those of a dog, the big teeth close together and uneven, the neck very thick and short, covered with bristling hair, extremely long and thick, with a black transverse band descending toward the shoulder, the hind-quarters rather resembling a wolf's, except for the huge size; the front legs shorter that the hind legs,*

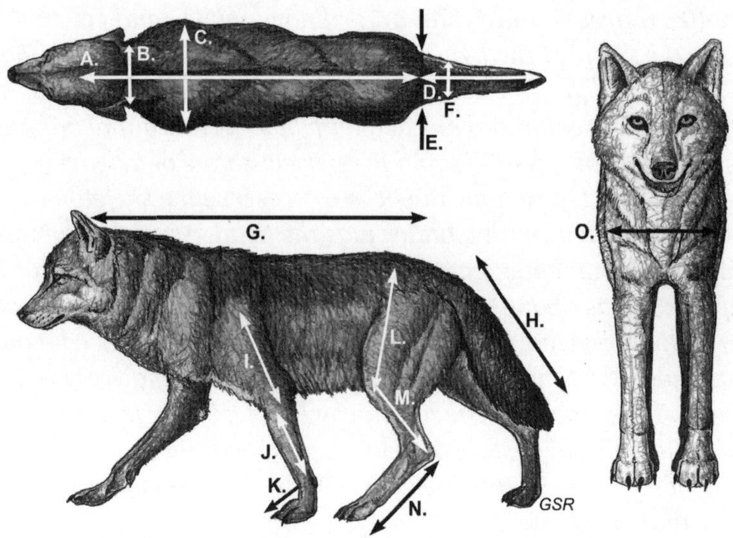

Notary Marin autopsy, body "proportions" for La Ténazeyre Canid (shot by Jean Chastel). Refer to text for data on measurements.

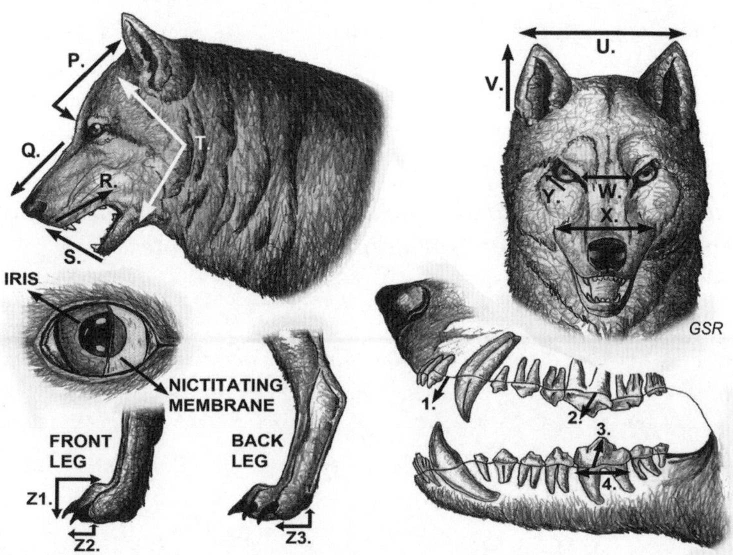

Notary Marin autopsy, head/legs "proportions" for La Ténazeyre Canid (shot by Jean Chastel). Refer to text for data on measurements.

more like a greyhound's than an ordinary wolf's, and covered, as well as the front of the head, with tawny hair, short and smooth, precisely the color of a deer's (. . .) The body hair very thick and long, grayish in color and mottled with black. The animal has on its chest a wide white spot, having the perfect shape of a heart (. . .)

We resolved to remove the flesh to preserve the skeleton (. . .)

What struck us with wonder was the head. After removing the common integuments, we spotted a bony ridge that began at the occipital; it was about 15 lines high (3.38 cm) and ended imperceptibly on the forehead, always decreasing (. . .) We removed a mass of muscular flesh, weighing over 6 lbs (2.9 kg), that covered the parietal. These muscles ended attached to the lower jaw and to the eyes. When all the fleshy parts were removed, this head, so monstrous in its natural state, merely consisted in a bony box, slightly bigger than a fist (. . .)

In Langeac, July 6, 1767

<u>Conversion notes:</u>
Measurements based on the official French units of the time ("royal units"), likely to have been used by a royal notary.

1 foot = 32.48 cm
1 inch = 27.07 mm
1 line = 2.25 mm
1 pound = 0.4895 kg

**Translation by Gustavo Sánchez Romero, corrections and complements by Alain Bonet, including conversion notes.*

Notes

The Main Characters

xiv: financial misdeeds: Phil Barnson, *dans l'Ombre de la Bête (In the Shadow of the Beast)*, www.labetedugevaudan.com.

Prologue

xxi: "six funerals and a wedding": Colin Jones, *The Great Nation: France from Louis XV to Napoleon* (London: Penguin Books, 2003), 73.

xxi: "ringmaster": Julian Swann, *Politics and the Parlement of Paris Under Louis XV, 1754–1774* (Cambridge: Cambridge University Press, 1995), 260.

xxi: two to three hundred animals: Jones, 85.

xxi: dogs by name: Mary Morton, ed., *Oudry's Painted Menagerie: Portraits of Exotic Animals in Eighteenth-Century Europe* (Los Angeles: J. Paul Getty Museum, Getty Publications, 2007), 6.

xxi: three thousand candles: James Breck Perkins, *France Under Louis XV, Vol. I* (Boston and New York: Houghton Mifflin Company, 1897), 6.

xxi: yew tree and she as a shepherdess: Tony Spawforth, *Versailles: A Biography of a Palace* (New York: St. Martin's Press, 2008), 129. Yves Carlier, *A Day at Versailles* (Paris: Flammarion, S.A., 2013), 142.

xxii: *voyeuses*: Alvar Gonzalez-Palacios, *The Age of Louis XV*, trans. Henry Vidon (London: Paul Hamlyn, 1969), 91.

xxii: and, almost, a re-directed river: A mind-boggling attempt was made to divert the river Eure, located more than fifty miles away; the project was abandoned but a gigantic aqueduct on the grounds of the Château de Maintenon (home of Louis XIV's second wife, Madame de Maintenon) still remains. Spawforth, 17, 18, 35.

Chapter 1: The Apparition

3: all cropping grass on the vertiginous hillside: Livestock were taken to graze in what was termed the *saltus*; that is, non-cultivated areas that included meadows, scrublands, heath, and forest. Pierre Goubert, *The Ancien Régime: French Society, 1750–1600*, trans. Steve Cox (New York: Harper & Row Publishers, Harper Torchbooks, 1974), 80.

5: Rambo-like sheep in the French mountains: Graham Robb, *The Discovery of France: A Historical Geography from the Revolution to the First World War* (New York and London: W. W. Norton & Company, 2007), 182.

Chapter 2. The Gévaudan

7: Historians hold: Jean-Marc Moriceau, *La Bête du Gévaudan* (Paris: Larousse, 2008), 20.

7: "like a wolf, yet not a wolf": Richard H. Thompson, *Wolf-Hunting in France in the Reign of Louis XV: The Beast of the Gévaudan* (Lewiston, New York; Queenstown, Ontario, Canada; Lampeter, Dyfed, Wales: The Edwin Mellen Press, 1991), 32.

9: "The famine was so terrible": Abbé Pierre Pourcher, *Histoire de la Bête du Gévaudan, veritable fléau de Dieu (History of La Bête du Gévaudan: True Scourge of God)*, trans. Derek Brockis (Milton Keynes, United Kingdom, and Bloomington, Indiana: AuthorHouse, 2006), 3. Abbé Pierre Pourcher, *Histoire de la Bête du Gévaudan, Veritable fléau de Dieu, d'aprè les documents inédits and authentiques* (Marseille, France: Éditions Jeanne Laffitte, 2006), 13.

9: guerrilla Resistance movement: Henry S. Ruess and Margaret M. Ruess, *The Unknown South of France: A History Buff's Guide* (Boston: Harvard Common Press, 1991), 180, 189–197.

11: "bleak fields": Robert Louis Stevenson, *Travels with a Donkey in the Cévennes* (New York: The Heritage Press, 1957), 33, 38.

11: "roaring blackness": Ibid., 38.

11: "Wolves, alas,": Ibid., 27.

Chapter 3: Lafont

13: "throttled and half-eaten": Moriceau, 23.

14: shorter goosefeathers: Joyce Irene Whalley, *Writing Implements and Accessories: From the Roman Stylus to the Typewriter* (Detroit: Gale Research Company, 1975), 24. (Whalleyalso tells us that the word pen comes from the Latin word for feather: *penna*.) According to historian John Fleming, "this was a world in which practically nobody who was anybody spent less than two hours a day conducting private correspondence, and some expended considerably more." John V. Fleming, *The Dark Side of the Enlightenment: Wizards, Alchemists, and Spiritual Seekers in the Age of Reason* (New York and London: W. W. Norton, 2013), 281.

15: "selfless": Moriceau, 26.

15: outbreaks: Moriceau, 97.

16: "ecclesiastical surveillance": Barnson.

Chapter 4: Count Morangiès

21: First Communion: Moriceau, 24.

21: "poor man's caviar": *Les lentilles du Puy*, French green lentils, grown in Auvergne.

23: four and one half grams of silver: Goubert, 62.

24: "able to 'read' the 'book' of nature": Ibid., 265.

24-25: small for his age, "*non naturelle*": Moriceau, 24.

Chapter 5: Le Petit Versailles du Gévaudan

28: "a year's salary": Moriceau, 27.

29: Could an animal cause a human decapitation?: Ibid., p. 30. Also Sylvain Macchi, Parc à loups de Gévaudan, Sainte-Lucie, France, interview by Phil Barnson, *dans l'Ombre de la Bête (In the Shadow of the Beast)* (Béziers, France: Myster B Improductions, 2011), documentary.

29: suicidal hanging from a bridge: Bao-Li Zhu, Kaori Ishida, Shigeki Oritani, Mari Taniguchi, Masaki Q. Fujita, Kazunori Fukita, Hitoshi Maeda, "Decapitation in suicidal hanging—a case report with a review of the literature." *Legal Medicine*, Vol. 2, Issue 3, October 2000, 159–162.

29: "*le petit Versailles du Gévaudan*": *Château de la Baume*, www.chateaudelabaume.org.

30: "a sort of fear": Pourcher, AuthorHouse, 15.

31: "lost their minds": Pourcher, Éditions Jeanne Laffitte, 43.

31: advised "fervent prayers," etc.: Pourcher, AuthorHouse, 66.

31: Winston Churchill: Daniel A. Baugh, *The Global Seven Years War, 1754–1763: Britain and France in a Great Power Contest* (Harlow, United Kingdom: Pearson Education Limited, 2011), 1.

32: France was in the midst of a "hangover": Jay M. Smith, *Monsters of the Gévaudan: The Making of a Beast* (Cambridge, Massachusetts: Harvard University Press, 2011), interview by Frank Stasio, "The State of Things," WUNC, North Carolina Public Radio, March 2, 2011.

32: His cavalry unit, called the Clermont-Prince Volunteers: Barnson.

32: About a quarter of the French army: Jones, 140.

33: Smartly outfitted, etc.: Barnson.

33: *dragonnades*: Jones, 20.

33: "There is no longer any doubt": Pourcher, Éditions Jeanne Laffitte, 22.

34: professional shepherds: Moriceau, 26.

Chapter 6: "Ferocious with Design"

35: growing commerce in news: as discussed by Smith, Fleming, Thompson, and Moriceau. Moriceau tells us that even Germany's "very serious" *Gazette de Cologne* picked up the story, 51.

36: print runs increased to three thousand: Thompson, 57n.

36: "ferocious with design": Pourcher, AuthorHouse, 27.

Chapter 7: "Inconsolable"

37: "inconsolable": Moriceau, 56.

Chapter 8: Wolf Month

39: "Wolf Month": Harting, 123.

43: Scarface: Thompson, 85.

43: yard accents: Louise E. Robbins, *Elephant Slaves and Pampered Pets: Exotic Animals in Eighteenth-Century Paris* (Baltimore and London: The Johns Hopkins University Press, 2002), 188.

43: "Even the peddlers": Pourcher, Éditions Jeanne Laffitte, 60.

43: "Its immense renown": Judith Devlin, *The Superstitious Mind: French Peasants and the Supernatural in the Nineteenth Century* (New Haven and London: Yale University Press, 1987), 75.

43: Moriceau has commented on how such coverage: Jean-Marc Moriceau, "Posters, Periodicals, and Newspapers: a Distorted Reflection?" *Man and Wolf: 2,000 Years of History*, http://www.unicaen.fr/homme_et_loup/_en/sources_presse.php.

43: By the King: Charles Dickens, "A Wonderful Wild Beast," *Household Words: A Weekly Journal*, Vol. 18 (November 20, 1858), 544–547.

45: this same day: Pourcher, Éditions Jeanne Laffitte, 112.

Chapter 9: Wolf-Stalk

47: flaxen-hued wheat bread: Bread was of the utmost concern, we are told by Colin Jones (148–149). The wealthy could partake of lighter wheat breads while peasants might only have the means to prepare or obtain unleavened black rye/barley loaves or a "practically indigestible chestnut bread," which sustained both humans and livestock.

Chapter 10: "An Old Norman Gentleman Who Has Grown Gray in the Pursuit of Wolves"

51: "An old Norman gentleman": Pourcher, AuthorHouse, 107.

51: a couple of weeks to bag the Beast: Smith, 141.

51: Young d'Enneval wrote: Pourcher, AuthorHouse, 110–111.

52: Duhamel did all he could: Pourcher, Éditions Jeanne Laffitte, 111.

52–53: Artificial Women and Little-Girl Lambs: Pourcher, AuthorHouse, 117–141; Pourcher, Éditions Jeanne Laffitte, 96–109. Thompson, 118–121.

Chapter 11: "Courage, Hunters of France"

55–58: the *femme* Jouve: She is also known as Jeanne Chastang, Moriceau, 112.

57: "seized La Bête": Pourcher, AuthorHouse, 234.

58: "see La Bête": Pourcher, Éditions Jeanne Laffitte, 133.

58: "The dragoons go on hunts": Pourcher, AuthorHouse, 154.

58: On March 19: Pourcher, AuthorHouse, 155–164.

60: "Courage, Hunters of France": Pourcher, Éditions Jeanne Laffitte, 118.

Chapter 12: "An Unfortunate Time"

62: "an unfortunate time!": Pourcher, Éditions Jeanne Laffitte, 89.

63: A spoof account: Smith, 116-117. A French response published in the *Courier* said, "The art of making witty spicy comments and of teasing with grace is rarely possessed by English authors. The oppressive climate and somber character of the nation is opposed to it." Pourcher, AuthorHouse, 243.

64: the story of the Beast, along with that of other creatures: Devlin, 79.

65–66: A Dickens of a Beast: Charles Dickens, "A Wonderful Wild Beast," *Household Words: A Weekly Journal, Vol. 18* (November 20, 1858), 544–547.

Chapter 13: The Royal Gunbearer

67: On June 1, 1765: Pourcher, AuthorHouse, 305.

68: the Beast attacked: Thompson, 160–161.

69: “a stick with a bayonet”: Pourcher, Éditions Jeanne Laffitte, 281.

69: “cried out very loudly”: Pourcher, Éditions Jeanne Laffitte, 281.

69: The intrepid Jeanne-Marie was an “Amazon”: Smith, 206.

71: demonstrated: Lynn, Michael R., “Fireworks and the Nation,” *The Ultimate History Project*, www.ultimatehistoryproject.com/fireworks-and-the-nation.html.

Chapter 14: Chazes

73: *carardière*: Moriceau, 177.

75: According to an October 3, 1765, letter: Horace Walpole, *The Letters of Horace Walpole, Vol. III*, 1759–1769 (Project Gutenberg, 2003, http://www.gutenberg.org/cache/epub/4773/pg4773-images.html), 427, 429.

75: pet spaniel: Robb, 280.

75: Mrs. Cavendish: Smith, p. 219.

76: Another Version: Andrew Lang, ed., H. J. Ford, illus., *The Animal Story Book* (1896; reprint, New York: Dover Publications, Inc., 2002), 167–173.

78: consumed “with such voracity”: Pourcher, Éditions Jeanne Laffitte, 336.

Chapter 15: “A Short Truce”

79: “a short truce”: Pourcher, Éditions Jeanne Laffitte, 336–337.

Chapter 16: Ténazeyre

85: pilgrimages: Devlin, 51–57. Devlin states that some yearly pilgrimages were considered a kind of primitive preventive medicine.

87: “in a spirit of piety”: Pourcher, AuthorHouse, 469.

Epilogue

89: document: Thompson, 235n.
89: Compiègne: Thompson, 231.
89: a July 7, 1767, communication: Moriceau, 246.

Afterword

91: Paul Le Blanc: Barnson. Thompson, 270–271.

Chapter 17: Hypotheses

95: "gloriously atmospheric": Roger Ebert, "The Brotherhood of the Wolf," (*RogerEbert.com*, 2002), www.rogerebert.com/reviews/the-brotherhood-of-the-wolf-2002.

96: "especially on the scale": Thompson, 263.

97: their reports spoke of an animal, not a human: Barnson.

97: helm of a gang of malefactors: Smith, 267.

97–98: Marquis de Sade: Barnson. Thompson, 264–265.

98: "armed truce": Emile F. Williams, *Undiscovered France* (Boston and New York: Houghton Mifflin Company, The Riverside Press Cambridge, 1927), 186.

99: "Catholics got the worst of it": Thompson, 268.

99: "settling his scores": Véronique Campion-Vincent, "The Return of the Wolf in France," *Journal of Indian Folkloristics, Special Issue, Islands and Narratives,* Vol. V, No. 1/2 (2003): 17n.

99: "easy grace": Fleming, 82.

99: Saint Severian: Thompson, 43.

99: "the wild beast of the Gévaudan was an allegory": Dickens, 545.

100: augur the time of the Apocalypse: Thompson, 59.

100: Pourcher and the Deception: Smith, p. 260.

100: Monsieur Ollier: Thompson, 195–196.

101: raised his gun, and killed the marauder: Father Pourcher obtained Chastel's gun in 1888. The gun, according to the Abbé, was purchased from Chastel by the Marquis d'Apcher. It was later sold to a man named François Duffaud, who converted it from a flintlock to a percussion gun. Duffaud's grandson sold it to Pourcher through an intermediary. Pourcher tells us it bore a little silver plate with the inscription "Jean Chastel." Pourcher, 477–481. Pourcher, AuthorHouse, 477–486; Éditions Jeanne Laffitte, 369–372. See also Barnson's website.

101: a living hyena among the animals: Franz Jullien, *La deuxième mort de la bête du Gévaudan* (Le Havre: Annales du Muséum du Havre, No. 59, 1998), 1–9.

102: a case in Marvejols: Barnson.

102: Some wolf leaders: Thompson, 175.

102: Cannibal Soldiers?: Barnson.

102–103: conspiracy theorists: Robert M. Sapolsky, "Mind & Matter" (*Wall Street Journal*, November 9 and 10, 2013).

103: famine pact: in French, *pacte de famine*, Jones, 264.

Chapter 18: Modus Operandi

106: "A very strange wild beast": Dickens, 544.

106: the Chazes wolf was a donkey: Smith, 207.

107: "flashing eyes": Pourcher, from a *Complainte*, or Lament, Éditions Jeanne Lafitte, 62–63.

107: "His eyes sparkled so with fire": Dickens, 547.

107: "cinnabar red": Autopsy, La Ténazeyre Wolf.

107: the stench of the Beast: Dickens, 547.

107: "singular cunning and inconceivable agility": Pourcher, Éditions Jeanne Lafitte, 148.

108: "lightning movements": Hugo and Jane van Lawick-Goodall, *Innocent Killers* (New York: Houghton Mifflin, 1971), 109.

108: "different from wolves": Pourcher, Éditions Jeanne Lafitte, 87.

109: "prepared to risk kicks": van Lawick-Goodalls, 168–169.

109: maps of the region: Moriceau, 6–11.

109: extent of movement: David L. Mech, *The Wolf: The Ecology and Behavior of an Endangered Species* (Minneapolis: University of Minnesota Press, 1970), 194–195.

110: "quick and efficient": van Lawick-Goodalls, 66.

111: "'This animal'": Pourcher, Éditions Jeanne Lafitte, 16.

112: Victims' Garments: C. H. D. Clarke, "The Beast of Gévaudan," *Natural History* (April 1971), 47.

Chapter 19: Werewolves of France

113: an ideal setting for werewolfery: Devlin, 73–74.

113: "a great dark night of the primitive": George Sand, *Légendes rustiques* (1858; electronic version, Project Gutenberg, 2006), http://www.gutenberg.org/cache/epub/17911/pg17911-images.html).

113: But these conventions are fairly recent: Chantal Bourgault du Coudray, *The Curse of the Werewolf: Fantasy, Horror, and the Beast Within* (London: I. B. Tauris & Co., Ltd., 2006), 78–79.

114: Calmeil enumerated: Devlin, 73–74.

114: medical definition of lycanthropy: Charlotte F. Otten, ed., *A Lycanthropy Reader: Werewolves in Western Culture* (Syracuse, New York: Syracuse University Press, 1986), 8.

114: More than a millennia ago: Ibid., 13.

114: no life without bread: Jones, 148-149. In some locales, it was required in death as well: Devlin says it was often the custom to inter deceased loved ones with a loaf of bread and a plate (in Auvergne and elsewhere), and perhaps wine or other items; "death was sometimes seen as a change of place . . ." (90).

114: celiac disease: Moises Velasquez-Manoff, "Can Celiac Disease Affect the Brain?" *New York Times Opinion* (October 11, 2014).

115: King Cnut: Otten, 5.

115: Fallen angels: Otten, 3.

116: "In Basse-Bretagne": Montague Summers, *The Werewolf in Lore and Legend* (1933; reprint, New York: Dover Publishing, 2003), .

116: Louis XV: Elliott O'Donnell, *Werwolves* (1912; electronic version, Project Gutenberg, 2008, https://www.gutenberg.org/files/26629/26629-h/26629-h.htm), 135. *Chamber's Edinburgh Journal*, Vol. 12, 124.

116: the word *vampire*: Paul Barber, *Vampires, Burial, and Death: Folklore and Reality* (New Haven: Yale University Press, 1988), 5, 14–17.

116: German werewolf Stubbe Peter: Otten, 53–54, 69.

117: "the rank foul weeds of werewolfery": Summers, 223.

117: a woman of Thiaucourt: Francesco Maria Guazzo, *Compendium Maleficarum, the Montague Summers Edition,* trans. E. A. Ashwin (New York: Dover Publications, 1988), 52.

117: "a leash of witches": Summers, 224.

118: "epidemic of sorcery": Ibid., 228.

118: newly buried cadavers: Bourgault du Coudray, 23–25.

118: "The clothes of the children": Otten, 88.

120: In the present-day region: author Sánchez in conversations with locals, November 2013.

120: "sham lycanthropy": O'Donnell, 11.

123: "red man": Devlin, 77.

123: a girl was discovered living wild: Ibid., 74.

123: Neanderthal: Robb, 11.

124: spectral black dogs: Trubshaw, 13, 84.

124: Sherlock Holmes: Crispin Andrews, "Sherlock Holmes and the Beast of the Gévaudan," *History Today,* Vol. 63, Issue 7 (2013), http://www.historytoday.com/crispin-andrews/sherlock-holmes-and-beast-Gévaudan.

124: skinwalkers: Hampton, 43.

124: spirit wolf: Stanley Young, *The Last of the Loners* (New York: The Macmillan Company, 1970), 250–274.

125: *Dracula* character Jonathan Harker: Bourgault du Coudray, 26–27.

126: "A French Werewolf in Kent, England": This tale may now be found in *The Best Werewolf Short Stories 1800–1849: A Classic Werewolf Anthology,* compiled by Andrew Barger (Collierville, Tennessee: Bottletree Books LLC, 2010).

128: immune to the power of silver: Lang, 169.

128: a case in the Vendée, France: Devlin, 199.

129: Memory and Story: Jonathan Gottschall, *The Storytelling Animal: How Stories Make Us Human* (Boston & New York: Mariner Books, Houghton Mifflin Harcourt, 2013), 167–176.

130: French rustics: Devlin, 198–199.

130: "War-wolves": Summers, 52n.

131: *loup-garou* (translated as "wolf-werewolf"): Thompson, 311.

131: a sermon: Sabine Baring-Gould, *The Book of Were-Wolves* (London: Smith, Elder, & Co., 1865), . The author adds that "the preacher alludes to this superstition in his sermon on wild-men of the woods, but translates his lycanthropists to Spain," 266.

131: "He who seeks a wolf at Candlemas": Candlemas is a holy day occurring on February 2. It is a commemoration of the purification of the Virgin Mary. Candles intended for church use are blessed on this day. Shrove Tuesday is a day of feasting day before Ash Wednesday, the first day of Lent; most of us know it as Mardi Gras today. Lent, from the Middle English word for "long" (a word that also indicated spring, when days begin lengthening) is a forty-day period of Christian fasting and penance to commemorate Jesus' fasting in the wilderness.

131: *Malleus Maleficarum*: Thompson, 338n.

132: warlock: Devlin, 198–199.

132: "reflected real fears": Robb, 175.

132: "a werewolf (in a waistcoat)": Devlin, 76.

132: bound through the air: Summers, 236.

132: "Scratching Fanny": Thompson, 138n.

133: "It talks, takes tobacco": Devlin, 76.

Chapter 20: Man-Beasts and Serial Killers

135: serial killer Joseph Vacher: Douglas P. Starr, *The Killer of Little Shepherds: a True Crime Story and the Birth of Forensic Science* (New York: Alfred A. Knopf, 2010).

136: man-beast hybrids: Anne Clark, *Beasts and Bawdy* (New York: Taplinger Publishing Company, 1975), 66.

137: the Skidi: Bruce Hampton, *The Great American Wolf* (New York: Henry Holt and Company, 1997), 50–51.

137: satyrs or men-goats: Clark, 62.

137: Saint Christopher: Bob Trubshaw, ed., *Explore Phantom Black Dogs* (Loughborough, England: Heart of Albion Press, 2005), 51–52, 56.

137: the wild man: Richard Bernheimer, *Wild Men in the Middle Ages: A Study in Art, Sentiment, and Demonology* (Cambridge: Harvard University Press, 1952), 1–20.

139: "the typical Edwardian face": Clark, 66.

139: Mother Nature: J. M. Gómez Tabanera, *Hunting in Prehistoric Times* (Madrid: Ediciones Istmo, 1980).

140: an era in which man gained more dominance over nature: J. L. Arsuaga, Kennis and Kennis, illus., *La saga humana* (Madrid: Edaf, 2006). See also www.atapuercatv.com.

141: They were also believed to drink the blood of the animal: Otten.

142: he seemed even to increase in size: Bob Curran, *Werewolves* (Franklin Lakes, New Jersey: New Page Books, 2009).

142: something more psychological: Ibid.

142: "human beasts" appear on the scene: Derek Brockis, "The Beast of Gévaudan," http://labete.7hunters.net/bete1.htm (website no longer active; see https://www.yumpu.com/en/document/view/10049286/what-was-the-beast-of-gevaudan-by-derek-brockis-a-great-).

143: He was so afraid after this vision: Ibid. (Brockis)

144: "'I think nothing should be ruled out'": Robert Dumont, "Notes on the book *The Beast of Gevaudan* by Pascal Cazottes," http://www.betedugevaudan.com/es/avis_cazottes_es.html

144: Fact, fiction, or imagination? Or human interference?: Brockis.

146: the only case of a werewolf sentenced to be executed by a national court of justice: "The Legend of the Allariz Werewolf," Galicia Holidays, www.paxinasgalegas.es/fiestas/la-leyenda-del-hombre-lobo-de-allariz-allariz-5466.html

146: under the influence of the moon: Gabriel Quiroga, director, del archivo reino de Galicia, Spain (personal communication with author Sánchez).

146: (body fat): Ibid.

146: devouring their flesh: *Reseña de la causa formada contra Manuel Blanco Romasanta, el Hombre Lobo de Allariz, Anónimo (Review of the case made against Manuel Blanco Romasanta, The Werewolf of Allariz),* (1858; reprint, Madrid: Bubok Publishing, 2012).

148: Ceuta, a Spanish city: "Blanco Romasanta died at age fifty-four in a prison in Ceuta, of stomach cancer and serving sentences," Ourense Digital, http://www.ourensedixital.com/_novas/11/10/31_01.htm

149: "Romasanta revealed symptoms": "Mañá García states that Romasanta could commit crimes under the hallucinogenic effects of Cornel," Ourense Digital, http://www.ourensedixital.com/_novas/11/10/31_02.htm

149: "I run about the country as a wolf": Sabine Baring-Gould, *The Book of Were-Wolves* (1865; electronic version, Project Gutenberg, 2004), https://www.gutenberg.org/files/5324/5324-h/5324-h.htm.

150: disappearances of children: Robert Eisler, *Man Into Wolf: An Anthropological Interpretation of Sadism, Masochism, and Lycanthropy* (London: Routledge and Kegan Paul Limited, 1951).

150: "Jean had often told her": Baring-Gould.

150: Jean was imprisoned for life: Eisler.

151: He died seven years later: Baring-Gould.

151: Clinical neurologist L. Illis: Otten, 195–199.

152: cases that link Garnier: Baring-Gould.

153: "Mr. Daniel d'Ange": Frank Hamel, *Human Animals* (New York: Frederick Stokes Publishing, 1977).

155: groups of armed hunters: Smith.

Chapter 21: Other Contenders: Prehistoric and Exotic Species

159: various carnivore species: The reader who wishes to expand his or her knowledge on the biology and natural history of the species covered here is strongly invited to read the following consulted sources:

- V.G. Heptner and N.P. Naumov, eds., *Mammals of the Soviet Union*, 3 vols. (Moscow: Vysshaya Shkola Publishers, trans. and published for the Smithsonian Institution Libraries, pursuant to an agreement with the National Science Foundation, Washington, D.C., by Amerind Publishing Co. Pvt. Ltd. 1961; reprint, New Delhi: Amerind Publishing Co. Pvt. Ltd., 1988).
- Don E. Wilson and Russell A. Mittermeier, *Handbook of the Mammals of the World, Vol. 1, Carnivores* (Barcelona: Lynx Editions, 2009).
- Luke Hunter, *A Field Guide to the Carnivores of the World* (London: New Holland Publishers, 2011).
- Jonathan Kingdon, *Kingdon Field Guide to African Mammals* (London: Christopher Helm, 2003).
- Richard D. Estes and Daniel Otte, *The Behavior Guide to African Mammals: Including Hoofed Mammals, Carnivores, and Primates* (Berkeley: University of California Press, 2012).
- Bjorn Kurten, *Pleistocene Mammals of Europe* (Chicago: Aldine Publishing, 2009).
- "Hyena Specialist Group," International Union for Conservation of Nature, www.hyaenidae.org.

- "Cat Specialist Group," Species Survival Commission, International Union for Conservation of Nature, www.catsg.org.

160: a wolf-dog version of the snow leopard: According to researcher Laura Wilkinson (personal communication with author Sánchez).

163: *Hundepanzer*: Robert C. Woosnam-Savage, *Brassey's Book of Body Armor* (Herndon, Virginia: Potomac Books, 2002).

168: The cave leopard: Darren Naish, "Tetrapod Zoology," *Science Blogs*, March 12, 2008, http://scienceblogs.com/tetrapodzoology/2008/03/12/european-cats-part-i/.

168: Indian leopard: Ronald M. Nowak and John L. Paradiso, *Walker's Mammals of the World*, 4th ed. (Baltimore: Johns Hopkins University Press; 1983).

168: Jim Corbett: Jerry A. Jaleel, *Under the Shadow of Man-eaters: The Life and Legend of Jim Corbett of Kumaon.* (London: Orient Longman, 2001).

169: "believed to be a leopard": Smith.

170: "a leopard probably prowled the hills around Langogne.": Ibid.

170: leopards were used for hunting: Gaston Phébus, *Le livre de chasse* (*The Book of the Hunt*) (1389), "Le livre de chasse per Gaston Phébus," Bibliothèque nationale de France, http://expositions.bnf.fr/phebus/. "There are several species of wild cats: specifically, some are as big as leopards, and are sometimes called lynx and sometimes wolf-cats; and this is incorrect, as they are neither lynxes nor wolf-cats. They should rather be called leopard-cats than anything else, as they have more in common with the leopard than with any other animal. They eat what other cats do, except they catch chickens and geese and a goat or a ewe, if they can find such on their own, because they are as big as a wolf and also have the shape of a leopard, except they do not have so long a tail; a greyhound alone could not engage one of these cats and detain him; it would rather take a wolf than a cat, because they have nails like a leopard's and, moreover, a very bad bite. They are seldom hunted unless by mistake." The term wolf-cat (in French chat-loups) could refer to species from the big cat family, such as lions or tigers (and possibly also to lesser known species), or perhaps was used to identify such a creature(unknown to most people in France in the eighteenth century) when seen for the first time. Phébus also speaks of wolves and how—when the predators are old, weak, and have lost their teeth—they might attack humans; how wolves might also consume corpses in times of war, the bodies of criminals fallen from the gallows, etc. Sánchez.

170: Big cats (especially leopards) were trophy animals: 16 "Factsheet: The Royal Menagerie at the Tower of London," *Historic Royal Palaces Enterprises Ltd.*, http://www.hrp.org.uk/Resources/The%20Royal%20Menagerie.pdf: Dating from the reign of King John (1199–1216), the former Royal Menagerie in London operated for more than six hundred years until its closure in the 1830s. Animals acquired included numbers of big cats for its Lion Tower. In 1235, the Holy Roman Emperor Frederick II sent three leopards to Henry III, a tribute to the Plantagenet coat of arms, a trio of lions. The Menagerie was opened to the public in Elizabethan times and became quite popular. In June 1704, its collection was said to include six lions, two leopards or tigers, two "Cats of the Mountains," a jackal, three eagles, and two Swedish owls "of great bigness." A 1741 guide listed many animals by name: lions Marco and Phillis and their son Nero; two lionesses, Jenny and Nanny; Will, a leopard; Jenny, a panther; and two tigers, Will and Phillis, and their son Dick. (Other creatures included a raccoon, a porcupine, vultures, eagles, an ape, and a warwoven, a bird from the East Indies.) Eighty years later, the Menagerie consisted of four lions, a tiger, a leopard, a panther, and a grizzly bear. In 1831 and 1832, animals belonging to the Crown were transferred to Zoological Society of London facilities in Regent's Park; the rest were purchased by an American showman.

174: The cats also had bad teeth: *"La Bête du Gévaudan.eu: Histoire et Enquête" ("The Beast of Gévaudan: History and Investigation"),* http://www.labetedugevaudan.eu/.

174: "Was he not fighting with a lion?": J. H. Patterson, *The Man-Eaters of Tsavo and Other East-African Adventures* (London: Macmillan and Co., Limited, 1952), 22.

175: The Marquis de Lafayette: Simon Schama, *Citizens: A Chronicle of the French Revolution* (New York: Alfred A. Knopf, Inc., 1989), 26.

176: archaic humans and giant hyenas: M. Patrocinio-Espigares, B. Martínez-Navarro, P. Palmqvist, S. Ros-Montoya, I. Toro, J. Agustí, R. Sala, "Homo vs. Pachycrocuta: earliest evidence of competition for an elephant carcass between scavengers at Fuente Nueva-3 (Orce, Spain)," *Quaternary International 295* (2013), 113–125.

180: Striped hyenas rarely attack: Craig Howard, "Hyaena hyaena, Striped Hyena," Animal Diversity Web, Museum of Zoology, University of Michigan, http://animaldiversity.ummz.umich.edu/accounts/Hyaena_hyaena/.

180: hyenas attacking humans: Heptner and Naumov.

181: located a museum-published pamphlet dating to 1819: Franz Jullien, "La deuxième mort de la Bête du Gévaudan," *dans l'Ombre de la Bête,* labetedugevaudan.com/pdf/deuxieme_mort_franz.pdf

183: key factors in Jullien's hypothesis: Ibid.

183: Folklorist and French researcher Michel Meurger suggests: "The Beast of Gévaudan Identified?" Virtual Institute of Cryptozoology, http://cryptozoo.sperso-orange.fr/actualit/1997/hyenegev.htm

184: "According to local lore": Smith.

184: Chastel's hyena/Beast: Buffon (Georges Louis Leclerc, comte de[count]) (1707–1788), intendant of the royal botanical garden (*Jardin du Roi*, King's Garden), also cataloged the natural history collections, an undertaking that led to the compilation of his exhaustive *Natural History (Histoire naturelle, générale et particulière*). He planned the *History* to include fifty volumes; he published thirty-six before he died. The Beast is not mentioned in Garden records of acquisitions. And, as far as is known, Buffon never directly referred to the Beast, although journalist Frédéric Melchior, also known as Baron von Grimm, reported in the April 1765 *Correspondance Litteraire* (406–407) that Buffon, reacting to the reports of the *Gazette de France*, believed the Beast was several large wolves (as in antiquity, the labors said to be those of Hercules were in reality the feats of several heroes), which would "disappear in the return of summer."

185: portraits of animals: Morton.

188: Became extinct: 9 Bermudo Meléndez, *Mamíferos* (Part 1), Book 3, Vol. 1, *Tratado de Paleontología* (Madrid: Editorial Paraninfo, 1990).

Chapter 22: What of Wolves and Hybrids?

191: forty degrees below zero: Barry Holstun Lopez, *Of Wolves and Men* (New York: Charles Scribner's Sons, 1978), 19.

191: "wolves hunt": David L. Mech, *The Wolf: The Ecology and Behavior of an Endangered Species* (Minneapolis: University of Minnesota Press, 1970), 196.

191: a female gray wolf: Associated Press, "Wolf travels hundred of miles to northern Arizona," *Rapid City Journal*, November 23, 2014, http://rapidcityjournal.com/news/latest/wolf-travels-hundreds-of-miles-to-northern-arizona/article_b4de25e8-d7d1-52df-9ec2-fb82a3fd10c0.html.

191: The animal was killed months later: Associated Press, "Wolf killed in Utah was from rare Arizona sighting," *Rapid City Journal*, February 11, 2015, http://rapidcityjournal.com/news/latest/wolf-killed-in-utah-was-animal-from-rare-arizona-sighting/article_4ec-7ce7b-fe63-5bbb-b85b-0da8700cfe9e.html

192: Optimal prey for wolves: Mech, 196, 237, 217.

192: carnassials, or "shearing teeth": Hampton, 15.

192: corpses of the English vanquished: James Edmund Harting, *Extinct British Animals* or *British Animals Extinct within Historic Times* (Buckinghamshire: Paul P. B. Minet, 1972), 133–134.

192: Centuries later, in the New World: Hampton, 54, 55, 58.

192: wolf-free islands off the coast: Harting, 182, 183.

192: "less of a threat to humans": Hampton, 56. In ancient Japan, farmers revered the wolf, the "Large-Mouthed Pure God," for protecting their fields and crops from deer, boars, and rodents. Brett L. Walker, *The Lost Wolves of Japan* (Seattle, Washington, and London: University of Seattle Press, 2005), 9.

192: "conversation of death": Lopez, 62, 94–95.

193: certain organs and parts: Pourcher, Éditions Jeanne Laffitte, 20.

193: a wolf pack cooperates: Stahler, Smith, and Guernsey.

193: "lobo wolves": Stanley Young, *The Last of the Loners* (New York: The Macmillan Company, 1970).

194: "gummers": Ibid., 279.

194: easier-to-chew portions: Ibid., 283–284.

194: A letter from a grateful stockman: Ibid., 223.

194: Custer Wolf: Ibid., 297–304.

194: "coming together of science and folklore": Jon T. Coleman, *Vicious: Wolves and Men in America* (New Haven: Yale University Press, 2004), 205.

194: ranchers raised longhorns: Gipson and Ballard, 735.

195: scientists studied famous wolves: Philip S. Gipson, and Warren B. Ballard, "Accounts of Famous North American Wolves,"

The Canadian Field-Naturalist, Vol. 112, Issue 4 (1998): 724–739. Philip S. Gipson, Warren B. Ballard, and Ronald M. Nowak, "Famous North American Wolves and the Credibility of Early Wildlife Literature," *Wildlife Society Bulletin*, Vol. 26, No. 4 (Winter 1998): 808–816.

195: "partially severed trachea": Hampton, 11.

196: a suspiciously large, three-toed wolf: Ibid., 736.

197: "surplus kills": Ibid., 737. The Beast bobtailed a sheep: Pourcher, AuthorHouse, 220; Éditions Jeanne Laffitte, 168.

197: wolf-dog hybrids: Ibid.

197: these types of animals: Gipson, Ballard, and Nowak, 808–816.

197: "attributions of kills to the wrong predator species": Ibid.

197: "hybrid vigor": Clarke, 71–72.

198: service animals: Hampton, 26.

198: hybrid incident: Ernest Thompson Seton, *The Coyote,* Vol. 1, Life IX, *Lives of Game Animals* (Garden City, New York: Doubleday, Doran, 1929), 401–402.

199: "undoubtedly somewhat warped": Thompson, 81.

199: Lupine predations: Harting, 144.

199: Hospitals: Ibid., 124–125.

199: "vast tracts of forest and moor": Ibid., 158.

200: Cromwell: Ibid., 204.

200: "If the he-wolf doesn't get you, the she-wolf will.": Robb, 91.

200: sharecropper: Devlin, 75.

200: indicative of clashes: Jean-Marc Moriceau, interview by Jacques Rochefort, *Mission Agrobiosciences, www.montpellier-agglo.com,* 2008, http://www.agrobiosciences.org/article.php3?id_article=2415:)

200: Gabalitan: Thompson, 31. Clarke, 68.

200: "twilight herding": Clarke, 68.

Chapter 23: Two Dead Beasts

202: de Beauterne: According to Barnson, de Beauterne was added to Robert-François's name, and not, as other historians believe, to the name of his father. The lands de Beauterne or of Beauterne were in Robert-François's future wife's dowry. He began using the name before he officially acquired it through marriage, essentially to avoid confusion with his father.

203: Speculative similarities: Smith.

204: summary of the reactions: Pourcher, AuthorHouse.

204: William Cole: William Cole, *A Journal of My Journey to Paris in the Year 1765* (London: F. G. Stokes, 1931).

204: "exceedingly large wolf": Horace Walpole, *The Letters of Horace Walpole, Vol. 3, 1759–1769* (electronic version, Project Gutenberg, 2003), http://www.gutenberg.org/cache/epub/4773/pg4773-images.html.

204: The king reacted: Smith.

207: Based on the weights recorded: François de Beaufort, *Le loup en France* (Paris, France: *Société française pour l'étude et la protection des mammifères,* 1987).

207: Average measurements and weights: Luke Hunter, *A Field Guide to the Carnivores of the World* (London: New Holland Publishers, 2011).

207: maximum "average" sizes: Don E. Wilson and Russell A. Mittermeier, *Handbook of the Mammals of the World, Vol. 1, Carnivores* (Barcelona: Lynx Editions, 2009).

207: an exceptionally large wolf: Geneviève Carbone, *La peur du loup* (Paris: Gallimard, 1991).

207: international researchers: Barnson, personal communication with author Sánchez: "The veterinarian I saw (in 2007) and asked to take a look at the report by maître Marin, told me that in his mind it was clearly a hybrid wolf and eastern dog, like the Leonberg, the Kangal, or other tough mastiff dogs . . . because of the measurements, and because of the fur, thick and quite long for a 'simple wolf.'"

207: morphological aspects: Stephen Spotte, *Societies of Wolves and Free-ranging Dogs* (Cambridge University Press, 2012): "The name *Canis lycaon* was given by von Schreber to a live specimen captured as a pup in Quebec, kept chained for a time, and eventually taken alive to Paris by a French naval officer . . . There it was seen by the renowned naturalist Georges-Louis Leclerc, Comte de Buffon, who published a description and illustration of a black wolf in 1761. What became of its remains is unknown. All physical traces have disappeared. Which is unfortunate because a tiny sample of skin might resolve much of the controversy discussed above. According to Buffon this animal was smaller than the European gray wolf, with larger ears. Its tail was also less bushy. A specimen observed by R. I. Pocock, an expert at the British Museum of Natural History, labeled *Canis lycaon, N. America*, similar to Buffon's and pointing out that its pelt was black too, the attendant skull short, and the teeth small for an ordinary wolf. The pelt had a white patch on the breast, a character that in later gray wolf x domestic dog admixing experiments would be attributed to dog genes. Over several years the Russian geneticist N. A. Iljin produced four generations' captive wolf-dogs through selective breeding and recorded their characters. Many had white markings that he suspected were derived from dogs, but wrote, 'However, the presence of the genes in wolves is also possible, since naturalists have sometimes (though rarely) recorded wolves with white spots on the chest.' An early Pennsylvania pioneer noted that wolves will intermix with dogs mentioning 'an old she-wolf [that came] into the settlement [to] entice away a number of dogs.' Of her six admixed pups, 'Two of them had spots on them exactly like one of the dogs.'" Reprinted with the permission of Cambridge University Press.

207: Such specimens may result: Ibid. "Pliny reported how the Gauls tied estrous dogs to trees so they might mate with wolves . . . Evidently this technique strikes a universal chord. Early explorers wrote that Eskimos occasionally staked out sled dogs in heat hoping wolves would mate with them, thereby enhancing the hardiness of their breed . . . To quote Glover M. Allen: 'There is much evidence, though of a somewhat uncertain character, that wild male Wolves will breed with female Eskimo Dogs at proper seasons, and the northern Indians are said to encourage such occasional crosses.'" Reprinted with the permission of Cambridge University Press.

208: Female and male wolves: Ibid.

209: The animal shows clear characteristics: Ibid. "Coydogs produced by Lee R. Dice had wider muzzles and shorter faces than coyotes, their skulls broader and ears typically lopped instead of erect like a coyote's . . . The coat might mimic the parent dog's in being spotted or mottled with shorter hair. All are phenotypic characters of domestication . . . Offspring of eastern coyote x purebred dog crosses looked like lop-eared mongrel dogs . . . This is not surprising because coat color, coat pattern, and morphology of wolf dogs render them easily mistaken for mongrel dogs too. Domestication, whether through admixing or captive breeding of wild canids selected for tameness, eventually results in distinctive, predictable changes in morphology. Foremost are shortening and broadening of the snout and palate causing crowding of the teeth and a reduction in tooth size, a steeply rising forehead and wider posterior cranial vault, and differences in the position and angle of the orbits. These features are used in attempts to distinguish fossil dogs from fossil wolves. A kink tail or tail that is curled forward, lopped ears, and color or pattern of the coat are other indicators of domestication." Ibid. Reprinted with the permission of Cambridge University Press.

211: new evidence: Morell, Virginia, "Evolution: From Wolf to Dog," Scientific American (July 2015), 60–67.

211: became primitive dogs,: Xiaoming Wang, Richard H. Tedford, and Mauricio Anton, *Dogs: Their Fossil Relatives and Evolutionary History* (Columbia University Press, 2010).

211: Anthropology professor Pat Shipman: Pat Shipman, *The Invaders: How Humans and Their Dogs Drove Neanderthals to Extinction* (Cambridge, Massachusetts and London, England: The Bellknap Press of Harvard University Press, 2015).

212: retained natural instincts and behaviors: Robert A. Willems, DVM, "The Wolf-Dog Hybrid, An Overview of a Controversial Animal" (US Department of Agriculture/National Agricultural Library *Animal Welfare Information Center Bulletin*, Vol. 5, No. 4, Winter 1994/1995), https://archive.org/stream/CAT10401495018/CAT10401495018_djvu.txt.

212: The adult behavior of hybrid pups: Ibid.

212: national statistics: Ibid.

213: statistics may be misleading: Ibid.

214: according to Willems: Ibid.

216: wolves and wolf-dogs make inappropriate pets: Spotte.

218: French dog breeds from the eighteenth century: Hélène Nunes and C. Degueurce, *"Les races de chiens dans la littérature vétérinaire française du XVIII e siècle"* ("Dog breeds in the French veterinary literature of the eighteenth century"), *Bulletin of the French Society for the History of Veterinary Medicine*, 4 (1) (2005).

Chapter 24: Cold Winters, Killer Wolves

222: "reminiscent of prey in distress": Jean-Marc Landry, *Le loup* (Paris: Delachaux et Niestlé, 2001).

225: twelve thousand wolves: Ibid.

225: three thousand to seven thousand specimens: François de Beaufort, *Le loup en France* (Paris: *Société française pour l'étude et la protection des mammifères*, 1987).

225: In parts of North America and Canada: Landry.

226: the record weight: de Beaufort.

228: From our sources: Landry: "In 1996, there were 76 animal attacks on children in India; 50 died. The victims were between two and four years old and weighed between 22 and 26.4 lbs. From each child, about 6.6 to 8.8 lbs was removed, incriminating a single animal: a large canid or possibly a wolf."

230: Such man-eaters: Patrick Newman, *Tracking the Weretiger: Supernatural Man-Eaters of India, China and Southeast Asia* (Jefferson, North Carolina: McFarland, 2012).

230: The Gévaudan case: In the wild, wolves may live up to thirteen to fifteen years; in captivity more than seventeen. The Beast was probably more than ten years of age if an individual; if the Beast consisted of a group of older males and females which managed to survive beyond fifteen years, they would probably die soon after from natural causes—illness, weakness, wounds, gunshots, natural accidents, etc. Sánchez.

231: the affected creature: Bill Wasik and Monica Murphy, *Rabid: A Cultural History of the World's Most Diabolical Virus* (New York: Viking, 2012), 3, 4, 7.

232: "kills nearly one hundred percent": Ibid., 3.

232: conditioned to recognize: Clarke, 46–47.

233: addictive: Bruce D. Patterson, *The Lions of Tsavo* (New York: McGraw-Hill Professional, 2004); and G. G. Rushby, *No More the Tusker* (London: W. H. Allen, 1965).

233: It is probable that: Spotte, "Most of white wolves captured in the twenties in the Canadian Subarctic, being aged animals, were found to have bad teeth, with in some instances, a few altogether missing." Reprinted with the permission of Cambridge University Press.

234: capable of finding natural prey: Landry, personal communication with author Sánchez, October 2010.

Chapter 25: Beasts Past and Present

246: "wheelbarrow": *Parisian Journal, 1405–1449*, trans. Janet Shirley (Oxford: The Clarendon Press, 1968), 332.

247: The Lunel-Viel wolf: Landry.

247: French historian Jean-Marc Moriceau: "Maps," *Man and Wolf: 2,000 Years of History*, http://www.unicaen.fr/homme_et_loup/cartes.php.

252: French researcher Michel Meurger: Michel Meurger, *"Les félins exotiques dans le légendaire français"* (*Communications*, 52, 1990), 175–196.

255: Modern French cases: Campion-Vincent, "Return."

256: Mijas (Malaga) Panther: Javier Resines, "¿ Alien big cats en Málaga?" *Andalucia: Land of Mysteries,* http://andaluciamisteriosa.es.tl/%BFAlien-big-cats-en-M%E1laga-f-.htm.

Chapter 26: The Beast and Wolves Today in France

260: A footnote to a story: "Sketch of a Fortnight's Excursion to Paris in 1788," *The Gentleman's Magazine*, Vol. 67, Part 1, 1797.

261: Wolves were indeed menacing: Devlin, 74–75.

261: Lozère in January 1951: Clarke, 58.

262: "spreads on all the Alps": "The Wolf in France," Regional Directorate of Environment, Physical Planning and Housing, http://www.rdbrmc-travaux.com/loup/index.php?lang=en.

262: Wolf populations today are monitored: "Loup and Lynx Network," *Office de la Chasse et de la Faun Savauge*, http://www.oncfs.gouv.fr/Reseau-Loup-Lynx-ru100.

262: taking over immense Soviet training grounds: "Could the wolf return to Western Europe?" (*Independent.co.uk*, July 12, 2013), http://www.independent.co.uk/news/world/europe/could-the-wolf-return-to-western-europe-8703910.html

262: "the strongest and most negative image": Véronique Campion-Vincent, "The Restoration of Wolves in France: Story, Conflicts, and Uses of Rumor," *Mad About Wildlife: Looking at Social Conflict Over Wildlife,* Ann Herda-Rapp and Theresa L. Goedeke, eds. (Leiden, Germany, and Boston: Brill, 2005) 99–122.

262: "launched a major rehabilitation campaign": Ibid, 100.

262: "symbolic bestiary": Ibid.

262: "of species formerly considered as pests": Campion-Vincent, "Return," 2.

263: The State provides compensation: Ibid., 5, 8.

263: not truly "natural": Ibid., 9.

263: stray dogs: Ibid., 10.

263: "conspiracy theories": Ibid.

263: As of 2013: "France at a Glance," International Wolf Center, http://www.wolf.org/wow/europe/France/.

263: wild dogs may be to blame: "French farmers try to keep the wolf from the door"(*Independent.co.uk*, October 20, 2013), http://www.independent.co.uk/environment/nature/french-farmers-try-to-keep-the-wolves-from-their-door-8891789.html

263: "The stakes of the manipulations": Campion-Vincent, "Return," 16.

264: "an indicator of relations": Moriceau, interview by Jacques Rochefort.

Appendix

265: Details of the Autopsies: Translation by Gustavo Sánchez Romero, corrections and complements by Alain Bonet, including conversion notes.

Bibliography

Books

Arsuaga, J. L. *La saga humana*. Illus. Kennis and Kennis. Madrid: Edaf, 2006. See also www.atapuercatv.com.

Barber, Paul. *Vampires, Burial, and Death: Folklore and Reality*. New Haven: Yale University Press, 1988.

Barger, Andrew. *The Best Werewolf Short Stories 1800–1849: A Classic Werewolf Anthology*. Collierville, Tennessee: Bottletree Books LLC, 2010.

Baring-Gould, Sabine, *The Book of Were-Wolves*. London: Smith, Elder, & Co., 1865.

Baugh, Daniel A. *The Global Seven Years War, 1754–1763: Britain and France in a Great Power Contest*. Harlow, United Kingdom: Pearson Education Limited, 2011.

de Beaufort, François. *Le loup en France*. Paris: Société française pour l'étude et la protection des mammifères, 1987.

Bernheimer, Richard. *Wild Men in the Middle Ages: A Study in Art, Sentiment, and Demonology*. Cambridge: Harvard University Press, 1952.

Bourgault du Coudray, Chantal. *The Curse of the Werewolf: Fantasy, Horror, and the Beast Within*. London: I. B. Tauris & Co., Ltd., 2006.

Carbone, Geneviève. *La peur du loup*, Paris: Gallimard, 1991.

Carlier, Yves. *A Day at Versailles*, Paris: Flammarion, S.A., 2013.

Clark, Anne. *Beasts and Bawdy*. New York: Taplinger Publishing Company, 1975.

Cole, William. *A Journal of My Journey to Paris in the Year 1765*, London: F. G. Stokes, 1931.

Coleman, Jon T. *Vicious: Wolves and Men in America*. New Haven: Yale University Press, 2004.

Curran, Bob. *Werewolves*. Franklin Lakes, New Jersey: New Page Books, 2009.

Delperrie de Bayac, Jacques, *Du sang dans la montagne*. Paris: éditions Fayard, 1970.

Devlin, Judith. *The Superstitious Mind: French Peasants and the Supernatural in the Nineteenth Century*. New Haven and London: Yale University Press, 1987.

Eisler, Robert. *Man into Wolf: An Anthropological Interpretation of Sadism, Masochism, and Lycanthropy*. London: Routledge and Kegan Paul Limited, 1951.

Estes, Richard D., and Daniel Otte. *The Behavior Guide to African Mammals: Including Hoofed Mammals, Carnivores, and Primates*. Berkeley: University of California Press, 2012.

Fleming, John V. *The Dark Side of the Enlightenment: Wizards, Alchemists, and Spiritual Seekers in the Age of Reason*. New York and London: W. W. Norton, 2013.

Gómez Tabanera, J. M. *Hunting in Prehistoric Times*. Madrid: Ediciones Istmo, 1980.

Gonzalez-Palacios, Alvar. *The Age of Louis XV*. Translated by Henry Vidon. London: Paul Hamlyn, 1969.

Gottschall, Jonathan. *The Storytelling Animal: How Stories Make Us Human*. Boston & New York: Mariner Books, Houghton Mifflin Harcourt, 2013.

Goubert, Pierre. *The Ancien Régime: French Society, 1600–1750*. Translated by Steve Cox. New York: Harper & Row Publishers, Harper Torchbooks, 1974.

Gougaud, Henri, and Colette Gouvion. *France Observed*. Translated by Genevieve Westham. New York: Gallery Books, an imprint of W. H. Smith Publishers, Inc., 1986.

Guazzo, Francesco Maria. *Compendium Maleficarum, Montague Summers Edition*. Translated by E. A. Ashwin. New York: Dover Publications, 1988.

Hamel, Frank. *Human Animals*. New York: Frederick Stokes Publishing, 1977.

Hampton, Bruce. *The Great American Wolf.* New York: Henry Holt and Company, 1997.

Harting, James Edmund. *Extinct British Animals* or *British Animals Extinct within Historic Times.* Buckinghamshire: Paul P. B. Minet, 1972.

Heptner, V. G., and N. P. Naumov, eds. *Mammals of the Soviet Union.* 3 vols. Moscow: Vysshaya Shkola Publishers, 1961. Reprint translated and published for the Smithsonian Institution Libraries pursuant to an agreement with the National Science Foundation, Washington, D.C., by Amerind Publishing Co. Pvt. Ltd., New Delhi, India, 1988.

Hufton, Olwen L. *The Poor of Eighteenth-Century France: 1750-1789.* London: Oxford University Press, Ely Press, 1974.

Hunter, Luke. *A Field Guide to the Carnivores of the World.* London: New Holland Publishers, 2011.

Jaleel, Jerry A. *Under the Shadow of Man-Eaters: The Life and Legend of Jim Corbett of Kumaon.* London: Orient Longman, 2001.

Jones, Colin. *The Great Nation: France from Louis XV to Napoleon.* London: Penguin Books, 2003.

Journal d'un bourgeois de Paris sous Charles VI et Charles VII. A Parisian Journal, 1405–1449. Trans. Janet Shirley. Oxford: The Clarendon Press, 1968.

Kingdon, Jonathan. *The Kingdon Field Guide to African Mammals.* London: Christopher Helm, 2003.

Kurten, Bjorn. *Pleistocene Mammals of Europe.* Chicago: Aldine Publishing, 2009.

Landry, Jean-Marc. *Le loup.* Paris: Delachaux et Niestlé, 2001.

Lang, Andrew, ed., H. J. Ford, illus. *The Animal Story Book.* 1896. Reprint, New York: Dover Publications, Inc., 2002.

van Lawick-Goodall, Hugo and Jane. *Innocent Killers.* New York: Houghton Mifflin, 1971.

Lopez, Barry Holstun. *Of Wolves and Men.* New York: Charles Scribner's Sons, 1978.

Mannix, Daniel P. *The Wolves of Paris.* New York: E. P. Dutton, 1978.

Mech, L. David. *The Wolf: The Ecology and Behavior of an Endangered Species.* Minneapolis: University of Minnesota Press, 1970.

Meléndez, Bermudo. *Tratado de Paleontología, Tomo 3, Vol. 1, Mamíferos (1ª parte)*. Madrid: Editorial Paraninfo, 1990.

Moriceau, Jean-Marc. *La Bête du Gévaudan*. Paris: Larousse, 2008.

Moriceau, Jean-Marc. *Histoire du Méchant Loup: 3000 attaques sur l'homme en France*. Paris: Fayard, 2007.

Morton, Mary, ed. *Oudry's Painted Menagerie: Portraits of Exotic Animals in Eighteenth-Century Europe*. Los Angeles: J. Paul Getty Museum, Getty Publications, 2007.

Newman, Patrick. *Tracking the Weretiger: Supernatural Man-Eaters of India, China, and Southeast Asia*. Jefferson, North Carolina: MacFarland, 2012.

Nowak, Ronald M., and John L. Paradiso. *Walker's Mammals of the World*, 4th Ed. Baltimore: Johns Hopkins University Press, 1983.

O'Donnell, Elliott. *Werwolves*. 1912. Electronic version, Project Gutenberg, 2008, https://www.gutenberg.org/files/26629/26629-h/26629-h.htm.

Otten, Charlotte F., ed. *A Lycanthropy Reader: Werewolves in Western Culture*. Syracuse, New York: Syracuse University Press, 1986.

Patterson, J. H. *The Man-Eaters of Tsavo and Other East-African Adventures*. London: Macmillan and Co., Limited, 1952. Also: New York: McGraw-Hill Professional, 2004.

Perkins, James Breck. *France Under Louis XV. Volume I*. Boston and New York: Houghton Mifflin Company, 1897.

de Planhol, Xavier. *An Historical Geography of France*. Cambridge: Cambridge University Press, 1994.

Pourcher, Abbé Pierre. *History of La Bête du Gévaudan: True Scourge of God*. Translated by Derek Brockis. Milton Keynes, United Kingdom and Bloomington, Indiana: AuthorHouse, 2006.

Pourcher, Abbé Pierre. *Histoire de la Bête du Gévaudan, Veritable fléau de Dieu, d'aprè les documents inédits and authentiques*. Marseille, France: Éditions Jeanne Lafitte, 2006.

Preston, Richard. *The Demon in the Freezer: A True Story*. New York Random House, 2002.

Reuss, Henry S., and Margaret M. Reuss. *The Unknown South of France: A History Buff's Guide*. Boston, Massachusetts: Harvard Common Press, 1991.

Robb, Graham. *The Discovery of France: A Historical Geography from the Revolution to the First World War*. New York and London: W. W. Norton & Company, 2007.

Robbins, Louise E. *Elephant Slaves and Pampered Pets: Exotic Animals in Eighteenth-Century Paris*. Baltimore and London: The Johns Hopkins University Press, 2002.

Rushby, G. G. *No More the Tusker*. London: W. H. Allen, 1965.

Sand, George. *Légendes rustiques*. Paris: A. Morel et Cie, 1858. Electronic version, Project Gutenberg, 2006, http://www.gutenberg.org/cache/epub/17911/pg17911-images.html.

Schama, Simon. *Citizens: A Chronicle of the French Revolution*. New York: Alfred A. Knopf, Inc., 1989.

Seton, Ernest Thompson. *The Coyote*, Vol. 1, Life IX, *Lives of Game Animals*. Garden City, New York: Doubleday, Doran, 1929.

Shipman, Pat. *The Invaders: How Humans and Their Dogs Drove Neanderthals to Extinction*. Cambridge, Massachusetts and London, England: The Bellknap Press of Harvard University Press, 2015.

Smith, Jay M. *Monsters of the Gévaudan: The Making of a Beast*. Cambridge, Massachusetts: Harvard University Press, 2011.

Spawforth, Tony. *Versailles: A Biography of a Palace*. New York: St. Martin's Press, 2008.

Spotte, Stephen. *Societies of Wolves and Free-ranging Dogs*. Cambridge: Cambridge University Press, 2012.

Starr, Douglas P. *The Killer of Little Shepherds: a True Crime Story and the Birth of Forensic Science*. New York: Alfred A. Knopf, 2010.

Stevenson, Robert Louis. *Travels with a Donkey in the Cévennes*. New York: The Heritage Press, 1957.

Summers, Montague. *The Werewolf in Lore and Legend*. 1933. Reprint, New York: Dover Publishing, 2003.

Swann, Julian. *Politics and the Parlement of Paris Under Louis XV, 1754–1774*. Cambridge: Cambridge University Press, 1995).

Thompson, Richard H. *Wolf-Hunting in France in the Reign of Louis XV: The Beast of the Gévaudan*. Lewiston, New York; Queenstown, Ontario, Canada; Lampeter, Dyfed, Wales, United Kingdom: The Edwin Mellen Press, 1991.

Trubshaw, Bob, ed. *Explore Phantom Black Dogs*, Loughborough, England: Heart of Albion Press, 2005.

Walker, Brett L. *The Lost Wolves of Japan*. Seattle, Washington, and London: University of Seattle Press, 2005.

Walpole, Horace, *The Letters of Horace Walpole, Vol. 3*. Project Gutenberg, 2003. http://www.gutenberg.org/cache/epub/4773/pg4773-images.html.

Wang, Xiaoming, Richard H. Tedford, and Mauricio Anton. *Dogs: Their Fossil Relatives and Evolutionary History*. New York: Columbia University Press, 2010.

Wasik, Bill, and Monica Murphy. *Rabid: A Cultural History of the World's Most Diabolical Virus*. New York: Viking, 2012.

Whalley, Joyce Irene. *Writing Implements and Accessories: From the Roman Stylus to the Typewriter*. Detroit: Gale Research Company, 1975.

White, Freda. *West of the Rhone: Languedoc, Roussillon, the Massif Central*. London: Faber and Faber, 1964.

Williams, Emile F. *Undiscovered France*. Boston and New York: Houghton Mifflin Company, The Riverside Press Cambridge, 1927.

Wilson, Don E., and Russell A. Mittermeier. *Handbook of the Mammals of the World, Vol. 1, Carnivores*. Barcelona: Lynx Editions, 2009.

Woosnam-Savage, Robert C. *Brassey's Book of Body Armor*. Herndon, Virginia: Potomac Books, 2002.

Young, Stanley P. *The Last of the Loners*. New York: The Macmillan Company, 1970.

Articles

Andrews, Crispin. "Sherlock Holmes and the Beast of the Gévaudan." *History Today*, Vol. 63, Issue 7 (2013). http://www.historytoday.com/crispin-andrews/sherlock-holmes-and-beast-Gévaudan.

Campion-Vincent, Véronique. "The Restoration of Wolves in France: Story, Conflicts, and Uses of Rumor." *Mad About Wildlife: Looking at Social Conflict Over Wildlife*. Herda-Rapp, Ann, and Goedeke, Theresa L., eds. Leiden, Germany, and Boston: Brill, 2005: 99–122.

Campion-Vincent, Véronique. "The Return of the Wolf in France." *Journal of Indian Folkloristics, Special Issue, Islands and Narratives*, Vol. V, No. ½ (2003): 133–162.

Clarke, C. H. D. "The Beast of Gévaudan." *Natural History* (April 1971): 44–73.

Dickens, Charles. "A Wonderful Wild Beast." *Household Words: A Weekly Journal*, Vol. 18 (November 20, 1858): 544–547.

Gipson, Philip S., and Warren B. Ballard. "Accounts of Famous North American Wolves." *The Canadian Field-Naturalist*, Vol. 112, Issue 4, (1998): 724–739.

Gipson, Philip S., Warren B. Ballard, and Ronald M. Nowak. "Famous North American Wolves and the Credibility of Early Wildlife Literature." *Wildlife Society Bulletin*, Vol. 26, No. 4, (Winter 1998): 808–816.

Jullien, Franz. "*La deuxième mort de la bête du Gévaudan.*" *Le Havre: Annales du Muséum du Havre*, n° 59 (1998): 1–9.

Meurger, Michel. "*Les félins exotiques dans le légendaire français.*" *Communications*, No. 52 (1990): 175–196.

Moriceau, Jean-Marc. Interview by Jacques Rochefort, Mission Agrobiosciences, www.montpellier-agglo.com (2008). http://www.agrobiosciences.org/article.php3?id_article=2415.

Moriceau, Jean-Marc. "Posters, Periodicals, and Newspapers: A Distorted Reflection?" from the website *Man and Wolf: 2,000 Years of History*. http://www.unicaen.fr/homme_et_loup/_en/sources_presse.php.

Morell, Mary. "Evolution: From Wolf to Dog." *Scientific American* (July 2015).

Nunes, Hélène, and C. Degueurce. "*Les races de chiens dans la littérature vétérinaire française du XVIII e siècle.*" *Bulletin of the French Society for the History of Veterinary Medicine*, 4 (1) (2005).

Patrocinio Espigares, M., B. Martínez-Navarro, P. Palmqvist, S. Ros-Montoya, I. Toro, J. Agustí, R. Sala. "*Homo vs. Pachycrocuta:* Earliest evidence of competition for an elephant carcass between scavengers at Fuente Nueva-3 (Orce, Spain)." *Quaternary International* Vol. 295 (2013): 113–125.

Resine, Javier. "¿ Alien big cats en Málaga?" from the website *Andalucia: Land of Mysteries*. http://andaluciamisteriosa.es.tl/%BFAlien-big-cats-en-M%E1laga-f-.htm.

Sapolsky, Robert M. "Mind & Matter." *The Wall Street Journal*, November 9–10, 2013.

"Sketch of a Fortnight's Excursion to Paris in 1788." *The Gentleman's Magazine*, Vol. 67, Part 1, 1797.

Stahler, D. R., D. W. Smith, and D. S. Guernsey. "Foraging and feeding ecology of the gray wolf *(Canis lupus):* lessons from Yellowstone National Park, Wyoming, USA" *Journal of Nutrition*, Vol. 136, No. 7 (July 2006): 1923S-1926S. Available online from the National

Center for Biotechnology Information, http://www.ncbi.nlm.nih.gov/pubmed/16772460.

Valasquez-Manoff, Moises. "Can Celiac Disease Affect the Brain?" *New York Times Sunday Review, Opinion* (October 11, 2014).

Willems, Robert A., DVM. "The Wolf-Dog Hybrid, An Overview of a Controversial Animal," US Department of Agriculture/National Agricultural Library, *Animal Welfare Information Center Bulletin*, Vol. 5, No. 4 (Winter 1994/1995): https://archive.org/stream/CAT10401495018/CAT10401495018_djvu.txt.

Zhu, Bao-Li, with Kaori Ishida, Shigeki Oritani, Mari Taniguchi, Masaki Q. Fujita, Kazunori Fukita, and Hitoshi Maeda. "Decapitation in suicidal hanging—a case report with a review of the literature." *Legal Medicine*, Vol. 2, Issue 3 (October 2000): 159–162.

Web Resources

www.labetedugevaudan.com: *dans l'Ombre de la Bête (In the Shadow of the Beast)*. Site of Beast researcher Phil Barnson. In French and English.

www.labete.7hunters.net: "The Beast of the Gévaudan." Site of Derek Brockis, English translator of Pourcher's book, *La Bête du Gévaudan,* in English. (Currently inactive.)

http://www.labetedugevaudan.eu/: *"La Bête du Gévaudan.eu: Histoire et Enquête" ("The Beast of Gévaudan: History and Investigation"),* Another informative website, in French and English.

http://www.ot-mende.fr/decouvrir/visiter/histoire-de-mende: A guide to the history of the city of Mende, France, in French.

Museum

Le Muse Fantastique de la Bête du Gévaudan, Saugues, France. Visit website for seasonal hours and contact information: www.musee-bete-Gévaudan.com.

Wolf Park

Les Loups du Gévaudan Wolf Park, Hameau de Sainte-Lucie, France. This forty-acre wolf preserve located in the region of the Beast is home to about one hundred wolves from Europe, Russia, and Canada. Visit website for seasonal hours and contact information: www.loupsduGévaudan.com.

Acknowledgments

Gustavo Sánchez Romero wishes to thank Phil Barnson and Alain Bonet, www.labetedugevaudan.com; Michel Binon, Muséum d'Orléans, France; Derek Brockis, translator, *The Beast of Gévaudan*; Xoan Domínguez, www.ourensedixital.com; Véronique Campion-Vincent, Fondation Maison des Sciences de l'Homme, Paris; David Gaussen and Pierre Yves Garcin, Editions Gaussen, Marseille, France; Blandine Gires, the Fantastic Museum of the Beast of Gévaudan, Saugues, Lozère, France; Franz Jullien and the staff of the National Museum of Natural History, Paris; Dr. Nicolas Kramar, Valais Nature Museum, Sion, Switzerland; Leon Klau, Le Puy-en-Velay; Jean-Marc Landry, IPRA SARL (Institute for the Promotion and Research on Livestock Guarding Animals) Switzerland and France; Christophe Matho, Editions CPE, Romorantin, France; Manabu Sakamoto and Rhian Rowson, Bristol Museum Galleries and Archives; Paolo Viscardi, Horniman Museum and Gardens, London; and the kind people from Saugues township, Lozère, France. I especially appreciate the encouraging help from Cory Allyn at Skyhorse Publishing, and S. R. Schwalb for guidance, support, and enthusiasm! Special thanks also to my partner Birgit, little Minki, and to my dear friend Coco, in memoriam.

S. R. Schwalb wishes to thank Gustavo Sánchez Romero; Cory Allyn, Skyhorse Publishing; Phil Barnson; Derek Brockis; David Lindroth; the staff of the Archives départementales de l'Herault, Montpellier; the staff of Bibliotheque nationale de France, Paris; the staff of the Westchester County Library System; Elaine Westwig and Gregory Raml, American Museum of Natural History; Emily Braker and Heather Christine Robeson, University of Colorado Museum of Natural History; Mark Madison, National Conservation Training Center Archives/Museum; Matt Trott, US Fish and Wildlife Service National Training Center Archives/Museum; Coi Gehrig, Denver Public Library; Véronique Campion-Vincent; Vicki Fischer; Andrew Lownie; Mark Beynon; Martin Griffiths; Val Wineyard; Jaap Rameijer; Roni Lubliner and Eric D. Chin, NBCUniversal; Agathe Theodore, Pathé; Massimo Moretti and Dominque Hascoet-Brunet, StudioCanal; Robbi Siegel, Art Resource; Melissa Goldstein, Bridgeman Images; Peter Kersten, Getty Images; Megan Foley and Joann Schwendemann, Dover Publications; and my family.

Index